Building a New Society

An Islamic Approach to Social Change

ZAHID PARVEZ

Revival

Published by
Revival Publications, Markfield Conference Centre, Ratby Lane,
Markfield, Leicestershire LE67 9SY, United Kingdom.
Tel: 01530–244944, Fax: 01530–244946
E-mail: revival@islamic-foundation.org.uk

ISBN 0–9536768–1–1

To

my parents and teachers
who inspired me to live by Islam
and to strive for a better society

In the name of Allah, the Beneficent, the most Merciful

Contents

PART II: THE CHANGE PROCESS: FRAMEWORK AND METHODOLOGY

Foreword

As humanity enters the third millennium of the Christian era, waves of globalisation and floods of information are forcing human beings in almost every part of the world to become citizens of the 'universal village'. A need for mutual understanding and dialogue between peoples belonging to different religions, cultures and ideologies was never as great and as pressing as it is today. It would not be going too far to suggest that this is now becoming a prerequisite for the very survival and sustenance of human society. No one can afford to live in isolation. We all have to learn to live with each other, as well as learn from each other, to build a better future for all. 'A Clash of Civilisations' is the worst scenario; co-existence, co-operation and the creation of a healthy confluence are definitely alternatives. As such, dialogue within and dialogue between religions, cultures and ideologies, constitute the most pressing needs of the future. Muslims living in the West can play a very important role in initiating and promoting this process.

Dialogue presupposes a readiness to think and talk, to discuss and even differ without conflict and confrontation. It can hardly flourish among those who choose to be deaf and dumb. For we can talk to each other with confidence only if we are clear about what we are, and what our vision of the future is. Muslims in the West can equip themselves to fulfil this historic and challenging responsibility by first talking to themselves and defining their position in the context of the contemporary world, even before they talk to others, which they must. I regard it a healthy development that young Muslim intellectuals are beginning to initiate debate and discussion on crucial issues relating to Islam's essential message and the strategies and methodologies of social change under its influence. To me this represents yet one more expression of Islamic resilience and global upsurge. It is all the more important that young intellectuals are trying to breathe some fresh air by trying to make inputs based upon the original sources of Islam, without discarding the tradition and simply replaying the drama of angry young men, a sight so familiar in our times.

Zahid Parvez is a young Muslim academic serving at the Business School, of the University of Wolverhampton. As an ex-President of The Young Muslims and of the Islamic Society of Britain, and an active member of the Islamic Movement, he has had full exposure to the intellectual and social challenges the two million strong Muslim community is facing in the United Kingdom. He is also aware of the contemporary Western context, both intellectual and cultural. He has tried to delve deep into the sources of the Quran and Sunna, along with availing himself of contemporary Muslim literature, to rediscover the message of Islam and to carry it to men and women struggling today to carve out a future that is spiritually and morally rich, along with being materially comfortable and socially just and honourable. He is concerned about the future of human beings, who are torn between the extremes of crass materialism and socially devoid spiritualism. He nourishes a vision of the future for humanity that is spiritually fulfilling and materially rewarding, along with ensuring freedom, justice, peace and well-being for all humans on the globe. He is convinced that the Quran and the Prophet Muhammad's (blessings and peace be upon him) model provide such an alternative, only if we understand them correctly and strive to live according to them assiduously. Moreover, he has tried to seriously explore the nature of this model and ventured to spell out as to how it can be actualised in the contemporary world. Simultaneously, he focuses on the nature of this model and its methodology for individual and societal change.

I regard this study as a creative and useful contribution to contemporary Islamic literature. I particularly value it as it can help the Muslims in the West in strengthening their own identity and in preparing them to be active participants in the dialogue between religions and cultures on which the future of humanity hinges. I also hope this will spur other Muslim intellectuals and activists, particularly younger ones, to come to grips with the challenges that beset the world of Islam in particular and humanity in general. It is only through integrity of faith, clarity of thought, creativity of approach and the cross-fertilisation of ideas that the challenges of today and tomorrow can be successfully met. This purposeful effort, of my younger brother and colleague, Zahid Parvez, however tentative and explorative, gives me great hope for the future. It is only through such efforts that the way can be paved for more elaborate and authoritative works to appear and influence the future development of Muslim thought and society in the West.

Essentially, Zahid Parvez's study on *Building a New Society – An Islamic Approach to Social Change*, represents a pioneering effort in the Muslim youth's search for a new paradigm to inspire mankind to emerge out of the cultural crisis of our times.

Leicester
June 2000

Khurshid Ahmad
Chairman,
Islamic Foundation

Preface

Two major concerns provided me with the idea and motivation for writing this book. The first of these relates to the growing fears and misunderstandings that are witnessed in the West regarding Islam and its upsurge in the world today. Fear of Islam is easily noticed from the attitudes of many ordinary people, and misunderstanding regarding it continually flow through the media, academic writings and from the views of numerous politicians. As viewed from a Muslim's perspective, these either exist due to a genuine lack of comprehension of the Islamic faith and mission, or are based on distorted or insufficient information, or even stem from deep rooted prejudices. Whatever the reasons for their existence may be, they simply contribute towards engendering suspicion and mistrust. They also foster negative attitudes and hostile responses, all of which are not conducive to social harmony nor world peace. As a saying goes: '*behaviour breeds behaviour*'. Mistrust and hostile responses initiated from one side is most likely to result in a similar behaviour from the other. The second concern, which is strongly connected to the first, relates to the negative, and in cases, extremist attitudes and approaches that are employed by certain Muslim groups in their efforts to free the Muslim world from secular-materialistic influences and take the message of Islam forward to humanity. Whether or not such attitudes are in response to the hostile conduct of certain Western governments, they only contribute towards reinforcing negative Muslim stereotypes and distract attention away from the true message of Islam and its grand vision for humanity.

Thus, to address both these concerns, a strong need was felt for a book in English that expounds the vision of Islam and the methodology it advocates for guiding and directing social and global change in a systematic and comprehensive way. Currently, however, little organised information is available in English on this important area. Whatever there is, is either dispersed through numerous books, or has primarily been translated from Arabic, Urdu and Turkish texts which were written a few decades ago and for different contexts. This book is, thus, a humble attempt aimed at fulfilling this need. The material covered is not new but is presented in a fresh, relevant and coherent way for a Western context. In particular, an effort has been made to present the vision of Islam for individuals, society and the state. A broad framework for guiding the process for realising this vision in society is also offered. Furthermore, an attempt has been made to extract the Islamic framework and methodology for guiding social change directly from the primary Islamic sources of guidance – namely the Quran and Sunna. Secondary sources, which includes historical sources, the views of scholars and experience, have been used wherever deemed appropriate to support and elaborate the primary sources.

It should be noted that the material provided in the book is not meant to be a step-by-step guide on the Islamic process for positive social change. On the contrary, it is intended to stimulate the reader's interest in the subject, and throw light on some of the major current debates, dilemmas, challenges and issues that are encountered by Islamic workers in their efforts for societal reform and change. Furthermore, only broad issues for effecting change are dealt with. These include the training and development of the change agents, their organisation into a social movement, key ingredients of the change process, the framework and methodology to guide thought and action, and the role of community and political institutions in the change process. More specifically, the book offers guidance on frequently encountered questions such as the following: what kind of change does Islam aim to promote in social life? How is this change different from other kinds of changes? Where does the process start from? What are the main principles and values that underpin the change efforts? Should change be introduced in a sudden way – through a revolution, or gradually? What should be the priority in the change process – to prepare and nurture good people prior to influencing change in social systems, or vice versa? Last, but not least, what strategies and methods should guide efforts for change in a given social context?

Organisation of the Book

This book is structured in two Parts, consisting of Eleven Chapters. Part One (incorporating Chapters One to Five) serves as an introduction. It depicts the Islamic vision, clarifies the purpose and mission of the Muslim people and attempts to highlight the major challenges that the Muslim world-community faces, both from within and without. Chapter One looks at some of the classical theories of social change from an Islamic perspective. It asserts that the world-view and moral condition of a people, the dimensions that are missing from the classical sociological theories, are important factors in producing social change and influencing its course. This Chapter also provides a brief overview of the Islamic process of social change. Chapter Two depicts Islam's vision for society and argues why a change based on Islam is greatly needed for our present day society and world. It also attempts to trace the historical roots to some of the present day misunderstandings and fears of Islam. Chapter Three elucidates the mission and purpose of the Muslim world-community. It concludes by suggesting how the Muslim world-community can revive and rebuild itself in order to play an active and constructive role in civilisational development. In Chapter Four, the ideological roots of Western civilisation are examined from a Muslim's perspective, and includes a critique of the existing order. In particular, it discusses the kind of attitudes, culture and way of life that have emerged from secular-materialistic thought and systems of society, and how these form an impediment to justice and peace. It is argued that an understanding of the ideological foundations of a society is an essential requirement for anyone who wishes to embark on a process for building a better social life. Part One concludes with Chapter Five which presents the major contemporary challenges that have to be addressed by the agents of change in the process of realising the vision of Islam.

With this basis established, Part Two (which includes Chapters Six through to Eleven) then builds on and describes how a change based on Islam should be brought about. In other words, this Part details the Islamic process for guiding and moulding social change. This includes the Islamic framework, which sets the broad parameters and principles for the change efforts (Chapter Six), the methodology, which guides the change process (Chapter Seven and Eight), and the most essential vehicle for influencing change – the Islamic movement (Chapter Nine). How the methodology can best be applied in a given context, together with the principles that should be observed and adhered to in efforts for change are also discussed. Chapter Ten examines the education, training and development of Islamic workers in the context of an Islamic movement. Finally, Chapter Eleven discusses more specifically how the Islamic methodology can be applied in a Western context and it offers a practical framework for advancing its Divinely ordained purpose.

It is hoped that the material covered will assist in clarifying the major problematic issues regarding the process of social change, and provide a correct direction for those who desire to build an integrated, moral and just society. The emphasis throughout the book is on employing methods and means that are based on Islamic guidance. These include a deep concern for humanity, justice, peace, public interest, and wisdom. Operating within a social context and employing a pragmatic approach during the change efforts are also emphasised. After all, this is the approach advocated by Islam in all human matters.

Finally, an attempt has been made to avoid the use of Arabic words and terms wherever possible, however, at times this has been unavoidable. Furthermore, 'God' and 'Allah' have been used interchangeably in this book solely for convenience and to facilitate understanding, although Muslims prefer to use 'Allah' because of its comprehensive and deeper meaning. Also the Translation of the Quranic verses are based upon *The Holy Quran* by Abdullah Yusuf Ali, and *The Meaning of the Quran* by Sayyid Abul Ala Mawdudi, with some minor modifications to further clarify their meaning.

Acknowledgements

This book is not the exclusive result of my own thoughts. Many people have contributed to the ideas contained in it, and they all deserve my sincere thanks.

First and foremost, a study of Quranic passages, an analysis of the life and sayings of Prophet Muhammad (peace and blessings of Allah be upon him), and a brief study of the life and works of Muslim revivalists, have all assisted in gaining an insight into the process for advancing positive social change based on Islam. In addition, a close look at the work and methodology of contemporary Islamic movements, reading books by many leading authors on the subject, and having countless discussions with numerous Islamic workers, scholars and leaders, have all aided enormously in the development of ideas, concepts and practical suggestions discussed in this book. I would, therefore, like to express my gratitude to all these people.

In particular, I am thankful to Muhammad Abdus Salam, former President of the Dawatul-Islam, for his encouragement in writing this book, and for providing me with his notes and a video on a lecture delivered by himself on the Prophetic Method of Change.

I would like to express my sincere gratitude to Professor Khurshid Ahmad (Chairman of the Islamic Foundation, Markfield) and Ustadh Khurram Murad (1932–1996, former Director General of the same institution) for what I have learnt from them over the years. Their immense contributions to the Islamic movement, together with their writings, translations, speeches, and my personal meetings with them, were very valuable – in particular their vision of Islam for the West. In fact many thoughts and concerns presented in this book have actually originated from them, either directly or indirectly. Professor Khurshid Ahmad also went through the first and second draft copies of this book and gave extremely useful suggestions regarding the clarification of concepts that are presented and the structure of the book.

My special gratitude also extends to Dr. Ataullah Siddiqui, Abdur Rashid Siddiqui, Dr. Anis Ahmed (Pakistan), Dr. Kamal Helbawi, Dr. Mawil Izzidien, Dr. Mashuq Ally, Arshad Malik, Robin Keen, Adnan Saif, Akhmed Hussain, Mehmood Anwar, Asim Hafeez, Dr. Abdur Rahim Kidwai, Dilwar Hussain and Dr. Muhammad Hanif who graciously reviewed the book in progress, and offered constructive and insightful advice and suggestions for improvements. Last, but not least, Brian Kemp, a senior lecturer at the University of Wolverhampton, deserves acknowledgement for making insightful comments from a non-Muslim's point of view regarding the contents and for suggesting improvements.

Further, all of my teachers who contributed much to the development of my knowledge and understanding of Islam deserve my gratitude. I would like to thank my first teacher, Maulana Munawar Hussain Mashadi, who was my main source of guidance and inspiration in the early years of my involvement in Islamic activities. I am also grateful to Maulana Shariff Ahmed, Maulana Sarfraz Madni, Maulana Saidur Rahman, Maulana Abdul Haq (Pakistan), Maulana Shamsul Qamar, and Maulana Mubarak Ali from whom I learnt and benefited a great deal.

Finally, and most importantly, I thank Allah, the Almighty, for enabling me to complete this book. May He accept my humble efforts, forgive any shortcomings on my part, increase my knowledge and understanding of His way, and enable me to serve the Islamic cause in a more effective way.

Wolverhampton
June 2000

Zahid Parvez

PART I

Islam and the Contemporary State of Affairs

CHAPTER I

Introduction

The Purpose of this Book

The need for putting together material on the Islamic methodology for guiding social change arose from a number of concerns, and it is these that make the contents of this book urgent and relevant. First, it is observed that many ordinary Muslims in the West, after a period of settling down in their new-found homes, are awakening to their Islamic duties and responsibilities. As a result they are becoming more enthusiastic, organised, assertive and active in efforts aimed at challenging secular-materialism, taking the message of Islam forward to the indigenous population, and striving for a more compassionate, fair and peaceful society for all citizens. However, the approaches adopted by the various Muslim groups differ. In cases these exhibit extremism, or are quite diverse and even conflicting. Such a state of affairs has given rise to much confusion and has unfortunately created tensions and inter-group conflicts to some extent. In addition, many activists, due to a poor understanding of the Islamic process of change (i.e. how a change based on Islam should be brought about), display impatience at times, become reactive, or frequently become entangled in side issues and insignificant details, or even find themselves easily distracted by the symptoms of social crises rather than remaining focused on the root issues and causes.

It is also observed that many activists are unable to work effectively in the West. They encounter difficulties in relating Islam to their contemporary Western, non-Muslim majority, context. Some also fail to distinguish between the ideals of Islam on the one hand, and the accretions added by history, customs and cultural practices on the other. This weakness is not only observed in efforts for change, but also encompasses other aspects of Muslim practices related to dress, rituals, family life, customs and so on. Unfortunately, at times a great deal is attached to the understanding and practices that originate from cultures and organisations operating in Muslim countries, even though some of these may conflict with Islamic ideals and values. In cases, even the operational strategies, terms, slogans, activities, organisational structures and ways of working are imitated and adopted with religious zeal, though they may not perhaps be appropriate or desirable in the contemporary Western context. Such blind imitation has led to inward-looking attitudes, inappropriate and irrelevant activities, and hence poor performance. In some cases these have also resulted in fanatical and extremist tendencies. Of course, Muslims in the West can, and should, learn from the experiences of Islamic movements operating in Muslim majority countries. However, the social and political context of these movements is quite different from that of the West, and hence an uncritical imitation may be counter-productive.

To counteract these negative tendencies, a balanced and comprehensive framework needs to be offered to the Muslim activists. Such a framework, based on a rich and balanced understanding of Islam and its methodology for positively shaping social life, will aid Islamic workers in distinguishing between the universal and fundamental Islamic beliefs and ideals on the one hand, and the evolved cultural and organisational practices found in Muslim countries on the other. Second, it will produce flexibility and enable the formulation of relevant and suitable organisational models, approaches and actions for the Western context. Furthermore, an understanding of the Islamic process of change will encourage the promotion of tolerance, harmony and co-operation between the various Muslim groups. Finally, it will enable Islamic workers, i.e. the change agents, to contribute creatively, positively and effectively towards the spiritual, social and moral development of their society.

In addition to these immediate concerns, an understanding of the Islamic framework for guiding and moulding social change becomes important because of the current socio-political circumstances that surround our global and local affairs. For example, prior to the collapse of the former Soviet Union, Communism was perceived by the West as an 'evil empire' and a great danger to the civilised world. However, due to the recent upsurge of the Islamic movements in many Muslim countries, Islam and the Muslim world-community are currently perceived as a potential threat to Western economic and political interests. In some quarters, intellectuals and scholars openly express their views and opinions about the threat of Islam. Some even predict that in the 21st century, the clash will be between Islam and the West[1]. Unfortunately, the fear of Islam is such that the Islamic revival in Muslim countries has come to denote radicalism, anti-Westernism and terrorism. At times, Islam is even grouped with Nazism. Such views and attitudes are obviously not based on true facts and are neither conducive to global harmony nor peace. Regrettably, views like these have, and are continuing to hamper the West's understanding of Islam, and they also condition and promote hostile political responses.

Furthermore, the Islamic world, since the 1980's in particular (with the Revolution in Iran), has, for some reasons, constantly become the centre of focus for the world's media. Issues such as Islamic fundamentalism, the rise of the Islamic movements, the defiance of Muslim people against the West, and the oppression and persecution of Muslims in their own homelands form the major topics of current affairs. Thus, in order to interpret such global events accurately, an understanding of the reasons behind the Islamic resurgence and the process of social change based on Islam, becomes imperative for politicians, journalists and political analysts.

Finally, owing to rapid technological developments, the establishment of international trade agreements and practices, and the drive towards globalisation, we are witnessing a substantial transparency between nations and an increase in the mobility of people. Subsequently, this has increased interactions and communication between nations and faith communities. Thus, ordinary Muslims today are in direct contact with the West, at all levels of life more than ever before. Also, presently there are many millions of Muslims who permanently reside in Western countries, where they are living as neighbours and share the work place, classrooms, hospitals and even businesses with their fellow non-Muslims. Further, there is a rapidly growing number of Muslims from the indigenous population of the West. This close contact makes it imperative for all parties concerned to have a better understanding of each others faith, culture and way of life.

Opinions and views based on prejudice, assumption and misinformation can be harmful, since they generally contribute towards increasing misunderstandings and mistrust. Therefore, to develop peace and harmony, and promote tolerance and co-operation, an understanding of Islam is required by the general public and policy makers in the West. Efforts need to be exerted to build bridges, and create understanding and trust between the various communities that make up our multi-cultural, multi-faith and pluralistic societies. The misrepresentations and fears about a social change based on Islam need to be dispelled, and it is hoped that this book will also contribute towards this aspect to some degree.

The Meaning of Social Change

The term 'social change' evokes different meanings and sentiments amongst different people. It is sometimes equated with social anarchy, radicalism, disruption and even revolution. Also, perhaps due to a culture of passivity that exists in most Western societies, collective social actions are not viewed favourably by some people and thus, efforts for moulding or advancing any kind of change in society are frowned upon. Owing to these negative connotations, it would be appropriate to briefly discuss and clarify what 'social change' actually denotes in the context of this book, since this term will be used quite frequently.

People who share common beliefs or ideas about what is desirable, right, good, wrong and bad, or who share common interests, tend to be drawn together in groups, communities, clubs, associations or political parties. This is implied by the proverb: '*birds of a feather flock together*'. Shared beliefs and ideas give rise to a set of social values (i.e. things considered good and beneficial), and on the whole, it is these that influence and mould the social life of a group or community and gives rise to a particular culture. However, social life does not remain static but undergoes change when influenced, either from within or without, by different sets of ideas or values. This is why the nature of community life, its traditions, social norms and language, change over time. Thus, when a group of people endeavour to change certain social and cultural norms, they are said to be exerting efforts for social change (or cultural change as some academics would like to refer to this). These efforts can be directed at changing certain long-held ideas or beliefs, modifying behaviours and attitudes, or altering political and economic practices, values and processes. If successful, change efforts can lead to modifications or alterations in the flow of information, social structures and practices, or in the laws and policies that govern social systems. The term 'process of social change', thus, refers to a transition or a series of transitions from one social condition to another[2].

Taking our contemporary context as an example, social change is produced, moulded or influenced through competing ideas, views, cultural beliefs and ethical values that a community or society comes into contact with. As an illustration, there are numerous political parties and social movements, organised in various forms and sizes, that are operating in present-day societies. These mass movements draw their inspiration and vision from certain ideologies. The current prevalent ideologies in Western societies include liberalism, capitalism, socialism and feminism as well as communism and fascism to a lesser degree; all these are founded upon a secular-materialistic world-view. Each movement endeavours to promote those political ideas, values, social structures and policies that have been derived from the ideology on which it is based, and strives to influence the direction of society and the state accordingly; either to preserve the status quo, or to introduce new ideas, practices, structures, institutions and laws, or even to revive traditional ones.

Besides the mainstream social movements, other organised efforts exists in society that intend to promote either small or radical changes in society, without intending to touch its core institutional structure. Amongst these are numerous 'pressure groups' or 'interest groups' which generally have a one-issue agenda. Some of these pressure groups aspire to improve the behaviour and attitudes of people, whilst others endeavour to alert and awaken the public about the environmental pollution and destruction that is taking place. Some even campaign for economic justice, or against crime, smoking, drugs, abortion, or other social problems. Indeed each such effort for change, being based upon a particular social concern, will promote different kinds of social values in society.

Recent years have also witnessed efforts targeted at rebuilding fragmented and shattered local communities through reviving civic and community values. For example, efforts for community policing, the formation of neighbourhood self-help groups, community-action groups, parent-teachers associations, tenants associations and so on are becoming popular in many towns and cities. These aim at involving and organising local communities in issues of common concern; to address and reduce crime, to improve the standards of education, and to ensure a better and safer neighbourhood. Such work facilitates community members in re-connecting with each other, organising themselves and working together to address their common problems and issues.

Additionally, the various groups and social movements that exist in contemporary societies, differ in their programme and scope of change, as well as in their strategy and desired pace for change. Some campaign to get into government, (i.e. for political power as a priority through which their change ideas and programme will be introduced – for example, political parties), whilst others strive to affirm their identity or to gain acceptance of their ideas, values or rights. Also some desire changes to take place gradually, in a flexible and adaptive way, whilst others prefer a swifter introduction or even a revolution.

With this background, Islam, which incorporates guidance on collective affairs, also aims to produce positive social change in society and the world. Indeed, it offers a comprehensive vision for individual and social life. As a matter of fact, the Muslim community is assigned by the Glorious Quran with a noble mission (which is detailed in Chapter Three). This is a mission for improving the human condition through building God-conscious and moral people, and establishing a just, virtuous and caring world order. Islamic faith demands that human life must be moulded in accordance with God's revealed guidance. This includes efforts for uprooting all forms of wrongs and injustices from society, and for building a social order based on Islamic values. These Islamic values include the following: worship and obedience of Allah, protection of human dignity, freedom of belief, respect for people, mercy and compassion, justice, equality in status, rights and opportunities for all citizens, stewardship of the natural environment, co-operation between people, moral behaviour, development of human potential, hard work, self-discipline, social progress, cleanliness and hygiene, and social welfare, care and support.

Thus, efforts for changing society according to Islamic ideals are not limited to addressing the symptoms of social crises, nor confined to problems and issues that deal with isolated individual cases, but they go further and confront directly the wrongs in society and the state; they attempt to address the roots of corruption and the processes of repression in order to improve the state of affairs. An Islamic social change, therefore, encompasses all aspects of life in their full varieties, complexities and dynamics. Islam demands a change from within – of hearts, minds, souls and attitudes – and a change in the external social environment. All this for a higher objective that transcends the limits of this worldly life – to win the pleasure of Allah and attain His Paradise (*Jannah*) in the life Hereafter *(Akhira)*. Put another way, Islam demands a fundamental change – a change that touches all levels and dimensions of society, one that reaches the core of societal institutions and functions.

Sociological Theories of Social Change

Having clarified what social change implies in the context of this book, the next important question that needs to be addressed as a way of introduction is: what factors cause change in societies and cultures? An understanding of these factors is crucial for those who desire to embark on efforts for introducing radical social and political changes. This section briefly looks at some of the major theories, put forward by sociologists, that attempt to explain the factors causing social change. The next section will discuss the Islamic perspective on this issue.

There are many sociological theories that attempt to explain the phenomena of social change, in particular the factors that produce social change and influence its course. Literature on social change suggests that the key areas of interest to those who endeavour to understand social change are[3]:

1. The factors and forces that initiate, direct and advance change in society.
2. The form that the change process takes (for example, linear, multi-linear, and cyclical, etc.).
3. The outcomes of the change (effects on individuals, family, community, institutions, etc.).
4. The time frame of change.

In broad terms, the various sociological theories, though based on differing assumptions and perspectives, attempt to explain why and how social change occurs. The classical theories in particular sought to identify the existence of general patterns or a direction in the past development of society. The belief was that if patterns can be identified then these could be used to predict future societal changes. The major (grand) theories of social change that have been presented by historians and sociologists can be broadly classified into the following categories:

1. Evolutionary theories (which suggest that societies evolve like biological organisms: for example, Social Darwinism. These ideas have been argued by people like Herbert Spencer 1820–1903 and Auguste Comte 1798–1857).
2. Historical determinism and the dialectical interpretation of change (as for example, by Karl Marx 1818–83).
3. Cyclical theories of change (which argue that social and historical change follows a cyclical process; it does not move along a linear path, but rather in a circle – growth, maturity and death. For example, these ideas can be found in the writings of Ibn Khaldun (1332–1406) and are more elaborately presented by Oswald Spengler 1880–1936).
4. System theories. These assume that societies are systems made up of numerous inter-related and inter-dependant subsystems. They contend that change is induced by multiple factors that originate within and without the systems (for example, as presented by Max Weber 1864–1920, Ferdinand Toennies 1855–1936 and Talcott Parsons 1902–79).

It is important to note here that the basic (materialistic and deterministic) premises and beliefs on which most of the above sociological theories of change are founded, do not entirely conform to the view put forward by Islam. Many are very simplistic and attribute a single major determining factor causing social change. For example, Social Darwinism compares evolution in the natural world with the development of human societies. It expounds a theory that all societies develop from simple to more complex forms. It argues that social organisations evolve by adapting to the changes occurring in their social environment, just as species adapt to their physical environment.

Accordingly, any social organisation that fails to adapt would eventually become extinct. Similarly, Karl Marx, believing that every society rests on an economic base, argued that change and development occurs through tensions, clashes and struggles between classes to control the forces of production. In contrast, the Islamic viewpoint, which is detailed below, rejects all forms of determinism. Social change, according to the Quran is not unidirectional; it is not a linear movement towards progress and equilibrium, and there is no concept of the end of history[4]. Reality points to the fact that social change is rather a dynamic and emergent process. It can either progress, stagnate or even retrogress. Social life can, thus, change direction: from good to bad and vice versa, and this being dependent on the moral condition of a people. A people can rise to great heights of social development and achieve wonders in material development. However, due to corruption, society and civilisation can also breakdown, suffer from great problems and conflicts and even sink into oblivion. With regard to this, Khurram Murad (1932–96) has very succinctly commented, in the light of Islamic guidance, on the classical theories of social change by stating:

> "The Quran, thus, radically negates all prevalent views of history. There is no determinism: historical, material, sociological or otherwise. History is not tied to any perpetually-revolving wheel of beginning, end, and return to the beginning. Societies are not biological: subject to birth, growth, decay and doom. Nor is there any inevitable linear march towards progress and perfection, either spiritual or moral and social."[5]

From the Quranic perspective therefore, some of the grand, materialistic theories of social change are too simplistic and misleading, because they either base their conclusions on wrong premises or on the symptoms of human problems rather than the causes. It is a fact that human societies do not evolve like biological organisms. This is too simplistic a proposition. Further, class struggle is a symptom of economic and social injustice (immorality) and not a cause. In view of this, it is an historical fact that the civilisations in India, China, Japan, and also the Islamic civilisation, did not rise or fall because of social evolution (a linear ascent) or tensions between classes for controlling the means of production[6]. Thus, materialistic interpretations of social change have great limitations and they fail to provide adequate explanations to what actually motivates people towards change. *Man does not live by bread alone, and the spiritual and moral conditions of a people cannot be ignored from the factors that cause and produce the dynamics of social change.* In view of this, evolutionary theories of social change such as Social Darwinism, deterministic theories of history, together with the dialectical interpretation of change as proposed by Karl Marx, are all incompatible with the reasons given by the Glorious Quran. These ideas and theories have also been criticised by latter day sociologists for their simplicity and flawed analysis of the human condition.

Latter day sociologists have moved on from grand theories to explore change at different levels, from individual and family to societal level, and have deliberated on more specific issues such as how change is guided and directed, what role is played by elite groups in imposing a direction on social change, and what role do ordinary people play in controlling the forces that shape their lives. In addition, different theories exist regarding what shapes human behaviour in society. Is behaviour shaped by individuals themselves (freedom to act), or is it influenced by the dominant societal structures, norms and values, or is it produced from the interaction and combined influence of both of these factors? Naturally, differing conclusions exist regarding these issues. However, present day sociologists tend to agree that change is a complex and non-linear process. A particular kind of social life is shaped and nurtured by the interaction and combination of multiple factors: historical, ideological, social, political, economic and technological. Sociologists have broadly divided the factors causing change into two main categories[7]:

1. Materialistic factors (such as economics, technological, environmental or biological), and
2. Idealistic factors (such as world-view, beliefs, ideology, religion, values, etc.).

These factors can be independent of each other, and may also, due to their interaction, influence each other as well as the course of society.

Islamic perspective on Social Change

In view of the above discussion, Islam also sheds light on the phenomena of social change. In actual fact, the central focus of the Quran is human beings, as individuals and collective bodies. The Quranic guidance deals with our material, spiritual and social condition, and it shows a path on how we can improve our inter-personal relations and interactions. Furthermore, it provides a framework of ideas for understanding the phenomena of social change in a more integrated and holistic way. In short, Islam offers an explanation for the rise and fall of civilisations, and it contends that the idealistic factors and the moral condition of a people are the fundamental factors that shape the course of social change. The core ideas of Islam regarding the phenomena of social change are summarised by the following two inter-related points: *levels of change and the Divine principle of change.* An understanding of these can assist the agents of change in making sense of the dynamics of the change situation.

1. Levels of Change

An analysis of the Islamic sources suggests that change in social life and human condition is affected at two levels:

1. *Primary level change.* This level of change relates to changes occurring in the idealistic factors on which a society is founded, such as a world-view, ideology, beliefs, vision, values, morals and attitudes.
2. *Secondary level change.* This level of change relates to the material factors and procedural changes occurring in a society – for example, change occurring in societal processes, mechanisms, procedures, laws and rules, roles, and also in technology, modes of production and services.

These two levels at which change can be instigated in social life are suggested by numerous verses of the Quran. For example:

> *"Allah has promised to those among you who believe and practise righteous deeds* [i.e. the primary level factors] *that He will surely establish them in the land* [i.e. lead to an improvement in secondary level factors], *as He established those before them ..."*
>
> (an-Nur 24: 54)

Secondary level changes are dependent upon, or occur within a framework provided by primary level factors. Thus, from an Islamic perspective, the overall human condition and direction of change in society is underpinned by primary level factors – that is, the world-views and assumptions about life and nature on which social life is founded. If there is no change at this level, then no fundamental change in society is possible. This is because the primary level factors provide the purpose, vision, values, interests, moral and social principles and motives that shape social, economic and technological policies and which drive society in a particular direction. *Therefore, anyone who wishes to bring about a fundamental change in social life, must initially target their efforts at influencing change at the primary level.*

Since Islam is primarily concerned with introducing fundamental changes in individual life and society, the Glorious Quran continually draws the attention of people towards the basic issues of world-view, beliefs, purpose of life and the inner dimensions of our being – motives, desires and emotions, etc. – since it is these factors that shape attitudes, drives (moral) actions, and provides the impetus and direction for societal change. Once the inner dimensions are affected positively, emotions and desires are channelled in the right direction, and Islamic values and morals are allowed to permeate into ones character, conduct and social systems, then a better person and a better society begins to develop.

2. *The Divine Principle of Change*

The Islamic sources also highlight that change in social life occurs according to the established Divine principle. This is summarsied in the following Quranic verse. A number of important points emerge from this verse which are discussed below:

> *"Verily, Allah does not change the condition of a people until they change that which is within themselves."*
>
> (ar-Rad 13: 11)

GOD IS THE CAUSE OF CHANGE

First, the verse states categorically that Allah is the cause of change, not people – change can only happen through Allah's Will, and humans are only the active agents of change. Islam proclaims that this universe is not a mechanical universe which is functioning by itself, rather Allah is ever involved in its administration, and the rise and fall of nations, or a positive or negative change in human condition occurs through His Will and Law – this however is dependent upon the moral, social and spiritual condition of a people. Allah will, by withholding His material and spiritual bounties, cause a negative change in peoples' social and physical environment as a consequence of their evil deeds and conduct. This is because, when human society goes against Divine laws and principles, it loses its natural norms and social balance. This inevitably results in social evils, and consequently the decadence and downfall of a society begins. In contrast, when sincere efforts for positive change are made, Allah showers His bounties on people by improving their social and material condition.

FREEDOM TO ACT

The Quranic verse suggests that people (groups and communities) possess free will, and hence they have the capacity to make a conscious choice regarding how they live and behave. They can choose to be either indifferent and let society steer itself – being tossed from one direction to another – or to exert efforts for positive social change (i.e. take responsibility for improving their social environment and establish a better social order), or even to drive society (due to their own corruption) towards its own decay and eventual ruin.

EFFORT AND STRUGGLE

The Quranic verse does not, however, imply that people should become passive or indifferent to their social condition as change is not within their power. On the contrary, it emphasises the point that people are only responsible and accountable for what they have power over. A people must strive to change and improve their personal and collective living, since they can choose to do this, before Allah will aid them in changing what they are powerless to accomplish. Put another way, it is people who are the main agents of change and who are responsible for constructing their own social environment and history – good or bad. Islam, thus, places the overall responsibility for a given social condition on the people themselves. People have a choice to make or mar their destiny. If they wish for a positive change, then they must first strive to raise their spirits, awaken their inherent human qualities, understand the underlying reasons and processes that are causing their deplorable social condition, and strive to bring about an improvement in their individual and collective living by adhering to the Islamic social code and striving against what is undesirable and unjust. Naturally, as more and more people strive together to improve themselves and their collective life, the social environment as a consequence, can be affected positively. In other words, a conscious decision has to be made for improving society. The current ills must be diagnosed thoroughly and a positive change planned and engineered.

UNIVERSAL MORAL LAWS

It appears that the dominant beliefs, values and moral condition of a people, which are important factors that mould social change from an Islamic perspective, have almost been completely overlooked from the sociological theories outlined earlier. Islam contends that there are certain universal moral laws, as there are physical laws, that determine the rise or fall of civilisations[8]. In fact, the Quran asserts that the decisive force in history, that is, the major force causing the rise and fall of societies, has been moral and not material or physical.

The line of argument from an Islamic perspective is as follows: if a people willingly choose to adhere to a moral code, founded on God's revealed guidance, in all aspects of their individual and social life, both private and public, then this choice will result in a better social order. This is because adherence to a moral code will direct people towards the fulfilment of their personal and social duties and responsibilities and promote a better order in relationships – at an inter-personal, inter-group, as well as inter-institutional levels. An order in relationships reduces inter-personal and social tensions and problems. As a result, personal and institutional energy becomes available for positive, creative and constructive work – for greater peace, prosperity, social development and societal progress. This view is supported by numerous verses of the Quran; two are quoted below:

"Has not the story reached them of those before them. The people of Noah, Ad, and Thamud; the people of Abraham, the men of Midian, and the cities overthrown. To them came their messengers with clear signs. It is not Allah who wrongs them, but they wrong their own souls."

(at-Tawba 9: 70)

"If the people of the towns had but believed and kept from evil ways, surely We would have opened out to them blessings from the sky and from the earth. But they rejected the truth and so We caused them to suffer for their misdeeds."

(al-Araf 7: 96)

In contrast to the above, corruption in faith and a slackness in adherence to a moral code will deteriorate the social order. This is because such choices and behaviour will inevitably give rise to tensions and conflicts in personal and group relationships. This in turn will lead to numerous behavioural and social problems and evils, thus, directing personal and institutional resources, attention and energy away from positive work. The greater and more rooted these problems become, the greater the energy and resources that will be required for addressing them. Continuing in this direction will, thus, inevitably lead a society towards its decay and ruin.

COLLECTIVE EFFORT

The Quranic verse under discussion also addresses people collectively. The Arabic word used in the text is *qaum*, which refers to a community or a collective body of people. This indicates that wider social change, positive or negative, is only possible with the support of the entire, or at least the majority of its population. If, for example, the majority of a people are good, moral and pious, then society on the whole cannot become corrupted due to the evil deeds of a few people. Similarly, if the majority of a people are immoral and corrupt, then the good and moral deeds of a few will not influence much positive change.

Therefore, for introducing wider positive social change, efforts must be collective, simply because unorganised individual efforts cannot influence change beyond a certain level. If, however, one's people, or community is not striving for a better society, as can commonly be the case, then individuals who are conscious of their mission in life must come together and launch a social movement for this purpose. This movement, through its work should awaken and involve the whole community and society for a better social environment.

> *"Let there arise from among you, a group, who would invite to all that is good, enjoining what is morally right, and forbidding what is unjust. They are the ones who would be successful."*
>
> (Ali-Imran 3: 104)

> *"And bind yourself firmly with those who call upon their Lord morning and evening, seeking only His attention. And let not your eyes pass beyond them seeking the pomp and glitter of this life ..."*
>
> (al-Kahf 18: 28)

To conclude, the Islamic view, on the phenomena of social change, contends that human nature and society are complex and dynamic. There are multiple factors and social issues that feed into the dynamics of change and which produce the emergent social conditions. A peoples' world-view, beliefs, values and the general level of moral conduct are the fundamental factors that determine how and why people initiate, direct, respond to, or adapt to change. A good and healthy society is nurtured by the adherence to a moral code by its members. Morals are in turn nurtured through a strong faith in God, and a strong faith is nourished through His regular worship and a sympathetic attitude towards humanity. This is why the noble Prophets of Allah inculcated faith in the hearts of their people, enjoined God's worship, righteous deeds, family, community, and justice so that better social conditions can be produced and sustained. Islam also indicates that positive change must be planned and engineered. There must be constant effort towards improving the social condition – in spiritual, moral, intellectual, social, economic and even material and technological terms.

An Overview of the Islamic Process of Social Change

Having discussed some conceptual issues regarding the phenomena of social change, we are now in a position to outline the process of change advocated by Islam. This section presents an overview of the framework and key elements and ingredients of the change process, based on Islamic guidance, for improving individual and social life. Chapters Six to Eleven of this book will look at some of these ideas in more detail.

It should be noted that the kind of change Islam aims to introduce in society is unique. The process it advocates to bring about this change is also unique. Thus, anyone who wishes to gain a deeper understanding of the Islamic process of social change must acquire a strong grasp of the following three points:

1. The objectives and vision of Islam. That is, have a clear picture of the kind of individuals, family and community life, society and the state Islam aims to build and for what purposes (Chapter Two).
2. The reasons why a change based on Islam is needed. That is, understand, from an Islamic perspective, the problems, contradictions and inconsistencies in the existing order, and the role Islam can play for changing and improving the state of affairs (Chapters Two–Five).
3. The change process itself, that is, how a change based on Islam can and should be brought about. In other words, the agents of change need a proper understanding of the framework and methodology for realising the Islamic vision in society (Chapters Six–Eleven).

Khurshid Ahmad, a leading personality in the international Islamic movement, offers the following major elements of a healthy social change based on Islam[9]:

a. Social change is not a result of totally pre-determined historical forces. The existence of a number of obstacles and constraints is a fact of life and history, but there is no historical determinism. Change has to be planned and engineered. Furthermore, this change should be purposive – that is, a movement towards the norm.
b. Man is the active agent of change. All other forces have been subordinated to him in his capacity as God's vicegerent (*khalifa*). Within the framework of the Divine arrangement for this

universe and its laws, it is man himself who is responsible for making or marring his destiny.

c. Change consists in environmental change and change within a man's heart and soul – his attitudes, his motivation, his commitment, his resolve to mobilise all that is within him and around him for the fulfilment of his objectives.
d. Life is a network of inter-relationships. Change means some disruption in some relationships somewhere, as there is a danger of change becoming an instrument of disequilibria within man and in society. Islamically-oriented social change involves the least friction and disequilibria, and enables a planned and co-ordinated movement from one state of equilibrium to a higher one, or from a state of disequilibria towards equilibrium. As such, change has to be balanced, gradual and evolutionary. Innovation is to be coupled with integration. It is the unique Islamic approach which leads to revolutionary changes through an evolutionary trajectory.

The above points stress upon a balanced approach, employment of wisdom, a planned and co-ordinated movement, and the introduction of change in society in a gradual manner. Further, efforts for change, according to Islam, should flow from a sincere desire to seek the good pleasure of Allah and to be successful in the life Hereafter *(Akhira)*. They should be motivated by a genuine concern and love for people, and be sincerely directed towards human welfare and dignity. Islam strongly condemns efforts that are motivated by evil intentions or hatred of anyone. Moreover, ends and means are both important. The means to advance certain changes in society need to be harmonised with the value-system of Islam. The Prophetic method of social change demonstrated that good and fair means were employed to achieve good ends. All these aspects are quite significant in understanding the Islamic process of social change.

The Direction of Change

A study of the following verse of the Glorious Quran will further assist in understanding the direction that an Islamic change must take.

"A Messenger, who teaches you the signs of Allah containing clear explanations, (so) that he may lead forth those who believe and do righteous deeds from the depths of darkness into the Light ..."

(at-Talaq 65: 11)

From a basic analysis of the above verse, the following points emerge:

1. The direction of change is from a society based on 'darkness' towards one that is based on Divine Light.

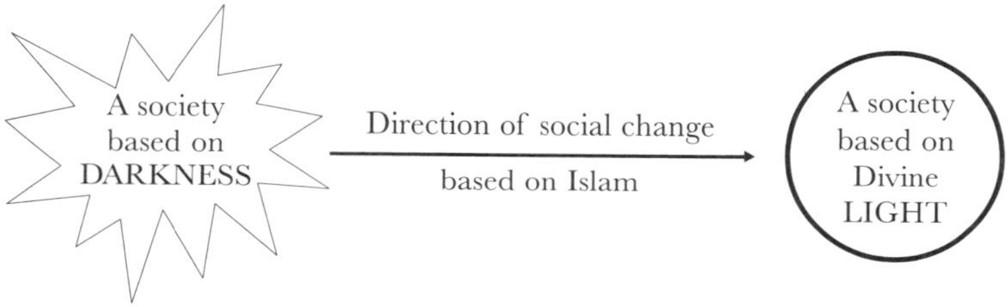

2. To be effective, agents of change need to comprehend the characteristics of a society based on 'darkness' and that based on Divine Light. This assists in producing a clear vision of the kind of change Islam desires in people and social systems. The word 'darkness', as used in the above verse, is significant and comprehensive in its meaning. It signifies disbelief, confusion, fear, immorality, social vices and injustices. Thus, according to Islam, any people or society that is characterised by these features is in a state of darkness, and Muslims, like the noble Prophets of Allah, have been ordained to work for changing such social conditions.
3. Furthermore, change agents require a full grasp of what actually leads people towards darkness and social crisis. This is important so that attitudes, practices, ways and means that can prevent this from happening can be promoted, nurtured and enjoined. This demands an insight into the Islamic sources of guidance, and a general analysis of history and of the contemporary social and global situation. In particular, an understanding of the dominant ideology and culture, and social and political structures that are entrenched in society becomes necessary. Also, the role played by key power brokers such as the media,

academics, business corporations, and political parties and institutions in society, and how they may work to maintain and promote their own interests need to be understood.

4. The Quranic verse also suggests that an understanding of the Islamic process to bring people and society out of a state of darkness into the Divine Light is crucial. This understanding must then be translated into socially relevant, strategic and organised actions for societal change. These of course will have to be carefully planned, executed and effectively managed.

Indeed, as the above discussion clearly indicates, influencing social change is a huge task. Simply basing a course of action on emotions, superficial analysis of circumstances and of current events, or on a few slogans only, cannot lead to positive change; on the contrary, this may result in more harm than good, which is something that conflicts with Islamic guidance.

Another important aspect of the Islamic process of social change, is that it follows a certain sequence. This sequence aids in bringing about a smooth change from one social condition to another, intending to cause least disturbances to individual and social life, and to allow Islamic ideas and values to be understood and rooted in behaviour and practices. This general sequence for moulding social and global change is outlined below:

Producing an Inner Change

The ultimate goal in life – the end of all endeavours – according to Islam, should be none other than to seek the good pleasure of Allah. This goal can only be attained through striving, sincerely and to the best of one's ability, to realise the Will of Allah in individual life, social life, society and the state, as shown by the noble Prophet Muhammad (peace and blessings of Allah be upon him) – that is, by striving to bring every aspect of life, both inner and outer dimensions of our being, into Allah's submission. In practical terms, this indicates that people must strive to establish Allah's chosen Way for humanity, Islam, in all affairs of human life, individual and collective, religious and secular. This is what the Islamic term *iqamat ad-Din* – or the establishment of Islam, signifies. Incidentally, the Quran stresses that whatever Allah has Willed for human beings, or has provided for our guidance, is in actual fact for our own good and benefit. In other words, striving to realise the Will of Allah in individual and social life is in the interest of all people.

Islamic work, thus, begins by exerting efforts to produce an inner change; building faith by inviting people, through appealing to their conscience, to believe in Allah as the sole Creator, Lord, Master and Sovereign of all that exists in the heavens and on earth, to commit themselves to live by His guidance, and strive sincerely to seek His good pleasure. The initial efforts, therefore, need to focus on clarifying for people the Islamic message and set of beliefs, and to root the love of Allah and humanity in their inner selves. These contribute in affecting a change in people's states of heart and mind, in perceptions, concerns, objectives, priorities and in attitudes.

Effecting Change in Family and Community Life

Simultaneously, efforts are directed towards cultivating Islamic values and morality, through the teachings and implementation of Islamic practices (for example, prayers, fasting, etc.), at the individual, family and community levels. This assists in creating mutual respect, tolerance, co-operation and affects a positive change in attitudes, behaviour and in inter-personal and inter-group relationships.

Effecting Socio-Political Change

As more people begin to respond to the call of living a moral, balanced and dignified life, efforts begin to be directed at influencing change in collective affairs; in the development and shaping of just and equitable social, economic and political policies. This includes the shaping of social institutions, the political economy and the state in general in line with the Islamic principles and values.

Effecting Change in Culture

All the above efforts contribute towards creating an Islamic culture. However, special attention is required for the gradual introduction and establishment of Islamic practices, traditions, values, principles and laws in social systems. These will enable the creation of a moral, caring and just culture and make the positive changes permanent in society.

Effecting a Global Change

Finally, a global programme for sharing Islam with humanity is initiated. This includes efforts for moulding and guiding global change; for playing a constructive role in world affairs.

The above steps indicate the general priority and order of the issues that need to be addressed by change agents for producing positive change. However, specific situations could demand this order of priority to be changed.

In short, the Islamic approach for societal change commences at the primary level by affecting an inner change in people as a priority; by introducing Islamic beliefs and world-view. Islam does not advocate a change through force, or using an approach that leads to more individual and social harm than benefit. On the contrary, Islam insists on building strong foundations, preparing people and creating healthy social conditions that are more amenable to the change ideas. Initially, therefore, Islam draws attention to the root cause of our personal and social problems as a change priority. It contends that the cause of our problems is not poverty, homelessness, unemployment, crime, lack of social services and so on. These are all symptoms. The root problem is more fundamental, and it stems from our perception of reality, our understanding of the meaning and purpose of life, and our attitudes towards life in general. In other words, the root problem arises from, and is related to, the crooked world-views and premises about life; premises that may directly conflict with the true universal reality, human nature and the high status conferred on human beings amongst God's creation.

Once Islam's solution to the root problem is understood and accepted, then people's perception of reality and social attitudes are gradually affected positively. As a result, the seeds to a better, moral and cohesive social life are sown. These seeds give rise to and promote desirable values that encourage moral behaviour, co-operation and the development of strong social relationships. From this process, a more natural, healthy, caring and just social system gradually evolves.

As a consequence, community life becomes revitalised, human potential is unleashed and a rich and vibrant culture evolves and begins to flourish.

An Islamic change is, thus, comprehensive, wide in scope, and is driven by a purposive and objective struggle; it stems from a clear vision and has a clear direction. It is a challenging task, a complex process, and it demands a multi-dimensional approach. This work brings people out of their small private worlds and engages them with societal powers for promoting and enjoining good and forbidding wrong.

> "*You are the best community raised for humanity, you enjoin good and forbid wrong, and you believe in Allah…*"
>
> (Ali-Imran 3: 110)

In conclusion then, Islam lays down a clear methodology for realising its vision in social life. This methodology provides a wider strategy for individual and social reform and change according to Islamic ideals. To gain a more clear understanding of what the Islamic methodology is aiming to propound, it may be helpful to consider an analogy of a journey to a specific destination. To successfully reach the destination, one will require a description of the route, an appropriate vehicle and also some essential resources for the journey. In a like manner, to attain the Islamic goal of establishing Islam (*iqamat ad-Din)*, the route that should be pursued by the agents of change is to bring their own life into the obedience of Allah (*ibada*), endeavour to awaken others from false consciousness and harmful influences and invite them to Allah's Way (*dawa*), and strive, in an organised and disciplined manner, against wrongs and injustices (*jihad*). In other words, the route for achieving the Islamic goal is *dawa* and *jihad*. The appropriate vehicle that has been strongly recommended by Islam for this purpose is to build an Islamic social movement (*jama'a*) – that is, the journey should be pursued collectively and in an organised and disciplined manner. Finally, the essential resources that are required for the journey include faith, God-consciousness, determination, moral behaviour, steadfastness, knowledge and understanding, fraternity, and power (intellectual and material).

The key components of the Islamic methodology for social change, thus, includes the building of a social movement (*jama'a*), *tarbiya* (nurturing of Islamic values and morals), *dawa*, *jihad* and *iqamat ad-Din*. *Dawa* helps in liberating individuals from the influences of false gods (see Chapter Six for a fuller discussion of the term 'false god'), whilst *jihad* directs efforts on addressing social injustices and towards liberating people from unjust systems, and the work of *iqamat ad-Din* focuses attention on improving the socio-political environment through establishing equitable and balanced systems of social life.

These key components and their application in a particular context are discussed in Part Two of this book (Chapters Six through to Eleven). Chapters Two through to Five of Part One elucidates the vision of Islam, the mission and purpose of the Muslim community and the challenges that secular-materialism poses for a change based on Islam. These provide a background and context for understanding the Islamic framework for guiding social change.

Notes

1. See Huntington, Samuel P., "Clash of Civilisations?", *Foreign Affairs*, Vol. 72, No. 3 (Summer 1993). For a more detailed discussion refer to: Esposito, John, L., *The Islamic Threat, Myth or Reality*, Oxford: Oxford University Press, 1992.
2. Gould, J. and Kolb, W. L. (eds), *Dictionary of the Social Sciences*, Free Press: New York, 1964.
3. See Sztompka, Piotr, *The Sociology of Social Change*, Oxford: Blackwell Publishers, 1993. There are numerous other books on this subject for example: Strasser, Hermann and Randall, Susan, C., *An Introduction to the Theories of Social Change*. London: Routledge & Kegan Paul, 1981.
4. See Fukuyama, Francis, *The End of History and the Last Man*, London: Hamish Hamilton Ltd, 1992.
5. Mawdudi, S.A., *The Islamic Movement Dynamics of Values Power and Change*, edited by K. Murad. Leicester: The Islamic Foundation, 1984. p. 47.
6. Giddens, Anthony, *Sociology*, 2nd edition, Oxford: Polity Press, 1993. p.656.
7. See Sztompka, Piotr, *The Sociology of Social Change*, Oxford: Blackwell Publishers, 1993.
8. See Mawdudi, S.A., *Nations Rise and Fall – Why?* Lahore: Islamic Publications, 1978.
9. Ahmad, Khurshid, "Economic Development in an Islamic Framework", in *Islamic Perspectives: Studies in Honour of Sayyid Abul A'la Mawdudi*, Leicester: The Islamic Foundation, 1979. p. 229.

CHAPTER II

Objectives and Vision

The first logical step in directing and moulding social change is to have a clear idea of what one wishes to accomplish. Thus, before embarking on efforts for shaping and improving society according to Islamic values and principles, it is essential to understand the objectives of Islam and have a clear vision of the kind of individuals and society Islam aims to build. The more clear a group of people are of these, the more effective they will be in their efforts for influencing positive change. In contrast, without a sound and clear vision, efforts and energies cannot remain focused, and may even bring more harm than benefit, or result in something other than what Islam intends.

A clear vision is produced from a deep understanding of Islamic beliefs, objectives and concepts. Questions such as the following need to be asked: what is the ultimate objective of Islam in human life? Is Islamic guidance limited to individual and personal matters only – confined to the private quarters of life – or does it also offer guidance for social and economic life? And more importantly, what kind of people and society would emerge from Islam? In addition, keeping our contemporary context in mind, questions such as the following also become important in clarifying the Islamic vision: Is Islam relevant today? Is it comprehensive enough to play a constructive role in present-day societies and the world, or is it an out-dated religion, limited in scope, rigid, and even incompatible with modern times? A thorough understanding of these questions is crucial for change agents since this will set the direction, underpin efforts for social change, and determine their effectiveness.

Unfortunately, due to the dominant influence of secular ideas in our world today, the very role of religion in society is generally questioned. Some people disapprove the idea of religion interfering, or having any say, in public affairs. Islam, however, opposes this view and maintains that religion should play a constructive role in the affairs of society. Islamic beliefs, values and principles cannot be restricted to the private quarters of life alone, but have to be pervasive in society. In fact, Islam offers a comprehensive vision of the kind of individuals, family and community life that should be built, together with the fundamental values that must be embedded in the social, economic and political processes and practices of society.

The Vision of Islam

Before depicting the vision of Islam, it is important to keep the following four points in mind. First, it should be clear that Islam does not aim to simply replace one form of government by another, or establish a society for Muslims only, or even make people believe in a few articles of faith, perform some acts of worship and follow a few rules and regulations. Neither does Islam only aim to change a corrupt and unjust political and economic system of a society and establish its own. Limiting the work of Islam to changing these few aspects would indicate a very mistaken and limited understanding of Islam.

> *"O believers enter into the fold of Islam completely and do not follow the footsteps of Satan, for he is indeed your open enemy."*
>
> (al-Baqara 2: 208)

Islam *has to be looked on as a whole and not in parts.* For instance, the political or the economic aspects cannot be studied in isolation from the moral and spiritual aspects and vice-versa. Islam is a complete and integrated code of life and its goal encompasses the whole of life, individual and society, this worldly and the Hereafter *(Akhira)*. All aspects of life are in fact interrelated and interdependent.

Second, faith, God-consciousness and Islamic morality underpin an Islamic way of life and are, therefore, prerequisites for a caring and just society. These cultivate compassion and social responsibility, balance in attitudes and practices, and a sense of mission and purpose. A deep conviction in Allah and a sense of accountability to Him, both contribute in enabling people to become upright and just. Without such a foundation in place, rules, regulations and laws on their own will not bring about a moral improvement in people. It is for this reason that an Islamic society is obliged to work for the spiritual, moral and intellectual development of its citizens. It must develop institutions and systems that will help in nurturing faith, morals, worship of Allah, and encourage educational development, social welfare and responsibility.

Third, the essential aim of Islam is to create a healthy, peaceful and dignified social environment that allows the development of human potential and ensures human well-being and progress. Islam stresses that people must be valued and their dignity, growth and development is considered to be far more important than any material consideration. As pointed out by Ibn al-Qayyim al-Jawziyya (691–750 CE)[1], the basis, or objectives, of the Islamic *Sharia* (law) is:

> "the basis of *Sharia* is wisdom and welfare of the people in this world as well as the Hereafter. This welfare lies in complete justice, mercy, well-being and wisdom. Anything that departs from justice to oppression, from mercy to harshness, from welfare to misery, and from wisdom to folly, has nothing to do with the *Sharia*".

Finally, since Islam is a universal message and way of life, it incorporates both permanent features and mechanisms for adapting to change. This can be verified from the following four major elements that make up Islam:

1. *Aqida*: a set of universal beliefs. These includes the basic articles of faith which expound the Islamic world-view. A world-view is a set of beliefs and premises that enables individuals to make sense of themselves and the world around them. It, thus, acts as a lens through which one perceives the physical and the social world. The Islamic message, '*Let there be no god but Allah and Muhammad is Allah's Messenger*', presents the Islamic world-view in a condensed form. This puts forth the vision of Islam, the mission of the Muslim people, defines the ultimate Islamic objective, its doctrine, and offers a meaning and purpose to life. (See Chapter Six, for a detailed exposition of the Islamic world-view).
2. *Akhlaq*: A set of universal values, morals and principles that aim to establish better relations between people and produce balance and harmony in human conduct and affairs.

3. *Manhaj*: A framework of programmes, priorities, methods and processes for developing and guiding all affairs of life according to Islamic values. This includes Allah's commands (*ahkam*) as to what is prohibited (*haram*), what is made obligatory (*fard*), what is important and recommended (*mandub)*, what is disliked (*makruh*) and what is permissible *(mubah)*.
4. *Usul al-fiqh* and *Fiqh*: A methodology and framework of rules and mechanisms, rooted in Islamic sources of guidance, for addressing personal and societal problems and for adapting to new situations.

These four elements assist in nurturing better people and in shaping social attitudes and practices in a positive way. They also anchor the Islamic way of life on a permanent set of values and principles. This makes Islam resilient and universal. At the same time, mechanisms are provided that enable Islam to adjust to the local, cultural, technological, economic and societal changes taking place in time and space. This makes it flexible, dynamic and relevant in the context of changing times.

With this background we now move onto elucidating the Islamic vision. The vision of Islam is rooted on, and produced from certain fundamental Islamic objectives and concepts. Taken together, these present a picture of the kind of people and society Islam aims to build. They highlight the Islamic view of human nature and provide the values, principles and priorities for shaping social life. The most important of these objectives and concepts that help in describing the vision of Islam are the following:

1. God's guidance as the Supreme Authority
2. Vicegerency of human beings (*khilafa*)
3. Justice
4. Disciplined political power and consultation (*shura*)
5. Social Responsibility

These are all powerful and comprehensive concepts that are unique to Islam. They are expounded upon below, and as the discussion will highlight, they give rise to the following values and objectives for individual and social life: God's guidance as the final authority in all affairs, worship of Allah, morality, freedom of choice, the preservation of human dignity, education, equality in status, rights and opportunities for all citizens, stewardship of the earth's resources, justice, consultation at all levels of collective affairs, the protection of society from elitism and abuse of power, and a positive contribution to society and social welfare. Each concept brings forth certain particular fundamental dimensions of Islam and taken together they will help in depicting the Islamic vision.

God's Guidance as the Supreme Authority

This concept forms the foundation of an Islamic society. Islam argues that this universe and all that it contains has been created by Allah Alone. After creating the universe, He did not go to rest (contrary to what is stated in the Bible – Genesis Chapter 2 verse 3) or leave it to run by itself. On the contrary, Allah is ever involved in its administration and management. He has set laws that regulate and provide order between the various elements and systems of the universe and He directs and controls their motion and determines their destiny. Regarding human life, Allah, through His Infinite Mercy has set moral laws to institute order and establish peace, harmony and co-operation in people's individual and collective affairs, so that they can live a life of fulfilment and develop their potential to the full. To explain and clarify these moral laws and to provide further guidance and values for all aspects of human affairs, He sent to all people, at different times, His Prophets and Messengers. All the noble Prophets of Allah brought the same message. This message declared that *Allah Alone is the Law giver and His guidance alone should shape individual and collective life and steer society.* Muslims are those who surrender themselves to Him Alone, and who strive to bring their collective life in accordance with His revealed guidance, for the sole objective of winning His good pleasure and attaining Paradise (*Jannah*) in the life Hereafter *(Akhira)*.

> *"He alone is the Sovereign of the Heavens and the Earth ..."*
>
> (az-Zukhruf 43: 84)

> *"The authority rests with none but Allah. He commands you not to surrender to any one save Him. That is the right way (of life)."*
>
> (Yusuf 12: 40)

Thus, Absolute Sovereignty (*uluhiyya*), that is, the Supreme Authority in society, or the absolute right to command, to define beliefs, laws, rights and wrongs, belongs only to Allah. It does not belong to anyone other than Allah; neither king, president, parliament, dictators or even to all the people of a society. However, political sovereignty – a limited, relative sovereignty (*mulk*), or the power to enforce the law, which has been derived from God's guidance, can be vested in an Islamic government, which in turn is accountable to the citizens[2]. In the light of this, the concept of the Sovereignty of God has spiritual, social and political implications. It identifies God as the sole source of guidance and offers a framework for guiding all the affairs of individual and social life.

The significance of this concept becomes apparent when one compares it to the opposing ideas and practices that are rooted in contemporary societies. Due to the dominance of secular ideas, present-day societies have shunned God from collective affairs. Sovereignty has either been attributed to the citizens, in theory at least, or it has been assumed by some elite groups. God's guidance is not allowed to influence or interfere in the processes of policy formulation or any public matter. Such ideas and practices are not, however, new, and can also be found to exist in many past civilisations such as the early Mesopotamian civilisations (for example, Sumerian, Elamite, and Babylonian), and Assyrian, Greek, Roman, Indian, and Chinese civilisations that were founded on similar, secular-materialistic ideas. According to Mawdudi[3], these civilisations may not have rejected Allah completely, but either due to ignorance or confusion, or even deliberately, squeezed Him out of collective human affairs by dividing Godhead into two main parts: one part they attributed partially or wholly to the real God (Divine Godhead) and the other (Sovereign Godhead) they claimed for themselves (again partially or wholly).

1. *Divine Godhead.* This part was assigned to the real God. He was more or less acknowledged as the Creator and Lord of the

heavens and the earth. Some idea of His worship also existed. However, in cases, even in this part of Godhead they associated certain spirits, angels, stars and planets and so on as partners or associates to the real God.

2. *Sovereign Godhead*. This part was assumed by, or attributed to some king, royal family, elite group, or to some other kind of political authority.

Put simply, a split of Godhead practically implied that Allah was not acknowledged as the sovereign in collective human affairs. Rather kings, or the ruling class of society were considered as sovereigns, having absolute power and authority over the lives of other people. And this power, as history indicates, was mostly abused and led to great wrongs. God's guidance had no say or involvement in the important domain of social life. Such ideas and practices directly conflict with the Islamic concept of God's Sovereignty because they inevitably, as will be argued later on, lead to the dominance of man over man, or class over class, to abuse of power, social injustice and human indignity. (See Chapter Six for further details on the social and political implications of this concept).

> *"Verily, associating partners with Allah (leads to) the greatest oppression."*
> (Luqman 31: 13)

In short, therefore, from an Islamic perspective, *Allah Alone is the Sovereign, the Lord and Master of all that exists in the heavens and on Earth* – in the physical universe as well as in human affairs. And this concept directly conflicts with the secular-materialistic thought that is prevalent in the world today.

Vicegerency of Human Beings (Khilafa)

How does Islam view human beings? This is an important question since civilisations are principally forged by their particular view of human nature. Are human beings an extension of the natural environment or are they different and have a special status in the universe? Are they like other animals on earth, devoid of any sense of good and bad, or do they have an innate moral consciousness?

According to Islam, human beings are different from the animal kingdom and have a special status in the universe. They did not come into the world through accident, but through design and purpose. They are made up of a body and spirit, and, hence, have both material and spiritual needs and aspirations. Both of these need to be nourished and a balance maintained between them. Moreover, human beings have been created by Allah as His *Khalifa,* i.e. vicegerents, trustees and representatives on earth.

> *"Behold, your Lord said to the angels: I will create a khalifa (vicegerent) on earth..."*
>
> (al-Baqara 2: 30)

The concept of vicegerency is comprehensive in its meaning and implications. It provides a number of values for shaping social life and it also clarifies the status of human beings and their position in relation to the rest of creation. Furthermore, this concept defines the nature of human relationship with Allah, with each other and also with the natural environment. The following important points emerge for the concept of human vicegerency:

NOBLE IDENTITY AND HUMAN DIGNITY

From an Islamic perspective, human beings have been created with an exalted and noble nature and they have the most dignified position in relation to the rest of Allah's creation. Islam teaches that Allah breathed His Spirit into human beings:

> *"And your Lord said to the angels: 'I am about to create a mortal out of sounding clay, out of dark slime transmuted; and when I have formed him fully and breathed into him of My Spirit, fall down before him in prostration'."*
>
> (al-Hijr 15: 28–9)

This spirit of Allah gives human beings a noble identity, it equips them with creative powers and gives them the ability to distinguish between good and evil. Human beings are, thus, not considered as animals, things or commodities. They have been given a dignified position and, therefore, their honour and dignity are sacred and must be nurtured through the social environment and culture, and protected by the law.

> "*We have indeed created humans in the best of moulds (stature).*"
>
> (at-Tin 95: 4)

> "*And indeed We have honoured the children of Adam...*"
>
> (al-Isra 17: 70)

FREEDOM OF CHOICE

Being vicegerents implies that humans should worship and obey Allah alone and turn to Him for guidance in all affairs of life, since He Alone is their Creator, Lord and Master. However, Allah has granted freedom in this matter – either individuals acknowledge Him as their Lord and Master and live a life according to His Will, or they follow themselves or someone else. On the Day of Judgement, all people will be held accountable by Allah for how they exercised their freedom and fulfilled their role of vicegerency during their time-span on earth. Human beings are, therefore, not evil, corrupt or sinful by nature. Nevertheless, they are imbued with a moral consciousness, and have a capacity to be good or bad, moral or immoral, and each person's ultimate destiny in the Hereafter *(Akhira)* is dependent upon how he/she chooses to live. Thus, no one can be coerced into believing in anything or following any particular way of life.

> "*And give glad tidings to those who believe and do righteous deeds, that for them will be gardens through which rivers flow (Paradise)...*"
>
> (al-Baqara 2: 25)

> "*Let there be no compulsion in religion (matters of faith and way of life). Truth stands out clear from error...*"
>
> (al-Baqara 2: 256)

Islam's civilisational framework is bounded in the principles of pluralism. In other words, Islam acknowledges other views including different faith communities in its system of society. Muslims may not agree with these, but they must accept them and show respect and tolerance. In relation to this, Islam gives special attention to the rights of non-Muslims in an Islamic society. The Prophet Muhammad (peace and blessings of Allah be upon him) stated:

> *"Beware, whoever is cruel and hard on such people (i.e. the non-Muslims living in an Islamic society) or curtails their rights, or burdens them more than they can endure, or realises anything from them against their free-will, I shall myself be a complainant against him on the Day of Judgement"*
>
> (Abu Daud)

EQUALITY IN STATUS AND RIGHTS

Since Allah Alone is the Master and all people are His vicegerents in the same way, this implies that men and women, black and white, are Allah's equal servants. No one is superior or inferior except on the basis of piety (*taqwa*) and character. Individuals and groups should not, therefore, seek to become masters of each other. This powerful concept cuts at the roots of oppression and racial discrimination. It suggests that no individual, group or nation should attempt to dominate or impose their will on others. Relationships should be based on trust, equity and justice. This also implies that men and women, both being vicegerents of Allah, are made from the same substance and have the same purpose in life. They should, therefore, not attempt to dominate or wrong each other – but rather co-operate and support each other towards fulfilling their role of vicegerency.

> *"O people, We have created you from a male and female, and made you into nations and tribes, so that you may know each other (not that you may despise each other). Surely the most honoured among you is the one who is most Godly..."*
>
> (al-Hujurat 49: 13)

> *"No one is superior to another except in point of faith and piety. All people are descended from Adam and Adam was made of clay."*
>
> (*Hadith* quoted by Ibn Kathir)

STEWARDSHIP OF THE EARTH

Furthermore, Allah is the real Owner and Master of the earth and not human beings. We are only its trustees and stewards. This establishes our relationship with the natural environment. We can utilise and consume the earth's resources for our benefit and harness the forces of nature, but at the same time we must exercise care and responsibility; extravagance, wastage or destruction of natural resources must be avoided. God has set a physical balance in the universe and this must not be disturbed.

> "*See you not (O people) that Allah has subjected for you whatsoever is in the heavens and on earth, and has completed and perfected His Grace upon you...*"
>
> (Luqman 31: 20)

> "*The world is green and beautiful and Allah has appointed you as His stewards over it. He sees how you acquit yourselves...*"
>
> (Muslim)

> "*....Eat and drink, but waste not by indulging in excesses; surely, Allah does not approve of the intemperate.*"
>
> (al-Araf 7: 31)

Justice

After the concept of God's Sovereignty and *Khilafa* (vicegerency), justice is the next important ingredient in forming the Islamic vision for human society. Justice is essential and crucial for social order and for a healthy and peaceful society. It is, therefore, the basic aim of the Islamic *Sharia*[4]. Islam stresses that justice should not only be rooted in the systems of society but should also flow through all levels of social life; in all relationships and dealings; from the family to the state. The Glorious Quran places much emphasis on this as is shown by the following verses:

> "*O Believers, stand firm for justice, be witnesses for Allah, even though it be against yourselves, or your parents and kinsmen, or whether the person be rich or poor.*"
>
> (an-Nisa 4: 135)

> "*Allah commands justice and kindness...*"
>
> (an-Nahl 16: 90)

> "*....And do not let hatred of any people dissuade you from dealing justly. Deal justly for that is closer to God-consciousness.*"
>
> (al-Maida 5: 8)

> "*And We sent our Messengers with clear signs, and sent down with them the Book and the Balance, so that people may establish justice.*"
>
> (al-Hadid 57: 25)

> "*surely Allah enjoins justice, and the doing of good and giving to kinsfolk, and He forbids all indecency, wrongs and rebellion.*"
>
> (an-Nahl 16: 90)

Islam enjoins that all citizens, irrespective of their race, language, colour or religious beliefs, be treated fairly and justly. Everyone must be guaranteed equal rights and opportunities for their basic needs of food, housing, education, health, transport and employment. No one should be discriminated against, wronged, abused or exploited in any way. Further, Islamic law gives full freedom of association, expression, criticism, belief and movement to all citizens – this is of course within the confines of preserving dignity, public safety and social peace. To ensure justice, the Islamic *Sharia* gives special attention to protecting the following basic human rights: *protection of people's faith, honour, life, property, family and intellect.* For example, Islamic guidance has prescribed particular kinds of punishments, some of which are very severe indeed so as to act as a deterrent, for murder (to protect life), theft and robbery (to protect property and wealth), adultery and fornication (to protect the family), slander (to protect honour) and intoxicants (to protect the intellect). In short, all human beings have a God-given right to justice and an Islamic state is commanded by the Quran to ensure that this is rooted in all social and economic policies and fully implemented.

Disciplined Political Power and Consultation (Shura)

Islam stresses that the concept of the Sovereignty of Allah, vicegerency and justice, should flow through all levels of human life; individual, family, community and society. All people are equal before Allah, no one can, therefore, impose their will on anyone else – only God's guidance should rule and direct the affairs of society. So in respect to this, how is power and authority exercised in an Islamic society? This is an important question and further discussion on it will help bring forward some important ideas that form part of the vision of Islam.

First, in order to administer justice and establish a peaceful society, political power is essential in the eyes of Islam. In fact, Islam obligates its followers to engage with power and enjoins social and political participation. It sees power as a moral and civilising force if it is utilised in accordance with God's law. A just social order cannot be established in society through sermons and preaching only. In addition, it requires political power to reform, improve and change social life. Power, submitted to Allah, can glue society together by improving and regulating inter-personal and inter-institutional relations. Regarding this matter, the Quran states:

> *'Surely We sent our Messengers with clear signs, and sent down with them the Book and the Balance, so that people may conduct themselves with equity; and We revealed iron, wherein is mighty power and (many) uses for humankind."*
>
> (al-Hadid 57: 25)

Iron, in the above verse according to scholars[5] symbolises political power. It is an essential requisite for building a system of governance through which social order can be maintained and society shaped for the common good. The Quran, thus, links power with faith and Islamic mission. However, Islam has transformed the nature, scope and processes of power, by placing it in an active moral framework[6]. Power is not something to be shunned, rather acquired, brought under God, and utilised for realising His Will in society and state; for reforming and transforming society and the state for the common good. In this respect, the Prophet Muhammad (peace and blessings of Allah be upon him) said:

> *"Allah brings to an end through the state what He does not eradicate with the Quran."*
>
> (*Hadith* quoted in Tafsir Ibn Kathir)

This saying suggests that wrong doings that are not eradicated through sermons and preaching of the Glorious Quran require the power of the state to eradicate them. It implies that the link between faith and power must be strengthened. This is because society moves along the direction set by those who hold the reigns of power, good or bad. Thus, as stated by Mawdudi[7]: 'those who have surrendered themselves to God should strive to wrest control of all centres of power and authority from those in rebellion against God, *not for themselves* but to bring them under God'.

Second, Islam does not recognise any form of religious, political or social elitism or hierarchy; this is to prevent power accumulating in a few hands. There is no clergy and priesthood in Islam since these lead to the formation of religious hierarchies. There is also no political elitism. In order to protect society from political corruption and dictatorship, Islam enjoins that leaders should be chosen by the people and no sensible and morally upright person can be barred from holding political office. The Prophet Muhammad (peace and blessings of Allah be upon him) stated:

> *"I enjoin you to fear Allah, and to hear and obey (your leaders) even if it be an Abyssinian slave."*
>
> (Abu-Dawud)

This saying indicates that political office is open to all Muslims, from any tribe or nation, whether they are rich or poor, and eligibility is based on God-consciousness (*taqwa*), knowledge and leadership skills.

Third, political power must be employed with wisdom and disciplined within the Islamic framework; subjected to God. Regarding the use of political power the Quran states:

> *"They are those who if We give them power in the land, they establish Prayer, and (the system of) Alms, and enjoin the good and forbid the wrong."*
>
> (al-Hajj 22: 40–1)

This verse provides a framework for utilising and channelling societal power. It suggests that power is not an objective in itself, but is a means for realising the Islamic vision in society. Power should, therefore, be controlled and guided within the framework of Islam; it should be tempered with justice so that it becomes a source of blessings and not an instrument of oppression and aggression. Moreover, the verse refers to power being given to the Muslim community as a whole and not an elite group or a class amongst them. This implies that power belongs to the whole community and should, therefore, not be allowed to accumulate in the hands of a few, or be abused in any way. Rather it should be employed to improve collective affairs; to fulfil the mission of Islam. Furthermore, political power should primarily be directed towards achieving the following:

1. Power should be used to establish the collective worship of Allah (*salat*, *sawm*, *zakat*, etc.). Acts of worship bring people together, provide common purpose and values, and assist in their spiritual and moral development. They further facilitate the social interaction of people and produce a more cohesive, caring and informed community life. All this contributes towards a greater social development of society and encourages the social and political participation of everyone.
2. To strive for establishing social systems that implement *shura* (consultation), and provide justice, social welfare, promote and enjoin good (*maruf*), and forbid all forms of wrong and social injustices that may exist in society.

Finally, Islam enjoins consultation (*shura*) at all levels of individual and social life: in the affairs of the family, community, society and the state. This concept further guides power towards realising the social benefit.

> *"Those who hearken to their Lord, and establish prayer; and who (conduct) their affairs by mutual consultation; who spend out of what We bestow on them ..."*
>
> (ash-Shura 42: 38)

Hasan[8] has defined *shura* as: '*a collective endeavour for seeking an objective truth*'. In it, the participants are involved in a free exchange of ideas and views to arrive at a decision or a solution to a problem, basing them on the Quran and Sunna. The discussion is not based on blind support of a person, group or party, but is rather intended to bring benefit and justice to society.

As mentioned previously, an Islamic form of government is bound within the framework provided by God's revealed guidance. No one can go against this framework. Second, consultation with the people is binding on a government because decisions cannot be imposed on anyone. In Islam, those who are affected by decisions or policies have a right to be consulted. Mechanisms must, therefore, exist for all people, including minority groups, to freely express their views on matters that affect them directly or indirectly, or to have a say in the general affairs of society. Differences of language, nationality, or status should not influence either who should participate or whose views should be accepted.

Furthermore, the system of government incorporates a leader (*amir*), who is chosen by the people, and a *shura* body (comprised of all citizens, or a body of representatives). The *shura* debates issues, addresses societal problems and is involved in the formulation of new legislation that is based on a framework provided by the Islamic guidance. The *shura* also gives consultation to the executive, which is led by the leader. In turn, leaders must consult the people on all collective matters, and are accountable to the *shura* body and to all the citizens of society. Mechanisms must, therefore, exist to allow people to participate in the decision-making process and to hold the leadership accountable for its work and actions.

Thus, *shura*, if implemented effectively, can ensure that an elite group does not emerge in society and take control of or dominate the political and social agenda. This is because social and political discussions and consultation (*shura*) on major issues should take place within designated public spaces or community forums (for example, in the mosques, which are the centre of community life and where everyone is obliged to attend), and all community members, or their representatives, have the opportunity to make their input in setting the social agendas. Further, leaders are obliged to formulate social policies and legislation based upon, and derived from the framework provided by the Quran and Sunna of the noble Prophet and not on their personal feelings, opinions, interests or fancies.

Social Responsibility

Social responsibility arises out of the above Islamic concepts. However, particular mention of it is made here because of its importance in understanding the vision of Islam for society.

Faith in Allah nurtures mercy and compassion towards fellow human beings. Furthermore, Islamic guidance brings about a balance between the rights of individuals and their duties and responsibilities towards others. It attempts to create a culture that binds individuals and families into a community so that a natural infra-structure for providing support and help to those in need is developed. Moreover, Islamic teachings stress on good treatment towards neighbours, while orphans, widows, the poor and needy should all be helped and cared for.

> *"It is not righteousness that you turn your faces towards the East or the West. But it is righteousness to believe in Allah, the Last Day, the angels, the Book, and the Messengers. And to spend your wealth out of love of Allah, for your kin, orphans, for the needy, for the wayfarer, for those who ask..."*
> (al-Baqara 2: 177)

Social care and welfare is, thus, not solely a duty of the government, but of all community members, particularly the well-to-do ones. Individuals are encouraged to sacrifice, give up, and spend their wealth on the poor and needy of society, expecting reward only from Allah. It is this sense of duty and spirit of sacrifice which Islam nurtures, that actually helps in removing self-centredness and covetousness and promotes compassion, care, co-operation and harmony between people.

> *"...As for him who gives (in charity), is God-conscious and believes in the truth – We will indeed make smooth for him the path towards ease. But as for him who is niggardly, behaves as if he is self-sufficient and denies the truth – We will indeed make smooth for him the path towards hardship."*
> (al-Layl 92: 5–10)

To sum up, the above discussion attempted to expound certain Islamic concepts that provide the Islamic vision for individuals and society. These concepts highlight the importance Islam gives to human dignity, social justice and disciplined power for shaping a healthy social environment and culture. These are all essential for nurturing a better person and society, and for developing human potential. The Glorious Quran contends that if its cardinal values and principles are understood, accepted and applied, both in personal and collective life, they will give rise to a rich and vibrant culture that will promote justice, compassion, protect human dignity and encourage positive progress.

The Quran further proclaims that success in the life Hereafter *(Akhira)* is dependent upon the sincere efforts a person exerts for a better individual and social life. This is what '*jihad*' or striving is all about. In Islamic terminology, *jihad* is not simply a holy war, or about fighting with the infidels only, as is commonly propagated. In contrast, it is about sincerely struggling against evil from within and without; it is about engaging with power; involving people in strategic and organised actions for eradicating oppression, corruption and social evil from society and the world; for liberating people from the domination of corrupt powers and nations, and for the betterment of their personal and social life.

> "*Do you think you can enter Paradise without Allah establishing who among you do Jihad and who are steadfast (in this work).*"
>
> (Ali-Imran 3: 142)

> "*Those who believe and suffer exile (Hijra) and strive (Jihad) in the way of Allah with their goods and their persons, have the highest rank in the sight of Allah. They are the people who are successful.*"
>
> (at-Tawba 9: 20)

Thus, working to realise the vision of Islam in individual life, social life, society, the state and in the world (i.e. building a civilised and just world), is part and parcel of being a Muslim – in fact a duty on every Muslim (see Chapter Three for a more detailed discussion on this point).

Islam and Contemporary Society

Having outlined the vision of Islam, this section moves on to explore whether or not this vision is relevant to our contemporary world.

Islam, being a universal guidance from God, is not considered by Muslims to be subject to the constraints of time and space. Rather, for each age, its guidance and principles remain fresh and relevant. It is as applicable, practical and needed today as it was in the past. History points to the fact that Islam guided humanity to emerge from the dark ages into an era of both human and material progress, and it still has the potential to do this today. As an example, the Prophet Muhammad (peace and blessings of Allah be upon him) actually established a society based on Islamic principles and values in his life-time. In this society people became more God-conscious, were morally transformed, spiritually elevated and social relations, based on tolerance and forgiveness, greatly improved between them. Mosques, schools, hospitals, societal infra-structure, and fair trade were established, and social welfare and care for all people became ingrained into social life. Furthermore, effective social and economic systems were developed and implemented. These, on the one hand, provided social and economic support and welfare to people, and on the other, kept a check on injustices and social evils. Due to these positive changes, great progress was made in trade, commerce, and in science and technology. New frontiers of knowledge were reached and political thought was developed and civilised. In short, a new and just civilisation was built, which stretched from Morocco to Indonesia, where on the whole, for over one thousand years people's lives, property and honour were protected by law[9].

Muslims established a brilliant Islamic civilisation in Spain that sustained itself for more than 700 years (714–1492 CE). During the height of its glory, this civilisation, having all the fascination of a rich culture, including its arts, sciences, politics, social organisation and technical superiority, attracted many students from all over Europe to its universities. In addition, merchants, tourists, and even religious and political leaders from neighbouring countries paid frequent visits to observe and learn. This interaction contributed significantly to the material, scientific and technological development and progress of the West. The following quotes from historians support this view:

> "For although there is not a single aspect of European growth in which the decisive influence of the Islamic civilisation is not traceable, nowhere is it so clear and momentous as in the genesis of that power which constitutes the permanent distinctive force of the modern world and the supreme source of its victory – natural science and scientific spirit."[10]

> "Muslim Spain wrote one of the brightest chapters in the intellectual history of medieval Europe...the Arabic-speaking peoples were the main bearers of the torch of culture and civilisation throughout the world. Moreover they were the medium through which ancient science and philosophy were recovered, supplemented and transmitted in such a way as to make possible the renaissance of Western Europe."[11]

Unfortunately, the West mostly took the material and technological aspects of the Islamic civilisation and developed them further. It totally failed to see the other aspects; most importantly the roots that gave rise to such progress – that of Islamic faith and culture. Although the world has moved on since that time, nevertheless, human nature and the roots to social problems and crises remain basically the same. Thus, Islam has the potential to re-construct a better, tolerant and just world today as it did in the past. It offers a moral, equitable and an effective framework for addressing our present day problems and issues. For example, Islamic values, principles and teachings for private and public life can assist in a balanced human and social development which is very much in need today. Islam's emphasis on religious tolerance, racial equality, social responsibility, strong families and communities, social and political participation and on collective morality, can all aid in improving social life dramatically. In addition, Islam's concern with establishing consultative processes for decision making at all levels, on minimal government intervention in local affairs, accountability of those in public positions, a usury free economic system, and its strong stance against economic and social injustices, are just some of the things it offers for creating a better and just society and world.

Today, however, many people do not view Islam in a positive manner. Indeed, due to misinformation and ignorance, some people are even horrified to imagine a society that would emerge from Islam. This is because Islam is mostly perceived in the West as 'evil' and 'barbaric', and Muslims in general are portrayed as 'oppressors of women', 'militant' and 'fanatic'. As a result of such perceptions, the present global resurgence of Islam has become a matter of grave concern for some political thinkers and governments, both in the East and West.

It has become common for some groups of people in the West (and what appears to be a very organised lobby) to see Muslims behind every tragedy and mishap in the world. They suspect Muslims to be behind most hijacking, bombing or terrorist activity. And it is such people who strive to portray ordinary Muslims around the world as 'fundamentalists' in a derogatory sense, 'terrorist', and 'uncultured', and exert efforts to create misconceptions amongst the general public about Islam. To achieve this, individual cases are deliberately highly generalised. In addition, efforts are made to constantly ridicule Islamic modes of worship, its family and social code and its laws. Even the Prophet Muhammad (peace and blessings of Allah be upon him), and everything else in history that is associated with Islam – the great Muslim heroes, Islamic history and traditions, arts and architecture – are all painted in a gloomy and cynical way. In short, whenever the word 'Islam' is mentioned to some people, it arouses fear and even disgust.

These perceptions and attitudes are not new, they are actually deep-rooted in history. Owing to the centuries long conflict between Islam and Christianity, and also due to the colonisation of Muslim countries by the West, various fears and prejudices about Islam and the Muslims evolved and were contrived. Amir Ali, in his book: *A Short History of Saracens*, quotes Denison Ross admitting:

> "For many centuries the acquaintance which the majority of Europeans possessed of Muhammadanism was based entirely on distorted reports... What was good in Muhammadanism was entirely ignored, and what was not good in the eyes of Europe was exaggerated or misinterpreted."[11]

Muslims have been referred to by various derogatory labels by Christian missionaries, Western institutions and writers since Medieval times – infidels, pagans, heathens and antichrists, to list but a few. Since that period, Islam has either been demonised and portrayed as the most cruel and barbaric of all religions, or is presented as an out-dated system of life. These images have filtered through from generation to generation, and are today generally accepted in the West to depict Islam and the Muslim people.

This gap in understanding considerably widened from the beginning of the 20th century as Muslims struggled to gain their independence from Western colonialism and imperialism. This gave rise to an organised propaganda by the colonialists to distort and misrepresent the value-system of Islam and its way of life. They aimed to weaken the Muslims by shattering their confidence in Islam, and hence their ideological and political unity. All such efforts have, therefore, contributed to the present day fears and misrepresentations of Islam and the Muslims in the West. Moreover, today, the West's perception of Islam is shaped, not only by historical events as have been outlined above, but also to suit its global political and economic interests.

This discussion should not suggest that the Muslims are wholly free from blame. In actual fact, some of the present day misconceptions that exist about Islam are being reinforced by the conduct of some Muslims themselves. Due to an ignorance of the Islamic social code, extremist tendencies and immoderate attitudes are being manifested by certain groups and these are continuing to reinforce the negative and dismal images of Islam. Having said so, it is still fair to affirm that the true nature of Islam, or of any other faith for that matter, cannot be understood if people view it with perceptions that are founded on assumptions, misinformation and historical prejudices. It is only right that opinions should be based on facts and correct information, and not on assumptions or myths. Thus, for a better understanding, an objective assessment of Islam and the social and political circumstances surrounding the Muslim people should be made. For Muslims, a societal change based on Islam is not about converting people and obtaining more followers, or about colonisation or conquering lands. Neither is it about oppressing people of other faiths or establishing a state run by dictators and kings. Nor is it about oppressing women, or enforcing cruel punishments. On the contrary, and as pointed out earlier, Islam is a thought, a hope, a vision, a concern and an integrated and coherent system of life that aims to cultivate human qualities and build a just and civilised society and world.

It is appropriate at this point to clarify a few important questions that are generally raised regarding the present day image of Islam as seen in Muslims countries. For example: Why are the benefits and blessings of Islam that are claimed not seen in many Muslim countries? If Islam is much against corruption and for establishing social justice, then why are there some societies where Muslims are in a majority, found to be corrupt?

These are important questions which demand answers. However, the answers actually require a lengthy discussion that would perhaps need a completely separate book. The rise, and the eventual downfall of the Muslim world-community needs to be analysed to bring out the reasons for its present state of backwardness and social and economic problems. How Islam was gradually squeezed out of public affairs and reduced to a few rituals, and how Muslim societies eventually became secular, both these issues require detailed discussion. Further, how the West, with its secular ideas and values, rose to become a world-power and began to colonise Muslim countries, and subsequently imposed its materialistic culture, secular institutions, legal systems and life-styles on Muslim peoples is also a major factor which led to the present situation of the Muslims. Moreover, the continuous interference of the West in some Muslim countries, even to this day, has resulted in numerous economic and political problems. It is also common knowledge that many dictators and rulers in certain Muslims countries have either been imposed or are sustained by the support of the West. Further, the poverty, backwardness and economic dependency of Muslim countries on other nations is to some extent, due to the huge interest re-payments they have to make on loans borrowed from the World Bank, IMF and other such bodies. A detailed discussion and analysis of all these factors are, therefore, beyond the scope of this book. However, in Chapter Three we shall examine a little more closely the situation of the Muslim world-community and throw light on some of these issues.

Islam, as a system of life cannot, therefore, be evaluated or judged either through the values that are deeply held by the West, or by the conduct of Muslims, since their actions and practices may not necessarily conform to the Islamic teachings. Undoubtedly, secular ideas and materialistic values, together with Western systems of education, economics and politics have dominated many Muslim societies since the period of colonisation. Therefore, Islam, as a system of life has not really directed Muslim societies for a long period of time. Because of this, ignorance of Islam has taken hold, and there has definitely been negligence in the observance of its teachings and social principles in individual and collective affairs.

In view of this, today one may come across many good and pious Muslims, as well as those who fail in their Islamic duties. There are even some Muslims who commit acts that are opposed to Islamic teachings and principles. Moreover, adherence to Islam is mainly limited to personal and spiritual aspects; it has generally been discarded from the social, economic and political affairs of Muslim societies, and subsequently the full blessings of Islam are not manifested. Also, throughout history, one can certainly find cases where Muslims, both as individuals and communities, have deviated and strayed from Islam to varying degrees. For example, some leaders have strayed so far that they even became oppressors and unjust rulers. However, as history bears testimony, such leaders have always been condemned by scholars and Muslims in general whenever such wrong deeds have taken place.[13]

Islam and Other World Religions

Some people may also argue that it is not only Islam that wishes for a better society and world, rather all the great religions of the world hope for the same. So what's so special about Islam?

First, many other great religions of the world, without doubt, have a similar vision for social life as Islam. They also share many of the Islamic values. This is why it is important for people of different faiths, who wish to build a better society and world to co-operate, support and work together for promoting positive change. In fact, Islam invites and encourages people of goodwill to join hands and work for the common good. Second, Islam is not a religion founded by the Prophet Muhammad (peace and blessings of Allah be upon him). Rather, it is the pure and unadulterated message of God brought by all the noble Prophets: Adam, Noah, Abraham, Moses, David, and Jesus (peace and blessings of Allah be upon them all) to name but a few. What Islam contends that after the great Prophets, people through the passage of time or due to wrong influences, either lost God's message, confused it, or it was diluted, distorted or even corrupted. Also, sometimes this message and way of life was reduced to a few rituals and rites, or even blended in with alien notions, polytheistic and secular ideas and practices that were not in line with its pure teachings. As a consequence, this led to certain religious and social practices that became the seeds of communal schism.

> "*(Their doom is) because Allah sent down the Book in truth but those who seek causes of dispute in the Book are in a schism far (from the purpose).*"
> (al-Baqara 2: 176)

This is why Allah, through His infinite Mercy, sent His noble Prophets and Messengers again and again to all communities, in order to bring them back to His chosen Way – Islam – which would lead to a better personal and social life. According to Islam, the Prophet

Muhammad was the last of God's Messengers. Islam claims that the Divine guidance revealed through the Prophet Muhammad preserves and encompasses all guidance sent by Allah for humans over the ages in its pristine purity – nothing lost and nothing added to it by human interpolation.

Though there are many common features found between Islam and other great religions, nevertheless, one difference stands out clearly. Islam views life in its totality and offers guidance for both personal and social life – for the religious and the secular, the private and the public. Other religions, in contrast, primarily focus on, and attend to, individuals or the private sphere alone. This is why their Scriptures and Holy Books do not contain any, or at most very little guidance on public conduct – on the political, legal, environmental, and economic aspects of society. If any guidance does exist, it is very limited in scope or is vague, and hence ineffectual for guiding social policy formulation. Their main emphasis is on inculcating love of God and love for humanity, imbibing moral values, good behaviour and spiritual elevation. On a collective level, however, guidance is limited to acts of worship, ceremonies, and some rules for a few aspects of life such as family life, being charitable, and assisting other people.

Such personal acts will no doubt help nurture pious people in their private sphere of life. However, pious people on their own will not necessarily lead to a better and just society. The collective systems of life, for example, the family, economics, politics, the law, etc., must also be founded on ethical principles. Therefore, due to a lack of comprehensive guidance, the followers of other religions are usually either found to shun political power, or if acquired, they on the whole adopt secular approaches to address social and economic issues and problems. As an example, Christianity, particularly after the conversion of the Roman Emperor Constantine, worked within the context of Roman systems of society and did not establish a society with its own peculiar political and economic systems derived from the Bible. The practice of Christianity mainly remained a personal and private concern – religious values did not impact much on political and economic life. Even today, in Britain, and in other European countries for that matter, the church and parliament work side-by-side, almost independent of each other, and only interact on very few issues and concerns.

In contrast, Islam at the outset worked to establish a culture and civilisation based on its own value-system. This civilisation remained at the height of its glory for more than a thousand years. This was possible because Islam provides a comprehensive framework and guidance containing principles for personal and collective life. It does not discriminate or distinguish between the material and spiritual, or between the political and religious aspects, but encompasses them all. Other religions undoubtedly desire a better social life, however, they do not offer a clear vision of such a society, or any comprehensive guidance on how to go about achieving it. Islam, in contrast, offers a clear vision and goes a step further and actually provides a methodology to guide thought and action for shaping social life.

Notes

1. Jawziyya, Ibn al-Qayyim al-, *I'lam al-Muwaqqi'in* in Vol. 3, p. 14, quoted by M.U. Chapra, in *Islam and the Economic Challenge*, Leicester: The Islamic Foundation and the International Institute of Islamic Thought, 1992. p.1.
2. Khir, Bustami Muhammad, 'Concept of Sovereignty in Contemporary Islamic Movements', in *Encounters, Journal of Inter-Cultural Perspectives*, Vol 1., No. 1, March 1995. Leicester: The Islamic Foundation, pp. 5–38.
3. See Mawdudi, S. A., *The Meaning of the Quran*, Vol. 1, al-Fatihah – al-Baqara: 291, also see al-An'am: 52, Lahore: Islamic Publications Ltd. 8th Edition, 1986.
4. See Murad, Khurram, *Shari'ah The Way of Justice*, Leicester: The Islamic Foundation, 1981.
5. See the commentary of Chapter Hadid by Mawdudi, S. A., *The Meaning of the Quran*, Lahore: Islamic Publications (Pvt) Ltd., 1987.
6. See the introduction to Mawdudi, S.A., *The Islamic Movement Dynamics of Values Power and Change*, edited by K. Murad. Leicester: The Islamic Foundation, 1984. pp. 48–53.
7. Ibid, p.11.
8. Hasan, A., *The Doctrine of Ijma' in Islam*, Islamabad: Islamic Research Institute, 1984. p.27.
9. See Mawdudi, S.A., *The Process of Islamic revolution*, Lahore: Islamic Publications Ltd., 7th edition, 1979.
10. Briffault, Robert, *The Making of Humanity*, Lahore: Islamic Book Foundation, 1980. p. 190.
11. Hitti, Philip, K., *History of the Arabs*, London: Macmillian and Co., 5th Edition, 1951. p. 557.
12. Quoted in Ahmad, Khurshid, *Islam and the West*, Lahore: Islamic Publications (PVT) Limited, 5th edition, 1986. p.22 (from Amir Ali, *A Short History of Saracens*, p.487).
13. Abdur Rauf, *Illustrated History of Islam*, Lahore: Ferozsons (Pvt.) Ltd, 1994.

CHAPTER III

Purpose and Mission

The Mission of God's Messengers

This Chapter takes a closer look at the Muslim world-community (*Umma*) particularly in terms of its purpose for realising the vision of Islam and its responsibilities towards humanity. It is hoped that what follows will place the current state of the Muslim world-community in its proper historical context, provide a sense of purpose and mission to Islamic workers, and indicate a way forward for the Muslim world-community in playing a constructive role in civilisational development.

Islam maintains that the Prophets and Messengers of Allah were sent with a noble and challenging mission. Their mission was not limited to building places of worship, or just to teaching people some aspects of faith and ethical principles, or even to sanctioning a few do's and don'ts, though these were all part of their noble work. More importantly, they came to realise the vision of Islam in society and history. The Quran, as shown below, mentions that all true Prophets of Allah brought the same Divine message and worked for the same purpose.

> *"Say, we believe in Allah, and the revelation sent to us, and to Abraham, Ishmael, Isaac, Jacob and the tribes, and that given to Moses and Jesus, and that given to all the Prophets from their Lord; we make no distinction between them and we submit to Allah (as Muslims)."*
>
> (al-Baqara 2: 136)

> *"The same way of life He has established for you as that which He enjoined on Noah – that which We have sent by inspiration to you – And that which We enjoined on Abraham, Moses, and Jesus: namely that you establish the way of life, and make no divisions therein: ..."*
>
> (ash-Shura 42: 13)

"It is Allah who sent His Messenger, with Guidance and the True Way, so that he may make it prevail over all other (corrupt) ways."

(as-Saff 61: 9)

Thus, the noble Prophets of Allah did not limit their work to preaching and delivering sermons only, since through such efforts individual and social life is not usually much affected. On the contrary, they actively invited their people to God's message, organised them into a God-conscious community and engaged with them in efforts to challenge corrupt powers and to reconstruct and reshape social life in accordance with God's revealed guidance.

According to Islam, the Prophet Muhammad (peace and blessings of Allah be upon him) was the last and final Messenger of Allah for humanity who brought a universal message:

"And We have not sent you but as a Mercy for all the worlds."

(al-Anbiya 21: 107)

After the noble Prophet, the Quran instructs the Muslim world-community to continue striving for building a just social order, locally and globally. The Muslim world-community is not formed of people who belong to a particular nation nor is it a religious cult. Rather it is a global community, drawing together people from all nations and races – transcending the boundaries of colour and language – all connected together into one brotherhood and sisterhood by the Islamic faith and vision. According to the Quran, this community exists for a particular purpose and mission – to live in accordance with Islamic principles and strive for building a better world for all people.

"You are the best community raised for humanity, you enjoin good and forbid wrong and you believe in Allah ..."

(Ali-Imran 3: 110)

"Thus We have made you into a world-community (Umma), justly balanced so that you be witnesses unto humanity and the Messenger a witness over you."

(al-Baqara 2: 143)

"*One who supports an oppressor and strengthens him knowing that he is an oppressor, has gone out of Islam* (i.e. he no longer remains a Muslim)."

(Mishkat)

As there is no priesthood or clergy in Islam, every Muslim is equally accountable to Allah for actively working to discharge his/her duties. Put another way, the Islamic mission is not only to be pursued by scholars, the pious and the pure, nor is it only for Islamic institutions or to be performed by paid workers – but all Muslims must be involved in this noble work.

"*O Believers, bow down and prostrate yourselves, and worship your Lord, and do good that you may prosper. And strive for Allah with the endeavour which is His right. He has chosen you and has not laid upon you in religion any hardship; the faith of your father Abraham (is yours). He has named you Muslims of old times and in this (Scripture) that the Messenger may be a witness over you, and that you may be witnesses over humanity. So establish worship, pay the poor-due, and hold fast to Allah. He is your Protector. A blessed Patron and a blessed Helper.*"

(al-Hajj 22: 77–8)

The Quran emphasises that the mission of Islam must be taken seriously and has to be carried out in all circumstances and under all personal and social conditions; whether Muslims live in a minority or majority situation; whether poor or affluent. There is no room for complacency or indifference towards social ills. A need to change and improve society should arise not only because Muslims are threatened, wronged or oppressed, but a call for change is explicit in the *Shahada* (Islamic declaration of faith). Faith demands that efforts for eradicating injustices and corruption from society should be continuous and ceaseless, as well as being intentional and planned.

"*If you do not (what you have been enjoined) there will be corruption in the Earth and tremendous disorder.*"

(al-Anfal 8: 73)

"*Enjoin good and forbid wrong, otherwise you will pray to Allah and He will not listen to your prayers ...*"

(Ibn Maja)

The Rise and Fall of the Muslim World-Community

Historical records indicate that the early Muslims were conscientious of their mission in life. The first generation of Muslims, in particular, established a strong attachment with God's revealed Book, the Glorious Quran, from which they drew their inspiration, motivation and guidance. Their personal and collective life became moulded according to Islamic guidance, and this enabled them to become exemplary witnesses of Islam before humanity. They were organised into a social movement by the Prophet Muhammad (peace and blessings of Allah be upon him) himself, through which they collectively strove, earnestly and vigorously, for a just social order. Within a short period (610–32 CE), under the leadership of the noble Prophet, their efforts gave rise to a better and organised social life. Through the help of Almighty God, they managed to transform their people and collective affairs[1]. The Islamic movement then turned its attention towards liberating humanity from tyrants and emperors who had dominated the world at that time, and had enslaved other nations under their oppressive rule.

After the death of the noble Prophet, his faithful Companions continued with the mission that he had started. They moved forward to liberate people from tyranny and oppression and established a social and political order based on God's guidance in neighbouring lands. Gradually, but within a few decades, such a way of life was firmly established in many parts of the globe: the Middle East, a great part of North Africa, Central Asia, the Indian sub-continent, in the far East, and parts of Europe, predominately in Spain. In all these areas, people of different races and religious beliefs lived together in social peace and harmony. Dignity was safeguarded by law and people were free to travel, live, trade and set up businesses anywhere in Islamic lands. Moreover, these societies made great progress in science, technology, mathematics, medicine, sociology, jurisprudence, and other branches of human knowledge. Great inventions and discoveries were also made. In fact, several modern day technological and social developments have actually evolved from the contributions made by a number of great Muslim scholars during this early period of Muslim history[2]. Regarding this, W. M. Watt writes:

"We sometimes belittle the extent and importance of the Islamic influence in our heritage, and sometime[s] overlook it altogether... We must acknowledge our indebtedness to the full. To try to cover it over and deny it is a mark of false pride."[3]

Scholars[4] point to many factors that played an important role in the rapid spread of Islam during these early centuries. The most important factors were religious, spiritual, moral and humanitarian factors. Also, factors such as the dynamism and resilience which are inherent in Islam, together with effective and sincere leadership, intellectual freedom and the tolerance shown to other religious beliefs and ways of life, all played a crucial role in the rapid spread of Islam.

Although these early Muslim societies did have their lapses, with occasional domestic conflicts, infighting, corruption in leadership, and the moral degeneration of some quarters of society, on the whole, social harmony, fair treatment, community spirit, social welfare and prosperity prevailed. Whenever the Muslims deviated, or slacked in upholding Islamic values, the great and honourable Muslim revivalists[5] did their utmost to bring them back to the right path and to keep Islam in its original form and purity. The great Muslim revivalists include amongst many: Umar bin Abdul Aziz (d. 719 CE), Imam al-Ghazali (1058–1111 CE), Imam Ibn Taimiyya (1262–1327 CE), Shaikh Ahmed of Sirhind (1563–1624 CE) and Shah Waliullah (1703–63 CE). However, it was not until the 11th century CE, that serious political stagnation, corruption and sectarian divisions began to take hold, and Muslims entered a phase of decadence and decay.

From 1095 CE till 1270 CE the Muslim world faced external aggression. During this period, eight bloody battles, known as the Crusades, were fought between Muslims and Christians from the West. These confrontations not only created calamities and suffering in social life, but also cultivated deep hatred of Islam in Europe. Many myths, fears and misunderstandings about Islam were contrived and vigorously propagated by the Christian crusaders. The 13th to the 15th centuries CE were also particularly marked as periods of great turmoil and the decline of Muslim societies. The violent attack by the Tartars from the East (1258 CE), and the slaughter and expulsion of Muslims from Spain by 1492 CE, both sent shock waves throughout the Muslim world. The Tartars devastated buildings and the infra-structure of society including mosques, schools, centres of learning and libraries. In Spain, hundreds of thousands of Muslims were either massacred or expelled, and thousands of mosques were destroyed or converted into churches.

Although these external attacks contributed to the weakening of the Muslim world-community, nevertheless, due to the tremendous efforts of Muslim scholars and revivalists, it managed to remain intact. At this junction, Islam captured the imagination of the Ottoman Turks (1299 CE), who not only took Islam further into Europe, but also provided a leadership to the Muslim world-community. However, despite these short intervals of upsurge, the Muslims did not fully recover. The political and social circumstances in the ensuing period created a feeling of apathy and pessimism amongst Muslims in general. Their will and confidence in themselves was weakened and moral degeneration took hold of society. By this period deep divisions and moral decadence had become widespread. Intellectual exertion and scientific progress was paralysed, and Muslim scholars were led to concentrate their work on re-discovering and preserving what was left, and they were, thus, restricted in their originality.

Finally, another onslaught from the West started around the late 18th century CE. This was quite ferocious and eventually resulted in the colonisation of Muslim lands and the devastation of their cultural and intellectual heritage during the 18th and 19th centuries CE. The West slowly introduced and promoted secularisation and its cultural values and way of life into Muslims societies. Immense efforts were made to remove Muslims from their faith, social code and culture. Many misconceptions were contrived so that Muslims would lose confidence in Islam. Further, a 'divide and rule' policy was employed to turn Muslims against each other, which shattered the little political unity that remained amongst them. Finally, the complete abandoning of Islamic political (Ottoman Rule) unity took place in 1924.

An understanding of the kind of plans and efforts that were made to secularise Muslims and other communities can be gained from the following statement made by Lord Macaulay, who was responsible for introducing a new education system during British rule in India:

> "We must do our best to form a class who may be interpreters between us and the millions whom we govern – a class of persons, Indian in blood and colour, but English in taste, in opinions, in morals, and in intellect"[6]

This statement says a great deal. Secular education and social systems were promoted and established so that through these the ideas and culture of the new generation, their thought and practice, could all be moulded and shaped, making them subservient to the colonial masters. It was hoped that through this process, the West could continue to govern indirectly and control these lands with little difficulty. Such manipulations and control tactics led to the present day situation of the Muslim world-community. Today, although Islam still exists in all Muslim countries, however, by and large, its following is limited to personal and spiritual aspects. It has been squeezed out of the political, economic and social areas of life and has been replaced by secular systems. This is why the full blessings of Islam in Muslim societies are not manifested.

What is the state of Muslim communities today? How far are they living by Islam? What is their global situation? Today there are just over one billion Muslims in the world. This approximates to about one-fifth of humanity. Muslims are found among all races and nations of the earth. In addition, there are over 50 countries where Muslims are in a majority. Together they cover more land than people of any other faith – spanning a large part of the world; from Morocco on the one hand to Indonesia on the other. It may also be interesting to note that some of these countries are geographically located at strategic points of the globe, and they possess many important resources, for example, oil, minerals, etc. The major trading and shipping routes also pass through Muslim countries.

Yet, despite all this, the Muslim *Umma*, particularly during the last three centuries, has faced numerous problems – from internal conflicts and colonisation, to oppression and the enforcement of kings and dictators in their lands. Today, they find themselves powerless, helpless and having little or no control over their own future in their own countries. They are economically and militarily dependent on the powerful nations of the West. Even after winning independence, most

Muslim countries are not free; they are caught in the complexities of a global world order and a global economy, over which they have no say or influence. In fact, Western political models of government and economic systems based on usury are operating in many Muslim countries, and cultural imperialism continues through satellite communication systems and the Internet. Some Muslims, at the time of writing, are being persecuted even in their own lands such as in Kashmir, Palestine, Kosova and Bosnia to name a few. That global community which was supposed to lead humanity out of darkness and injustice towards the Light of Islam has, itself, lost direction and is immersed in ignorance and social problems.

Today, Muslims generally have little contact with the basic sources of Islam. The Quran, a life-giving and a revolutionary Book of guidance, is recited by a vast majority of Muslims, but without them understanding it. Due to this attitude towards God's revealed guidance, ignorance has become deep-seated and Islam has been reduced to a few rituals and practices. Many Muslims today are holding onto whatever they understand to be Islam. There are some who concentrate on the spiritual aspects, whilst others focus their efforts on acts of worship and some do's and don'ts. Still a few have ignored the spiritual aspects and focus their attention solely on political issues. Such attitudes have led to extremism on the one hand, and apologetic attitudes on the other. Furthermore, several anti-Islamic practices such as saint worship, priesthood, superstitious beliefs, astrology, myths and legends, tribalism, nationalism, sectarian conflicts, and other social diseases can be found amongst Muslim communities around the world. All these afflictions have resulted in countless social weaknesses. These include passivity, indifference, blind-following, lack of tolerance and as a result many have become devoid of a spirit to stand against injustices and immorality.

The Reasons for the Downfall of the Muslim World-Community

Here, it is worth pausing and reflecting over the reasons for the downfall of the Muslim world-community. Those who aspire to re-build the Muslim *Umma* as a vehicle for positive global change should understand the factors responsible for its degeneration.

Was the downfall due to political corruption followed by intellectual stagnation? Was it because of an abandoning of the Islamic mission, a weakening of faith, or internal political and sectarian conflicts? Was it lack of spirituality, or due to a blind following (*taqlid*) of the practices of early Muslims by latter day Muslims? Were external factors the cause of their downfall? Was it because Islam had become out-dated and inadequate to address the new social and economic phenomena? Or could it be a combination of these reasons and factors? Scholars have differed in their views and give various reasons for the downfall of the Muslim world-community. However, they are all unanimous in stating categorically that it was not Islam, but Muslims themselves who were responsible for their own downfall. Muslim revivalists and thinkers of the 20th century, for example, Hasan Al-Banna (1906–49), Mawdudi (1903–79), Sayyid Qutb (1906–66), Khurram Murad (1932–96), Khurshid Ahmad and Rachid Gannouchi suggest a number of factors as the primary causes[7] for the current miserable state of affairs. These factors can be grouped into the following categories:

Lack of Capacity to Cope with the Rapid Expansion of Islam

As Islam spread rapidly in different directions, to new lands, the small city-state in Medina became an almost global-state within a short period. This change constituted serious administrative and management challenges. The government was suddenly overwhelmed with an increase in population whose needs had to be catered for. The emerging needs and social issues and problems related to administration, security, training and education, and the development of an infra-structure in these new areas all demanded a great deal of attention and resources. This new situation, therefore, created a strain on the central administration and called for rapid changes in, and a re-structuring of the polity. In other words, it demanded innovation in the political and administration structures and processes. Also, to maintain the unity and cohesion of the Muslim *Umma*, the new situation necessitated the involvement of people from the surrounding areas that had become part of the Islamic land at the centre of power.

Although, the pious leaders at the time did their best to cope with this complex situation, however, innovation and development in these areas was slow. The state, thus, did not develop the capacity, and the appropriate structures and mechanisms to respond rapidly and effectively to the increasing complexity of the newly arising situation, and to monitor and co-ordinate its administrative functions. Also, the involvement of people from far away Muslim lands at the centre of power was over-looked, and, hence, these people were not fully accommodated into the consultative and decision-making processes. As a consequence, dissension, tensions and numerous other social problems slowly began to grow, and finally these developed into a widespread rebellion that surfaced towards the end of Caliph Uthman's period of administration. In fact, the rebellion and uprising initially started in response to the inadequacy of the state to monitor governors in remote provinces, some of whom were involved in corrupt acts and luxurious life-styles. They were further fuelled by the frustration of many people who felt that they were not being heard and involved in the decision-making processes. Thus, a lack of capacity and inadequate political structures to cope with the rapid expansion of Islam were amongst the important factors that led to internal conflicts.[8]

Internal Decadence

The above weakness also contributed to some degree to the shift from an Islamic form of leadership to a kingship based on tribalism. Political decadence was, thus, sown with the emergence of hereditary rulers. This gave rise to increasing bureaucratisation and the centralisation of power and administration in the hands of elite groups and dynasties, and the Muslim *Umma* gradually began to split into a federation of tribes. Such events led to numerous internal tensions and inter-tribal conflicts, for example, between the Umayyad's and Abbasid's, and between the religious scholars and political rulers, and these occupied so much energy that gradually the Muslims collectively, although not on an individual or small group level, abandoned the Islamic mission. In other words, less emphasis was given to *dawa* and *jihad*, and more energy was either spent on power struggles, or on meaningless religious debates and the exaggeration of sectarian differences. These internal divisions weakened the Muslims, kept them away from playing a leading role in world affairs, and made them inward-looking and passive to social evils. Internal issues occupied them so much that they failed to address the external challenges. Even some activists and scholars began to fall into a number of camps: literalists, rationalists and spiritualists, and differences amongst them led to numerous religious divisions.

Imitative Attitude **(Taqlid)** *and Inflexibility*

Another major factor that prevented the Muslim *Umma* from playing a constructive role in world affairs was a reluctance by latter day Muslim scholars to exercise their judgement in the light of Islamic guidance to address problems and deal with new situations (*ijtihad*). This reluctance was due to a number of reasons, including the political leadership's loss of commitment to Islam in general, a lack of confidence amongst the scholars themselves for this task, and genuine fears of diluting Islam and even deviation from its fundamentals. Whatever the reasons, the *Umma* '*lost its ability to give birth to new ideas, to update its institutions, and to produce the planning, means, and policies essential to further progress at the civilisational level*'[9]. This reduced the practice of Islam to small spheres of life and gradually retreated it to the confines of the mosques.

External Aggression

Finally, external aggression further weakened the Muslim *Umma*. Major aggressions came from the Christian Crusades, the massacre and expulsion of Muslims from Spain, the invasion and devastation of Muslim lands and heritage by the Tartars, and the rise of the Western colonialism. Also, intellectual and cultural influences came mainly from Greek philosophy, scholastic rationalism, mystical ideas from Christian, Hindu and Buddhist philosophies, together with secular-materialistic thought and culture arising from the West. Although great Muslim scholars and revivalists did their utmost to address these challenges, they lacked however the full backing of the Muslim world-community due to its internal conflicts and divisions.

All these factors led to intellectual stagnation and sectarian tensions within Muslims. Coupled with the resulting ignorance of Islam that had grown amongst the masses, numerous religious innovations evolved and these became a source for further religious schism and social fragmentation. Many of these innovations conflicted with the pure message of Islam and, hence, Muslims began to deviate from God's way. Muslim revivalists and scholars of the recent past, for example, Mawdudi, Hasan Al-Banna and Sayyid Qutb, emphasise the point that the downfall and the continuing humiliation of the Muslim world-community is primarily due to a simple fact: Muslims have collectively neglected their prime responsibility – that of becoming witnesses of Islam before humanity. They state that the problems started when Muslims became so engrossed and occupied with their internal affairs, and this made them oblivious to their primary duty and mission – that of bringing humanity out of darkness into the Divine Light. In Spain[10], for example, after the first few generations of Muslims who took Islam there, the later generation became so engrossed with building magnificent mosques, castles and the like, addressing their internal political differences, or so preoccupied with their internal issues, that they became totally oblivious to their mission in life. This attitude prevented Islam from moving forward, and as a result Muslims failed to win the hearts of the people of Spain for Islam.

Muslims' Response to Their Situation

Given this background, one may wonder what may be the way out of this predicament. Muslim scholars and leaders have been responding to this complex situation and the challenges they face from secular-materialism in numerous ways. Most of these approaches can be broadly categorised into the following three, each having multiple sub-approaches[11]:

Traditionalists

Muslims belonging to this category advocate the preservation and protection of Islamic traditions that have been inherited from earlier generations – including knowledge, opinions, experience and cultural practices – whilst at the same time they encourage a rejection of almost everything that has originated from the West – including ideas, social systems, culture, language, etc. Although the contributions made by traditionalists towards safeguarding the Muslims from wrong influences and in reviving certain aspects of Islam have been enormous, their approach, however, has placed undue emphasis on the imitation of earlier Muslims (*taqlid*) and on the religious aspects of Islam. As a result, this has led to a tendency to divorce Islam from social life, and a frustration of efforts to address contemporary challenges. These have, in turn, created an inability to keep abreast of the times and hence, for Muslims to play any constructive role in world affairs.

Modernists

These scholars, at the other extreme, adopt an apologetic approach and attempt to use a rational interpretation of Islam to align and conform its ideas and practices to the modern day world. However, this is done at the cost of undermining the role and importance of tradition in Islamic history and culture. Some, in the name of 'modernisation', even advocated a close imitation of 'Westernisation' and secularism, in particular the adoption of the West's political and economic models, as a viable way out of the present-day backwardness and poverty that Muslims are facing. Nevertheless, due to the apologetic nature of this approach and its inherent compromising with un-Islamic ideas, it has gained very little support from Muslims in general.

Revivalists

This approach has avoided the pitfalls of the above two. Scholars belonging to this category, for example, Mawdudi and Hasan Al-Banna, launched Islamic movements for reviving Islam in its entirety in human life. These movements aim to shape individuals and systems of life according to Islamic values, principles, traditions and ideals so that a better, moral and just social life comes into being. Proponents advocating such an approach draw their inspiration and guidance directly from the Quran and Sunna, whilst at the same time attempting to learn from the rich Islamic tradition and history. They are striving to re-establish the link between faith and power which the influence of secularism has broken, so that power can be brought under the Islamic moral framework and be utilised for establishing justice in the world. They encourage Muslim intellectuals to gain insights into the contemporary dominant ideologies and systems of life in order to challenge them in the light of Islamic guidance, as well as to learn from anything that may be good and beneficial. The programme of work of the Islamic movements is multi-pronged, it includes[14]:

1. To examine thoroughly the roots of contemporary human problems, social conditions and power structures in light of Islamic guidance. To use the insights gained to develop and articulate a powerful critique of the ways of life based on Godlessness and secular-materialism. Also to use these insights to formulate effective and pragmatic strategies for advancing Islamic change.
2. To awaken a people from false consciousness (i.e. from a false understanding of reality), invite them to Islam, and assist them in grasping the relevance and importance of the Islamic message and mission. Furthermore, to build God-conscious and good people through shaping their ideas, moral view-points, attitudes and conduct into the Islamic mould.
3. To reconstruct family and social life according to Islamic ideals.
4. To introduce radical reforms in government so that it enjoins worship of Allah and morality, promotes good, protects human dignity, ensures justice to all citizens, and keeps a check on corruption and social evil.
5. To liberate Muslim nations from all kinds of imperialism, colonisation, and secular-materialistic influences.
6. To build wider co-operation and solidarity between Muslim nations.
7. To initiate a programme for sharing Islam with humanity at large and play a constructive role in world affairs.

Future Prospects

Today, for the Muslim *Umma* all is not doom and gloom. This present age, despite all the problems, is both an exciting and a challenging one. It is exciting because Muslims, after centuries of subjugation, degeneration and decay, are once again rising and responding to the call of Islam. Due to the tremendous efforts exerted by the Islamic revivalist movements, there is a renewed missionary zeal and aspiration for shaping their individual and collective affairs according to Islamic ideals. As a result, the gloomy trends and attitudes discussed earlier are disappearing fast. Islam is re-emerging as a potent global force. Today, we find Islamic movement leaders either holding key positions in a number of countries, or as the leading opposition figures in others.

Many young Muslims are recognising the fact that all other ideologies and systems of life have brought them nothing but misery and injustice, and the same to humanity at large. After Islam has been presented to them in a fresh way, many find its message and system of life appealing, logical, powerful, inspiring and motivating, and it has greatly raised their hopes. They are realising that it was not Islam that caused their downfall and their present miserable situation, but rather their own attitudes towards it, and their abandoning of the Islamic mission. They are returning to Islam in large numbers, beginning to assert their faith and are desirous of becoming emissaries of Islam and agents of change wherever they may be.

However, at the moment such people are not sufficiently organised and lack resources. But still, due to the powerful appeal of the Islamic message, they have the potential to awaken the rest of the Muslim world-community from its slumber, and humanity in general from the harms of secular-materialism. If this is achieved, then one can imagine the tremendous positive and creative energy that can be released to re-shape and re-build our world. No doubt, Islam, as in the past, has the potential to shape world events once again; it could again enable those who take up its mission to rise and make an unimaginable impact on society, achieve social and economic development, attain global leadership, and assist in building a just and civilised world.

Looking at contemporary Muslim societies, one sees that more and more young people are becoming involved in Islamic activities and programmes. There are talks and discussions, in homes, mosques, public gatherings, study circles, schools and universities, and even in the corridors of power, about bringing Islam back to their personal and social lives; about changing Godless societies and establishing justice for all people. This awakening of the Muslim global community, is very inspiring for anyone who wishes to see peace, social harmony and justice prevail in society. The enthusiasm of young people and the desire they have for Islam is very encouraging and motivating. In fact, a whole new generation, from Morocco to Indonesia, is being prepared and enthused with a sense of Islamic mission.

Numerous research institutions, professional bodies and think-tanks have been established by Islamic movements to take up the intellectual challenges that are presented, both from secular-materialism and for re-constructing the social life of Muslims in their respective countries. In addition, social welfare organisations, media bodies and publication houses, labour and professional unions, Islamic banks, schools, colleges and universities, health care centres, community development and support groups, women, youth and student organisations, and so on, are being established all over the Muslim world to face and address challenges at the practical level. Furthermore, organised efforts are being made for sharing Islam with humanity and for playing a constructive role in world affairs.

To sum up, the above discussion has attempted to elucidate the purpose and mission of the Muslim people. It stresses that Muslims have a responsibility towards humanity and, thus, they cannot remain indifferent to the affairs of society and the world. They must organise themselves and strive to realise the vision of Islam in society and the world. They must endeavour together to rid social life of injustices and wrong practices, and work for the moral, social and economic development of society and the world.

Notes:

1. See Mawdudi, S.A., *The Process of Islamic Revolution*, Lahore: Islamic Publications Ltd, 7th Edition, 1979.
2. See Ahmed, K. Jamil, *Heritage of Islam*, Lahore: Ferozsons, 1956.
3. Watt, W.M., *The Influence of Islam in Medieval Europe*, Edinburgh University Press, 1972. pp. 1–2.
4. See for example Nadwi, Abul Hasan, *Islam and the World*, Kuwait: International Islamic Federation of Student Organisations, 1977.
5. See Mawdudi, S.A., *A Short History of the Revivalist Movement in Islam*, Lahore: Islamic Publications Ltd. 5th Edition, 1981.
6. Lord Macaulay, Minutes of February 1836, quoted by Mahbub Kamal in *Islamic Movement, Why?* 1984.
7. See for example: Mawdudi, S.A., *Witnesses Unto Mankind. The Purpose and Duty of the Muslim Ummah*, edited and translated by Khurram Murad, Leicester: The Islamic Foundation, 1986. And Al-Banna, Hasan, *Memoirs of Hasan Al-Banna Shaheed*, translated by N.M. Shaikh, Karachi: International Islamic Publishers, 1982.
8. See Tamimi, Azzam, 'Democracy: The Religious and Political in Contemporary Islamic Debate', in *Encounters, Journal of Inter-Cultural Perspectives*, Vol. 4, No. 1, March 1998. Leicester: The Islamic Foundation.
9. Abu Sulayman, Abdul Hamid, *Crisis in the Muslim Mind*, translated by Yusuf Talal DeLorenzo, Herndon: The International Institute of Islamic Thought, 1994. p.32.
10. See for example Nadwi, Abul Hasan, *Muslims in the West The Message and Mission,* edited by Khurram Murad, Leicester: The Islamic Foundation, 1983.
11. See for example Ahmad, Khurshid, 'Islam and the West: Confrontation or Co-operation', *The Muslim World*, Vol. LXXXV, No. 1–2 (January–April 1995). pp. 67–8. Siddiqui, Atauallah, 'Muslims in the Contemporary World: Dialogue in Perspective', in *World Faiths Encounter*, No. 20, July 1998. pp. 24–30. Abu Sulayman, Abdul Hamid, *Crisis in the Muslim Mind*, ibid., p. 32.
12. For further details see Hawwa, Saeed, *The Muslim Brotherhood*, translated by Abdul Karim Shaikh, Kuwait: International Islamic Federation of Student Organisations, 1985.

CHAPTER IV

The World Today

This chapter examines the contemporary social and global context. This examination attempts to highlight, from a Muslim's perspective, the historical and ideological roots from which Western values, priorities and social life have evolved. The discussion will help in identifying the contemporary challenges that have to be addressed for introducing positive social change. These challenges must be understood, prioritised and effective strategies formulated for meeting them.

A superficial understanding of the state of affairs in contemporary Western societies may lead one to conclude that humanity has never had it so good as today, and hence there is no need for any kind of change. However, others may not agree with this view and desire to see improvements in a few aspects of their lives. Some may even be very unhappy with the status quo and wish to introduce fundamental changes in society. Still, a few other people may perhaps question the very basis of our social life and be actively looking for alternatives to the established social order. It is only when people begin to realise that there is something essentially wrong with the current state of affairs and feel a strong need for changing the status quo, that they will really look for alternatives and begin to exert efforts for change. This Chapter, therefore, takes a critical look at our present day society and world, and discusses why, from an Islamic perspective, social change in a particular direction is needed.

Gaining an understanding of the social context implies that one diagnoses the ideological roots, and the way of life that has emerged from these. An analysis of how a society is structured and functions is also necessary; this includes the role played by the government and business corporations, together with the media, academic, financial, social and religious institutions in society.

The Contemporary State of Affairs

Perhaps it would be correct to say that today we are living in an age of tremendous material and technological progress. People are able to travel in space, the world has become a global village, and our whole way of life has been revolutionised in recent decades. Great headway has been made in most areas of human life; in science, technology, health, mass communications, management practice, and so on. We can communicate with people on the other side of the world, and get to places faster than our ancestors could ever have imagined. All these achievements cannot be denied or belittled. They must be acknowledged, appreciated and developed further.

Furthermore, the unprecedented and tremendous material advances, together with social and economic policies to employ these, have indeed greatly raised the standard of living of some nations. In most Western countries, these have contributed to the establishment of an effective societal infra-structure, efficient business processes, and effective domestic services. Manufacturing, communication and information technologies such as computers, CAD/CAM, e-mail, video-conferencing, Internet and satellite, all these have transformed business operations and social systems, made work more efficient and provided many material comforts. In short, these developments in systems and technologies have brought significant prosperity to some nations, and contributed much to their political and military power.

However, at the same time, with all the benefits and positive aspects of these developments, they have also brought us to an age that is characterised by individualism, social alienation and social turbulence. People today are driven by a change rooted on materialism, and no country or nation can exclude, or even slow down the radical metamorphosis and alterations that are taking place in social life. There is a continuous change in consumer goods, in material products and technology, in modes of communication and transport, and in social values. These, in turn, cause continuous change to life styles, work practices, and in laws and policies that govern society. In fact, the way people live and work, how they interact and socialise, and even their beliefs, values and interests, are all being influenced in one way or another, by these social transformations.

The pace of material and technological change, and the accompanying change in social values, is so rapid, that for many people adaptation is only achievable at huge emotional, social and financial costs. This may be one of the reasons why many people fear change. Consequently, these changes adversely affect the physical and mental health of people. A rise in stress, depression, anxiety and mental illnesses is witnessed. To cope with the pressures of change and to drown their anxieties, people increasingly resort to alcohol, drugs, smoking, seclusion, and anti-social activities. Such practices have in like fashion led to many social problems. Along with the positive effects therefore, it would be a folly to overlook the harmful direction our society and world is taking – particularly in areas where people interact as human beings; in the socio-political arena of life. There is definitely a gloomy side to the way our society is structured and functions, and these cannot be disregarded from our analysis.

Are the social transformations we are facing, for the better or worse? One cannot overlook issues such as the breakdown of the family, community fragmentation, escalating delinquency and crime, increasing distress in inner-city areas, racial discrimination, drug addiction, alcoholism, immorality, economic and political corruption, falling educational standards, and so on. Along with technological and material progress, has there been an equal effort towards human and social development? Do our societies provide protection to peoples' lives, property and honour? Do people live in dignity because of the abundance in consumer goods? Is there a sense of trust and care, social cohesion, peace and harmony in society? The need of the hour is to boldly and honestly face such questions and re-explore the moral basis of society.

For the agents of change, these and related questions are momentous and cannot be brushed aside. Such questioning can actually assist in critically assessing and evaluating the current state of affairs, and also aid in identifying the causes of our social problems. Thus, from an Islamic perspective, though technological, material, and the resulting economic progress has brought numerous benefits to personal and social life, nevertheless, human and social development is more crucial and essential since it underpins the general health of a society. In view of this, material progress on its own, without being guided by moral values, cannot lead to a more dignified social life. In fact, moral values and just social principles are a prerequisite for society. Thus, behind all the glamour and glitter and the hype of modern technology, it is quite apparent that our societies today are degenerating. The polity lacks a firm ethical base and a just framework to guide social and economic policy. The societal changes that we are currently witnessing, since they are not wholly guided by ethical principles, love and justice, but rest more on greed, selfishness and market values, are influencing and affecting social relations in a harmful way. They are leading to particular social attitudes, behaviours and life-styles that are not very conducive to social cohesion and harmony.

The Rise of Secular-Materialism

What went wrong? Historical analysis by Muslim scholars in the 20th century, for example, Mawdudi, Nadwi and Muhammad Qutb[1], indicate that somewhere along the journey, in pursuit of personal pleasures and material progress, the balance was tilted towards the material and technological, at the cost of spiritual, moral and social development. This imbalance led to the processes of industrialisation and urbanisation, since these increased the efficiency and capacity of production and, hence, brought more material wealth and power. Over time, Western societies, through these processes, became increasingly differentiated (i.e. evolved a specialised division of labour) and more complex. Division of labour and increasing functionalisation of industry and society, in turn, led to greater class divisions, fragmentation and erosion of community life, and gradually developed greater individualism. The spiritual and moral dimensions of life were successively over-looked, and increasing value was placed on individual freedom and rights at the cost of duties, responsibilities, family and community.

Secular-materialistic ideas gradually evolved and developed over the last five or more centuries in the West. They were sown during the Renaissance period, around the 14th and 15th centuries CE, and started to grow and take shape during the Reformation and throughout the Scientific Revolution, the 16th and 17th centuries CE, and finally matured and crystallised during the Enlightenment, in the 18th century CE. They emerged firstly as a revolt against the oppression of the Church and the corruption of the clergy. Moreover, a discontentment with superstitious beliefs and practices that conflicted with scientific observations, gave further impetus to these ideas. Initially, therefore, development of secular thought started as a revolt against religion itself and it continued evolving in that direction. It was people like Descartes (1596–1650) who placed emphasis on reason and for seeking truth in the sciences. Hume (1711–76), Kant (1724–1804), Voltaire (1694–1778) and Goethe (1749–1837) stressed the preference for human reason and rationality, and people like Feuerbach (1804–72), Marx (1818–83), Darwin (1809–82), Freud (1856–1939), Nietzsche (1844–1900 – who expressed to the notion that 'God is dead'), Sartre (1905–80) and Wittgenstein (1889–1951) discredited revealed knowledge and commitment to any religion[2].

Thus, the seeds of imbalance towards materialism in Western civilisation were sown when greater belief and confidence was placed in human reason and empirical scientific findings in preference to the Divine guidance. This produced less and less confidence in 'religion' and gradually gave rise to secularism, materialism, liberalism and popular sovereignty, which all placed more value on material and physical aspects, than on moral and social ones. Theories and concepts such as Evolution, Dualism, Existentialism and Positivism, together with Determinism, Newton's Laws of Motion and Mechanisation, which hinted at a universe regulated by physical laws only, and hence a redundant God, Freudian Psychology and so on[3], all gave further impetus to materialistic and Godless ideas. These concepts subsequently shaped beliefs, social values and policies, together with attitudes, behaviours and life-styles. Consequently, social and political models and structures were forged in line with the rooting and maturing of secular-materialistic ideas. Additionally, human progress and well-being was mostly measured in terms of material gains.

All these developments in thought and practice have brought us to our present-day situation. Today, secular-materialistic thought is firmly rooted in the West, and it also dominates the whole world in practical terms. Though many people today do hold religious beliefs and values, and lead a moral life, however, these are generally restricted to the private quarters of their lives. Religion, in real concrete terms plays very little role in public life.

The above discussion illustrates that the core issue facing those who desire to build a better and just world, is that of the dominant world-view. Simply because a particular world-view, which embodies assumptions about reality and a set of beliefs, impacts on how people perceive and interpret the world around them. It guides personal and social life in a particular direction. Peoples' goals, aspirations, concerns, commitments, and likes and dislikes, are all, on the whole, influenced and forged by the world-view and beliefs they hold. Furthermore, a world-view shapes social and political beliefs, and, thus, underpins social and economic policies and the culture of a community.

As an illustration, a person having a secular-materialistic world-view would undoubtedly have different goals and life-styles as compared to a person having some other world-view. It follows, and this is what Islam contends, that a world-view that does not embody reality in its fullness, or is based on wrong assumptions of our true nature, will inevitably cause imbalances and inconsistencies in our personal and social life, and would definitely lead to numerous social problems and injustices in society. Such a world-view would lead to flawed perspectives and incoherent and disassociated social values, and, thus, affects attitudes and social conduct in a negative way. Thus, a*ny efforts for social change must, therefore, begin by analysing the dominant world-views in society, and the arising social principles and ideas that are influencing social life.*

According to Muslim scholars, ideologies, systems of society and cultural values that are prevalent in the world today, actually stem from the following three world-views: *Materialism,* that is, embracing the world and making it the sole goal in life, *Pseudo-Spiritualism* or monasticism, which involves disengaging or withdrawing from the world, and *Islam.* The first two are discussed below from a Muslim's perspective, together with the kind of society that emerges from each. This discussion will assist in understanding the roots of contemporary social problems, and why a world-view on which social life is founded must be challenged before an Islamic change is possible.

Materialism

> *"And they say, There is nothing except the life of this world. And we shall not be raised again (after death)."*
>
> (al-Anam 6: 29)

Materialism supports the view that only the material or physical universe exists. Matter and energy are the ultimate reality and, hence, the spiritual realm of our being and that of the universe is rejected. Materialism, therefore, either rejects or is indifferent to God, angels, the life Hereafter (*Akhira*), Paradise and Hell and everything else that cannot be sensed by humans or instruments. Materialism, in the ordinary sense of the term, has been defined as:

> "a primary concern for the acquisition of material goods and the enjoyment of physical satisfactions, and as a consequent rejection of or indifference to the spiritual, aesthetic, or ethical..."[4]

Such ideas definitely nurture a materialistic outlook on life and society. On the whole, they are likely to give rise to people having material objectives. Thus, if the present life is the only life, as this philosophy asserts, then it makes sense for people to strive for maximum pleasure, happiness and the enjoyment of material luxuries. In order to enjoy life to the full, materialism logically encourages people to endeavour for wealth acquisition, material goods, power and fame, and be involved in self-gratification. People holding such views are most likely, with some exceptions of course, to desire more money, better jobs, important positions, high status, more authority, be concerned about their self-image, prestige and self-recognition as their goals in life. The level to which one has attained these will determine his/her status, since material achievements are the things that are most valued. As a matter of fact, in today's society material well-being, power and prestige are the most desirable things in life, and these have become the criterion for respectability and honour.

> *"Fair in the eyes of people is the love of things they desire: women and sons; heaped-up hoards of gold and silver, horses branded, cattle and well-tilled land. Such are the possessions of this world's life; but with Allah is the best of goals."*
>
> (Ali-Imran 3: 14)

As there is no limit to human desire, the pursuit of pleasure and material goods can continue. In reference to this, the Prophet Muhammad pointed out that if a man has a valley of gold, he would most likely wish for another one (al-Bukhari). Thus, if greed is not controlled, ultimately it can lead people into a senseless chase after pleasures, material goods, wealth and power, never reaching a point of satisfaction. It is regrettable that the whole edifice of our society today and our way of life is raised on these foundations. Materialistic thought will, therefore, give rise to a culture where individuals are most likely to be indifferent to the problems of others, since each person becomes mainly concerned about their own pleasures. In general terms, a society based on materialism will lack people with a responsible, caring and sharing attitude. It will breed individualism, weaken social relationships and eventually disconnect people from each other. The social tensions, conflicts and evils emerging from such a world-view are not, therefore, difficult to comprehend.

It logically follows that on a collective level, a society based on materialistic beliefs is most likely to favour nationalism, imperialism and the exploitation of weaker nations, since these safeguard and promote a nation's selfish interests for acquiring more material goods and resources. This is why materialism was denounced by all the Prophets of Allah and pious people throughout the ages. They have all taught that man cannot live by bread, that is, material things, alone. Besides material needs, our spiritual thirst has also to be quenched in order to bring tranquillity to our souls. Can a compassionate, just, peaceful and moral society emerge from a materialistic world-view? One only needs observe present day societies which have been built upon a secular-materialistic thought to realise how they are full of confusion, contradiction, injustice, social tension and disharmony.

Social Crises Arising from Secular-Materialism

As mentioned earlier, despite the tremendous material progress made in the last few decades, today there are strong indications that our communities and societies are disintegrating and decaying rapidly due to a weakening in human relationships. There is a strong trend towards the erosion of morals, a general feeling of emptiness, and a lack of spiritual joy and inner peace. Official published statistics on social trends clearly point out that such social problems are a grim fact of life. The moral fabric of society is being ripped apart. Many concerned citizens, thinkers, social scientists, religious leaders and even some politicians and government officials, are deeply alarmed at the harmful direction present-day societies are taking. As an example, Hans Küng and Karl-Josef Kuschel state the following:

> "Our world is experiencing a fundamental crisis: a crisis in global economy, global ecology, and global politics. The lack of a grand vision, the tangle of unresolved problems, political paralysis, mediocre political leadership with little insight or foresight, and in general too little sense for the commonweal are seen everywhere... Hundreds of millions of human beings on our planet increasingly suffer from unemployment, poverty, hunger, and the destruction of their families. Hope for a lasting peace among nations slips away from us. There are tensions between the sexes and generations. Children die, kill, and are killed. More and more countries are shaken by corruption in politics and business..."[5]

Several other scholars have painted similar pictures of the present day world. Indeed, we are amidst a profound social crises. One philosopher has expressed his thoughts on the present day situation as:

> Man has learnt how to fly in the air like birds, and how to swim in the oceans like fish. But how to live on the earth, he does not know.

Let us look more closely at a few examples of a society born out of materialism.

FAMILY CRISIS

A normal family comprising both parents and children, which was considered as the most valued institution of community life amongst most religious traditions, is now beginning to disintegrate. Divorce rates in many Western societies are surging, and consequently a one parent family is now considered a social norm. Today, though there are more cars, washing machines, microwave ovens, TV's, computers, and other domestic appliances per household, yet peace, love, tranquillity and trust are fast fading from family life.

From an Islamic perspective, the major causes of family breakdown are: a weak hold of family values, confusion in gender roles, lack of marital responsibility, together with alcoholism, adultery and fornication. Today, motherhood is not valued by society – rather it is seen with contempt. A woman working for other people in a restaurant or office is valued and her job is trumpeted as a career. In contrast, a woman who cares for and looks after her own family is viewed as a backward woman, and her work is seen to be oppressive. Regrettably, these attitudes and practices have become so widespread and common, that they are not even considered destructive to social life. In some areas, women place advertisements in papers and magazines to find men to father their children without having to go through marriage. Owing to such depraved acts, many children are born and grow up never knowing who their fathers are. This, in turn, produces numerous identity, emotional and psychological problems amongst children, and as a result many grow up to be delinquents and offenders. Lifestyles and practices as these have led to countless personal and social problems such as poverty, unwanted children and crime.

In cases of one parent families, or where both parents are in full-time employment, there is usually a lack of proper parental attention and care towards the young. This familial deficiency generally leads the young towards social vices and crimes. Their energies instead of being directed along healthy channels, are either being wasted away or expended in socially harmful activities such as drug abuse, gambling, illicit sex and crime. In addition, a growing fascination with the latest consumer goods, films, video games, discos, fashion and leisure activities are all creating huge financial pressures and communication gaps between young and old, and between family and community members. Such interests and past-times, and the resulting attitudes and lifestyles, are also giving rise to discontentment, disorder and to general communal decay.

CORRUPTION IN PUBLIC LIFE

Similarly, at the public level, despite measures for increasing efficiency, cost-cutting, and developing more effective communication and information systems, public values are generally on the decline. The long process of industrialisation and bureaucratisation, has predominantly been the cause in our opinion, of over-looking personal and public values. In the public scene, one, therefore, can find that organised crime is on the increase, and social inequalities are becoming more manifest and deep-seated. Public institutions, that were expected to support and hold communities and society together, are themselves decaying from within.

The number of cases being reported of malpractice found in financial, legal and political institutions are increasing by the day. Tax evasion, manipulation of share prices, squandering of public money, loyalties and commitments to partisan policies rather than public welfare, and government secrecy and lack of accountability, are just some of the corrupt practices beginning to sprout in public life. Similarly, with lawyers fees reaching unaffordable levels, there is a growing scepticism of whether the judicial system is able to deliver justice – obviously the rich and powerful are able to gain advantage. In addition, while the rich have opted for private healthcare, education and pensions, the poor are at the mercy of under-resourced and ineffective public services.

MASS MANIPULATION

Furthermore, manipulation of ordinary people is taking place through social engineering, moulding of language, and through the mass media.

The movers and shakers of our societies, who influence the financial institutions, the mass media and policy making, are able to shape, whether intentionally or not, our social condition and common future. They have, to some extent, become the 'gods' of society. They control money, the flow and quality of information, and they influence public opinion, lifestyles and social systems. Social conditions are engineered by elite groups through employing various strategies and methods. Some of the means by which this is being achieved include erection of social and political hierarchies, influencing educational and social policies, and by indoctrinating people through advertisements, entertainments and the media in general. All this aids in the ideological conditioning of people, in manufacturing public consent and emotions, in generating revenue to support capitalist enterprises, and in cases rooting processes of repression. A 'false consciousness' (i.e. a false picture of reality) is produced and people are constrained in discovering the multiple dimensions of their social existence.

Moreover, by influencing and manipulating language, the attitudes of ordinary people can be affected, and their perception of the world around them altered. Language is a powerful means of regulating thought and practice. It is a means employed to manipulate people's emotions and feelings. Language is also directed towards giving new or different meanings to words and terms, and hence introducing, changing or modifying ideas, concepts and values. In this way, practices which people once found offensive or morally wrong, begin to be tolerated and accepted by them. Thus, it is through employing such techniques that values are continually being altered. As a result, today, there remain very few permanent values and guiding principles to direct the affairs of social life.

In addition, certain cultural values and lifestyles are constantly promoted, via the television and radio, into every home, creating a desire in individuals to adopt and follow. Furthermore, films, advertisements, magazines, night clubs, gambling shops, and the like, all promote certain social habits and re-inforce social structures, assisting in maintaining certain people and groups on top of the social hierarchy and in promoting consumerism. Coupled with all this, mass communication technology has enabled cultural imperialism to reach global levels.

INTERFERENCE WITH NATURAL PROCESSES

Likewise, materialism has embedded passivity, greed and selfishness in social attitudes and practices. To satisfy our greed, we are corrupting and polluting the air, water and fruits and vegetables, which are essential for human survival. In pursuit of increasing productivity, efficiency, and improving material well-being, we are disturbing the ecological balance. Even animals, fish, plants and trees, basically all creatures great and small, are not safe from human corruption and violence. In order to make big profits quickly, domestic animals are injected with chemical hormones and given feed that is not natural to their bodily systems in order to speed up and boost their growth. Scientists are just beginning to realise the long-term detrimental effects these interventions with natural processes are having on animals and subsequently on people who consume their meat. Foods, contaminated with all kinds of chemicals and preservatives, are changing the chemistry of our bodies to some extent; making some of us more temperamental, or less sensitive to social wrongs. Society is even using genetic engineering for cloning. What this will lead to, only Allah knows.

EROSION OF MORALS AND SOCIAL ALIENATION

Whilst all this is going on, ordinary people, most of whom have been isolated from their communities, and who possess meagre resources, sit helplessly and watch, powerless to intervene. Some have been totally extracted from their social base, and then separated from all moral reference points. Others have been slotted into production-consumption, money borrowing and entertainment processes in which they have virtually no power. Though living standards for some individuals have improved, the quality of human relations, in general, has deteriorated. Many people are lost and disillusioned, and as a result have opted to resign from communal affairs. Some have effectively become the cogs and wheels of an exploitative economic system. Many others have become indifferent and passive, and society has turned them into the lowest of the low. A few cannot make sense of life or distinguish much between right and wrong. They consume whatever they are fed with. They believe whatever comes through the TV, and have lost their values and sense of judgement. They are unable to think, reason, choose or decide for themselves. This begs the questions: are people really free, free to choose and decide; or are they just made to believe that they are free?.

Compassion, altruism and morals are slowly eroding. Worship of the 'self' has become a major driving force in our present day information age. Many are investing a great deal of their time, energies and abilities in gaining self-pleasure, material gain, wealth, pomp, fame and power for themselves. More cars, more houses, more luxuries, and 'loads of money' seem to be the motto of the day. This has led to a 'me-society' and to a people who can be classified into 'mad', 'bad' and 'sad' categories. With self-indulgence and self-pleasure as their aim, many people have little time or care for anyone else. They live their daily lives unconcerned where they are heading. Many love their money, belongings, and even their dogs, cats and teddy bears more than they love and respect their fellow human beings. As a matter of fact, paternal affection, respect for one's elders, care and affection for the young, marital fidelity and co-operation and care between people are not considered by many to be important issues for the health of our society.

Today, drugs have entered the schools which our children attend. We are witnessing poor education, an increase in crime in our neighbourhood, over-crowded prisons, and increasing pollution of our environment. Indeed these trends, a direct consequence of materialism and the secularisation of life are disturbing and the future looks bleak and uncertain.

The following Quranic verse clearly, concisely and comprehensively depicts our situation today, while at the same time it places the responsibility of the sad state of affairs on no one other than human beings themselves:

> *"Corruption has appeared on land and sea, by the actions of people. That Allah may give them a taste of some of their deeds: in order that they may turn back (from evil)."*
>
> (ar-Rum 30: 41)

GLOBAL CRISES

The vast powers of technology that were supposedly harnessed to bring happiness and abundance to all, have on the contrary actually been employed more for destructive purposes – for enslaving and exploiting weaker nations. Technology has been used to derive maximum comfort and control of power and resources for particular groups, classes or nations. It is in pursuit of these aims that the present day global conflicts, poverty, misery and other problems have resulted. As an example, both World-Wars, fought during the earlier part of the 20th century, were devastating and they led to the annihilation of many millions of people and the destruction of many societies. In fact, over a 100 million lives have been lost in the 20th century owing to wars and conflicts. Such human devastation has never before been witnessed in human history. Interestingly enough, during the First World War, most monarchies were put to an end, and during the Second World War, nation-states were weakened. Today, the world is ruled by multi-national banking and industrial enterprises. They dominate world affairs; they control the sources of information and the world's natural resources, and have established a complex and exploitative world economy. Developing and Third World nations, even though some of them possess an abundance of natural resources, have no, or little, control over them – they live at the mercy of the powerful nations and international banks.

On the whole, all this has led to complex social, economic and political problems and global crisis. Man is turning against man, and nation against nation. There is a struggle for world domination between nations and industrial enterprises. Competition for developing weapons of mass destruction is fierce. Genocide, the expulsion of peoples from their own homelands, political corruption, exploitation and oppression make the everyday news. It appears as though our world is on the brink of a great catastrophe. Does this state of affairs not compel people of good will, to leave aside their small differences, join hands and endeavour to put an end to this barbarity and change the course of history?

> *"Do they not travel through the earth, and see what was the end of those before them. They were superior to them in strength, and they tilled the earth and populated it in greater numbers than these (present people) have done. There came to them Messengers with clear signs (who they rejected to their own destruction). It was not Allah who wronged them, but they wronged themselves. The evil was the end of those who did evil, for that they rejected the signs of Allah and made mock of them."*
>
> (ar-Rum 30: 9–10)

> *"They were a people that have passed away. They shall reap the fruits of what they did and you of what you do..."*
>
> (al-Baqara 2: 141)

Solutions Based upon Secular-Materialism

From an Islamic perspective, such deteriorated social and global conditions have arisen from the inherent contradictions, inconsistencies and functional differentiation of systems of life, that were developed and shaped by secular-materialistic thought. Unfortunately, a good majority of political leaders do not see the connection between these social and global problems and secular-materialistic ideas. This is why numerous thinkers, intellectuals and politicians, who hold secular-materialistic beliefs and values, from time to time, have offered solutions to our social problems, and which initially sounded very promising, but as expected, have not been of much avail. In fact, most of these solutions, since they were based on faulty premises, material considerations, and addressed the symptoms rather the causes of our problems, have failed to reconnect people and bring peace, social harmony and justice to our world.

By carefully analysing the solutions derived from a secular-materialistic framework, it is not difficult to see that at the very best these address the symptoms of our personal and societal problems. They largely attempt to cater for the material and physical needs, but the more fundamental issues and concerns of individuals and community are generally overlooked. The need for love, dignity, family, community, mutual support, justice, and satisfying our other emotional and spiritual needs, which are essential for a healthy and balanced personal and social life, are not given the attention they deserve. Moreover, due to the limitations of human reason, such solutions are often narrowly focused and lack far-sightedness. They also usually tend to rely on external resources, agencies and control mechanisms for their implementation rather than on inner control mechanisms, i.e. self-discipline, self-motivation, self-adjustment and self-control. Thus, solutions to social problems are based on either incomplete knowledge of the problem's sociological, psychological, medical, geographical, political and economic context, and their inter-relationships, or are perhaps more politically and economically motivated, rather than being concerned with the common good.

Furthermore, by merely providing an abundance of consumer goods and technological-bureaucratic-mechanical type solutions, though these maybe beneficial to a certain extent, the causes of our social problems are not addressed in a comprehensive way. Such problems are often dealt with putting more money and resources into social services, health, education, police and so on. However, this makes people more dependent on the state and further cultivates individualism and alienation, which in turn gives rise to more personal and social problems. Perhaps, this is why loneliness, boredom, deterioration in relationships, spiritual emptiness and other social diseases that arise from moral and spiritual crises, continue to grow in our society and world.

Capitalism, communism, socialism, and fascism, all based on a secular-materialistic world-view, are among the recent social remedies applied to our societies. Although all these 'isms' have evolved through time, and today can be found in several variants, including many shared points between them, yet their distinct impact on Western thought and societies is still quite significant; socialist and capitalist ideas in particular. But how effective have they been in addressing the crises that face humanity?

COMMUNISM

The communist experiment in China and the former Soviet Union promised equality and prosperity to all, however, it totally failed to deliver these. Communism aimed at eliminating class oppression and putting a nation's resources and capital under public ownership. However, the centralised control of the state led to the concentration of power in fewer hands, and as a consequence, caused many social tensions and corruption, both in government and society as a whole. Moreover, the planned economy with its centralised control killed individuals' initiatives and thus, stagnated material and technological progress. All giving rise to many social problems and ills. It is for these and related reasons that the communist systems have recently collapsed in the former Soviet Union and in Eastern Europe.

SOCIALISM

Similarly modern socialism incorporating democratic ideas and with some revision of the basic tenets of Marxism, preaching a classless society, the emancipation of labour, a welfare state, prosperity, justice, and the public ownership of the fundamental means of production, also failed to deliver its promises. Socialist governments have, in general, led to inefficient social systems and a highly bureaucratic state system. They are also commonly known for creating a greater dependence of citizens on the state, and high public borrowing to fund public welfare and services, which subsequently produce a rise in inflation and taxes, and hence in unemployment. Ultimately, their policies created enormous societal problems in Western countries during the 1960's and 1970's. Because of these drawbacks, many present day socialist parties, for example, the Labour Party in Britain, have been compelled to reconsider their traditional socialist policies, and some are moving more towards the centre ground of politics on many issues.

CAPITALISM

Likewise, capitalist secular democracies are in crisis too. Capitalism, by its very philosophy, encourages greed, selfishness, and the exploitation of consumers and poorer nations. It values profit, efficiency, mass production, increases in market share and control, above human dignity. Capitalism has for the most part led to the accumulation of wealth in fewer hands and created economic and power inequalities. By constructing and enforcing classes of producers and consumers, it has created social hierarchies, tensions, conflicts, and poverty in society. Capitalism has indeed created social polarisation. The powerful and rich rule such societies simply because they have managed, by hook or by crook, to accumulate wealth and capital for themselves. Furthermore, in a capitalist society the market dominates and people are at its bidding. Enterprises are set-up and new products enter the markets irrespective of whether they are harmful to society or not.

Usury, a notable constituent of a modern-day capitalist system, is one of the major causes of economic injustice and exploitation, for example, the Third World Debt today. Above all, banking, commercial and industrial enterprises are all thriving on usury. Moreover, borrowing money has become almost a necessity of modern life, and the great majority in capitalist societies live in debt. They are financially enslaved and feel powerless to break out of this deplorable condition. There is no doubt that today the poisonous fruits of capitalism and usury are being harvested both in the East and the West.

"But Allah has permitted trade and has forbidden usury..."
(al-Baqara 2: 275)

"And whoever is saved from the greed of his ego will attain success."
(at-Taghabun 64: 16)

COMMUNITARIANISM

Other approaches for social change have been put forward during the latter part of the 20th century, particularly in the US. Amongst these is communitarianism and its various derivatives. These desire the empowerment of local communities through community building and organising, citizen's participation in socio-political affairs, and the accountability of all power-bases in society, so that a better social order can be established. Although these sound more promising, nevertheless, they do not address the fundamental issue: that of the world-view, beliefs and ideology on which society and the world are founded. Furthermore, most of these approaches adopt secular ideas, and their concerns are mostly to involve people and establish their co-operation in order to bring about an improvement in the material condition. The inner dimensions of people's lives are, therefore, generally over-looked or neglected.

Due to the failure of these social remedies, alternative efforts are being made by various religious groups and humanitarian bodies to promote love and justice, and hence improve social relationships and cohesion. However, these are mostly limited to the level of individuals and small communities, and have made little social and political impact.

Pseudo-Spiritualism (or Monasticism)

Let us now turn our attention to the second major world-view that exists in our world; pseudo-spiritualism or monasticism. This view goes to the other extreme of materialism. It differentiates between the religious and secular; the material and spiritual. Such views, in an extreme sense, teach that people should disengage and withdraw from, or shun the material world and curb desires and pleasures of the flesh in order to achieve spiritual elevation.

People with such views believe that the material and spiritual are somehow incompatible, disconnected or have very little relationship between them.

Individuals holding such ideas usually live their life in seclusion, practice monasticism, engage in ritual worship, favour celibacy and keep out of worldly and social affairs as much as possible. They consider time spent in mediation, chanting and in prayer as important and a means to spiritual upliftment. This is why many go through strict self-control and self-discipline exercises in order to gain control over bodily desires, lighten the soul's burden, make it pure, and experience spiritual ecstasy.

> *"But the monasticism which they invented for themselves, We did not prescribe for them..."*
>
> (al-Hadid 57: 27)

From an Islamic perspective, such a concept and beliefs are incompatible with human nature. They inevitably benumb, socially and politically, those who base their life on it. Such ideas lead to a culture of passivity and social exclusion, and also withdraw good and pious people from the affairs of society, giving way to the wicked to dominate. In regard to this, Ismail Raji al-Faruqi has stated:

> "The 'Kingdom of Allah' became an 'another world' and this world became the temporary theatre of Caesar, the devil, the 'flesh', 'where moth and rust doth corrupt, and where thieves break through and steal'."[6]

Furthermore, social affairs and societal progress are not considered important by people who hold such beliefs and attitudes, and material and technological progress is not encouraged. Is it possible then to create a compassionate culture, or to build a just and thriving civilisation based on this world-view?

On analysis, one will find that many of the world religions today, fall more or less into this category. Although some do not go to the extreme as that sketched above, nevertheless they do concentrate mainly on personal morality, worship and rituals and exert little or no influence on the political and economic affairs or direction of social life. They have reduced religious practice to the private sphere and have surrendered to the secularisation of public life. In fact, some religions have very little to say on the general conduct of society. This is why, most of the major religions can only play a very limited constructive role in society and the world.

Conclusion

The Islamic view of life is fundamentally different from what has been discussed above. Islam represents a complete antithesis to such world-views – materialism and pseudo-spiritualism. It teaches that human beings did not come to the world through accident, but through design. The world is an opportunity and a trial; humans, therefore, have a purpose and responsibility. Islam advocates balance and integration between the spiritual and material, individualism and collectivism, and between rights, duties and responsibilities. Humans are made up of a body and soul, and both of these require nourishment in order bring about peace and tranquillity in human personality. Spiritual upliftment is not possible by discarding the body and our material needs. In fact, effective spiritual development according to Islamic guidance should generate a force for positive social change. An inner peace and purity motivates a person to bring about peace and purity to the external social environment, and vice versa. Allama Iqbal has so elegantly stated:

> "Political action is the expression of Islam's spirituality."[7]

Throughout the ages, whenever people have rejected God's balanced way, they have either adopted materialism or similar ideologies on the one extreme, or pseudo-spiritualistic and monastic tendencies on the other. These extremes also incorporate atheism, polytheism, and asceticism since they all lead to similar attitudes towards life when compared to those depicted above. And it is these world-views that are also prevalent in our world today, and hence they continue to contribute to social and global problems.

In summary, this Chapter has highlighted two world-views at odds with each other, namely secular-materialism and pseudo-spiritualism or monasticism. One or the other is dominant in different parts of the earth today. It was argued that the underlying reason for the current unfortunate state of affairs is that humanity has adopted these world-views, and the ideologies emerging from them, but which are not compatible with our human nature. As a consequence, the emerging social and economic solutions have led to imbalances and inconsistencies in personal and social life. These, in turn, have given rise to particular attitudes and behaviours, which are not conducive to social harmony, welfare, peace and justice. They have produced a culture in which greed and selfishness are firmly rooted. An understanding of these world-views can, thus, provide Islamic workers with insights to the fundamental reasons for the existence of certain social attitudes and ailments in society. This understanding is crucial for formulating effective strategies to reshape ideas, beliefs and social values in accordance with Islamic guidance. This also implies that change agents should not reject everything that is found in the West, but should recognise the merits and contributions that the West has made towards the advancement of knowledge and civilisation. They should not hesitate to learn from those aspects of the prevailing civilisations which can, or have brought real benefits to humanity. However, at the same time, the problems created by secular-materialism and pseudo-Spiritualism should not be over-looked.

Notes:

1. See for example Nadwi, Abul Hasan, *Islam and the World*, Kuwait: International Islamic Federation of Student Organisations, 1977; Qutb, Muhammad, *Islam & the Modern Materialistic Thought*, Delhi: Hindustan Publications, 1985; and Mawdudi, S.A., *Come Let Us Change this World*, compiled by Kaukab Siddiq, Lahore: Islamic Publications Ltd., 1982.
2. See for example Baumer, Franklin Le Van (ed.), *Main Currents of Western Thought*, 4th edition, London: Yale University Press, 1978.
3. For the meaning of these terms, see Holroyd, Stuart, *The Arkana Dictionary of New Perspectives*, London: Penguin Group, 1989.
4. Holroyd, Stuart, *The Arkana Dictionary of New Perspectives*, ibid. p.19.
5. Küng, Hans and Kuschel, Karl-Josef (eds.), *A Global Ethic, The Declaration of the Parliament of the World's Religions*, London: SCM Press Ltd., 1993. p.17.
6. Quoted from Ahmad, Khurshid, and Ansari, Zafar Ishaq (eds.), *Islamic Perspectives, Studies in Honour of Sayyid Abul A'la Mawdudi*, Leicester: The Islamic Foundation, 1979. p.188.
7. Iqbal, Muhammad, *Reconstruction of Religious Thought in Islam*, Lahore: Muhammad Ashraf, 1960.

CHAPTER V

Contemporary Challenges

This chapter concludes Part One of this book. It draws together material covered in the former Chapters in order to highlight some of the major contemporary challenges that have to be addressed by the Islamic movements, both from within and without. By understanding these challenges and striving to meet them effectively the Islamic movements will be able to move towards realising Islam's vision and play a positive and constructive role in world affairs. This chapter also suggests a way forward, and emphasises the importance of rekindling the vision of Islam and the adherence to Quranic guidance.

Contemporary Challenges

Ideological Challenge

This, in our opinion, is the biggest challenge facing the Muslim world-community. As mentioned earlier, today we find that the dominant ideas the world over stand for the secularisation of life. Such ideas imply a separation of faith and politics. As a result, they have led to a complete or partial divorce between science and ethics, and law and morality. In fact, secularism has caused the uncoupling and differentiation of all aspects of life. It has squeezed religion or God's guidance from the mainstream society. Karel Dobbelaere states:

> "The higher the degree of functional differentiation the more advanced secularism will be, and the less impact religious organisations will be able to exert on the culture. Functional differentiation produces social sub-systems in polity, economy, education, family etc. They are increasingly autonomous and

> specialised. Religion is reduced to a sub-system of society rather than an overarching system of values and beliefs. Secular values replace religious ones."[1]

Put another way, secularism has divided life into water-tight compartments – into the private and public; spiritual and material; religious and mundane. This has gradually led to a separation of nearly all parts of human life and affairs – home life from work life, education from home life, family from community, judges from those executing their verdicts, politicians from the bureaucrats, management from operations, thought from action, news and information from their context, leaders from their followers, mass media producers from their audience, even mothers from their role of mothering, people's inner selves from their outward persona, and our bodies from our souls.

Unfortunately, due to the dominance of secular ideas, religious values and practices are having little impact on social life. This is why, in general, selfish interests or financial and material gains are the main motives behind social policies rather than the moral health of society. For example, economic policies are made with little consideration to their likely effects on the moral and social well-being of society. Similarly, educational policies, commonly have economic and material considerations at their focus rather than the personal and social development of students.

Thus, by advocating a separation between faith and politics, secular systems of life have, to all intents and purposes, rejected God's guidance in the social, economic and political areas of life – indeed God has been squeezed out from the corridors of power and public life. His following has been restricted to the churches, mosques and to the private quarters of personal life only. As a result, those who hold certain values can only act on them in their private life but not in public affairs. God can be praised and worshipped all day long, however, He is not allowed to intervene in the way we live and conduct our collective affairs. In other words, secularism in practice discourages God's guidance from directing public life or steering the formulation of laws and policies for society – according to this view, only human reason and experience, the god of secularism, has the right to exert its influence in this very important domain.

In contrast, Islam takes an integrated view of life and asserts that life cannot be compartmentalised or disconnected into separate components and elements – spiritual and moral conditions impress upon social and economic conditions, and vice-versa. Also, God is One and Indivisible. He rules the heavens and the earth, and He should also rule human affairs. Thus, secularism is the antithesis to Islam and poses many intellectual and practical challenges for Islamic thinkers and leaders. Indeed, the very perception of life and society are different between these two world-views. The challenge therefore, is that the whole way of thinking, reasoning, working, and the processes for the formulation of social and economic polices that exist in contemporary societies need to be addressed, influenced and changed in order to improve the existing social order. In other words, Muslim intellectuals and leaders have to address secular ideology and practices, and find mechanisms through which systems of life can be reintegrated in order to meet this challenge

Moral and Social Challenges

Similarly, secular-materialistic views and systems also pose numerous moral and social challenges. Although our world today has technologically become a global village, in reality it has increased the human distance between people in terms of respect, care, and love. There are really no permanent morals, rules, or principles in contemporary societies to ensure some kind of order in human relations and affairs. This is why immorality, shamelessness, crime, lack of social responsibility and other social evils have taken hold of present-day societies. Falsehood, cheating, fraud, deceit and other social vices are saturating community and public life, and such practices are not even considered wrong by many. In fact, the very distinction between right and wrong is obscured. This has given rise to numerous social problems. These include: the plight of the family, a lost and bewildered youth, disintegrated communities, the decay of social institutions, racial tension, rising crime, bribery and corruption, discrimination and economic exploitation. Indeed, public institutions and social systems need to be re-built on moral foundations and just principles so that social problems can be addressed effectively and equitably.

Global challenges

By making Allah redundant or by totally rejecting His guidance from collective and global affairs, secular systems have, and are continuing to lead our contemporary societies into numerous global problems and injustices. For example, the Third World Debt and the economic exploitation of poorer nations by the developed world, nuclear and other weapons of mass destruction, pollution and the devastation of the environment, cultural imperialism, ethnic cleansing, racial tensions and conflicts, and so on, are some of the poisonous fruits of these systems. Moreover, the mass media and communications' technology, advanced military machinery, and economic muscle are employed to maintain and enhance such unjust policies. One can imagine the challenges these will pose to establishing a just social order which Islam stands for.

Challenges for Islamic Jurisprudence (**Fiqh**)

In addition to the above challenges posed by secular-materialism, Muslim scholars and intellectuals must address some important issues regarding Islam and its relevance to the present day world. Some of the major issues in our humble opinion are:

1. Undoubtedly, Western civilisation has caught humanity, and Muslims in particular, in a web of secular-materialistic discourse and ideas. The framework for addressing issues, together with the political agenda and the language to be used, are all set and shaped by the dominant secular forces. They have power over language and over defining concepts and issues. Islamic scholars and intellectuals, therefore, need to challenge this framework and language, and introduce an alternative framework derived from Islamic sources. These efforts should be directed towards influencing change in contemporary discourse; from secularisation, functionalisation, reductionalism and materialism, towards justice, community, morality, virtue, holism and integration of thought and life. Further, existing vocabulary has to be redefined in light of Islamic guidance in order to convey the rich Islamic concepts in contemporary language and

in a meaningful and convincing way. This entails overcoming historical and cultural barriers so as to present the message of Islam more effectively in a contemporary context.

2. In addition, there are countless key practical issues that require urgent attention if Muslim societies are to become role models for humanity. These include addressing problems of crime and disorder, widespread poverty, unemployment and the general development of the economies of Muslim countries. Furthermore, thought and resources are required for addressing challenges such as the development of usury-free banking systems, providing adequate levels of education, and developing general societal institutions (for example, hospitals, police, public administration and welfare) and infra-structure (for example, transportation, sanitation and fuel needs).
3. More immediate legal and intellectual challenges that require attention include the following:

    i. The articulation in contemporary political language of Islam's stand on pluralism, power sharing and participation in democratic systems.
    ii. The complex global economy founded on usury (*riba*) and exploitation need to be challenged and the Islamic economic model presented and established.
    iii. The Islamic viewpoint on moral issues revolving around the use of modern media need to be offered, particularly guidelines on issues of illusion, entertainment, acting, and the use of drama and films in society.
    iv. The numerous issues faced by Muslims living in a minority situation in the West need to be addressed. For example, their views on citizenship in a non-Muslim society, what their priorities and role in a such society should be, together with on-going legal and moral issues and dilemmas related to food, clothing and social interaction with non-Muslims.

All these issues need to be viewed intellectually from many perspectives and in a balanced way, and Islamic responses and viewpoints formulated. Taking on this challenge is essential if Islam is to be seen as relevant in the present day world. Although a framework and even answers to these challenges and issues are contained in the Islamic sources of guidance, they do, however, need to be brought out, re-packaged and articulated in the language of the contemporary world.

Facing the Challenges

The above are, in our humble opinion, the major challenges that need to be addressed in the process of social and global change. How can these, being so huge and complex, requiring enormous resources, be faced? Agents of change need to realise that such challenges are not really new to our time or situation. Every Prophet of Allah met similar, if not greater challenges, during their efforts for building a better social life in their times. These challenges should not, therefore, frighten Islamic workers. They have to be faced, since it is only then that our societies can be brought out of the deplorable and lamentable states they are in. If Muslims fail to attend to this task now, and with a sense of urgency, humanity will inevitably sink into oblivion like the earlier communities and civilisations mentioned in the Quran, not least the people of Noah, Hud and Lot. To begin towards addressing these challenges effectively, the following suggestions are made:

1. First, the enormity and complexity of the task of societal and global reform and change has to be acknowledged. This gigantic task of directing and shaping society, a task for which Allah sent His mighty Messengers, cannot be accomplished merely through a few demonstrations, or by simply shouting slogans, distributing leaflets, attending a few study circles or working to achieve political power alone. The process of social change is much more complex and a thorough analysis of the social situation, a pragmatic approach, and huge human and material resources are required for this purpose.
2. A deep and balanced understanding of Islam is required. This will assist in generating strong confidence in Islam as the way forward for humanity. An understanding of the

social and political circumstances of contemporary society and the world will also be of help. Such an understanding can aid in producing an effective approach and strategic thought. Furthermore, an objective assessment of secular views, and the role played by those who wield power in shaping society is necessary. This assessment will aid in determining social and political actions and for building strategic alliances.

3. In addition, thought and efforts for advancing positive change have to be guided by a framework and a methodology. The Islamic framework and methodology for guiding social change are detailed in Part Two of this book (Chapters Six through to Eleven). Applying these to present-day societies will guide Islamic workers and leaders in moulding society and in meeting the challenges that are posed.
4 More importantly, to face current challenges, the purpose for which Muslims exist as a community must be constantly reinvigorated. This is a very powerful way of awakening a nation, motivating people and creating a collective commitment. This point is explored below.

Re-kindling the Islamic Vision

The starting point for inspiring and reviving a people is to cultivate in them a clear vision of Islam; a vision of what is required to be accomplished. However, history points to the fact that communities and movements, through the passage of time, or after the founding members have passed away, commonly tend to lose sight of their vision and begin to stray from their original objective. For example, after the great Messengers of Allah passed away, their people, in due time, became heedless towards the mission which they were left to pursue. This generally happens either when people begin to put too much emphasis on certain rituals, practices or aspects of the work and gradually these become the goals in themselves. Put another way, the goals become confused with the means and, hence, people begin to deviate from the right path. People also become distracted by material and mundane matters and as a result they lose sight of their vision.

The Muslim community is not immune to this pitfall. It is essential, therefore, that the agents of change do not lose sight of their Islamic vision. They must have this vision constantly in mind and even dream constantly of realising it in their life time. This is why a regular reading of the Glorious Quran is essential, and it is also important that from time to time, a thorough review, evaluation, and stock-taking of the efforts made is carried out. Serious questions should be asked such as: are we moving towards our goal? Is the current programme of work enabling us to move in the right direction? Are we doing the right things? Are we influencing change? Such questions are a key in keeping efforts focused in the right direction.

The Prophet Muhammad frequently made attempts to keep his Companions' minds focused on the vision of Islam. He took every opportunity to remind them of their purpose and objective. As an example, he advised one of his Companion, Khabbab Ibn al-Arat, when he complained about the persecutions the Muslims faced in Makka, during the early years of their mission, with the following words:

> *"By Allah, He will complete this mission until a rider will travel from Sana to Hadramawt* (both are places in Yemen) *and will have no fear but of Allah, and no worry but about a wolf that might harm his cattle – but you make haste."*
>
> (Bukhari)

This saying presents the vision of Islam for society and reminds Muslims that they must keep on working, irrespective of the adversities, for a better society that ensures peace and justice for all people. Further, the noble Prophet said to the leaders of his people:

> *"I have brought you a message (Kalima), if you accept it, then through it, the Arab world and the Ajam* (non-Arab world), *would be under your feet."*
>
> (Ahmed and Tirmidhi)

This indicates that, if they accept God's message, and ceaselessly work to realise the Islamic vision, God will ultimately honour them with leadership of the world. Taking another example, during the migration (*hijra*), when the enemies of Prophet Muhammad were determined not to let him reach Medina, a person called Suraqa Bin Malik came very close to capturing the Prophet. However, every time he approached close to the noble Prophet, his horse stumbled and threw him down. After a number of attempts, he soon realised that he could not achieve his objective, so he called out to the prophet asking him to stop, assuring him that he just wished to speak to him. During the conversation the Prophet said to him:

> "*What will be your feeling when you would be adorned with the bracelets of Qisra?* (the Emperor of Persia)."
>
> (Baihaqi)

Thus, even in such a fearful situation, when they were only two, Abu Bakr being the other person, escaping from their persecutors, the Prophet of Allah presented his vision with confidence; that a just social order would prevail even in the lands ruled by Qisra, which was a world power at that time. Incidentally, this prophecy was fulfilled during the time of the second Caliph, Umar. Furthermore, it is reported from Bara ibn Azib by Baihaqi and Abu Naim, that in the course of digging the trench around Medina, in preparation for the Battle of the Trench, a very hard rock was encountered which was difficult to break. The noble Prophet was called, and he attempted to break it. With each strike to the rock he said the following words:

> "*I am assigned the keys of the treasures of Syria. ... I am assigned the keys of Persia...I am assigned the keys of Yemen.*"
>
> (Baihaqi and Abu Naim)

Syria, Persia and Yemen were seats of power at that time. Thus, the Prophet was reminding his Companions, that even in these lands people will be liberated from injustices and a better social life established if they continued pursuing the vision of Islam with perseverance and fortitude. These examples should suffice. The point being emphasised is that for successfully connecting individuals in a cohesive movement and inspiring them to action, a clear vision and a sense of purpose and mission is required. These must be constantly reinvigorated. Generally, a lack of vision and mission are the main cause for people breaking away from each other, or for low morale. By keeping the Islamic mission constantly alive in the minds of people, unity, inspiration, motivation and commitment will be created, which in turn will strengthen the efforts for societal change.

The Role of Quranic Guidance

Finally, this Chapter concludes by highlighting the importance of adhering to the Quranic guidance during efforts for positive social change. It is our belief that a strong adherence to the Quran will enable Islamic workers to face contemporary challenges effectively and with confidence.

A Book of Guidance

The Glorious Quran, the Word of Allah, offers comprehensive guidance on introducing positive social change. It was by strongly adhering to this Book and following its guidance, that the Prophet Muhammad and his noble Companions were able to bring about a successful change in their social environment. The Quran moved and inspired them to action, and guided them through all the phases of change successfully. It gave them a clear vision, which extended beyond the boundaries of this worldly life. The Prophet and his Companions put their full trust in God and believed that success and failure are in His hands alone. They were convinced that success is not solely determined by material resources or military power, as a materialistic person might assume.

The Quran is, thus, not a story book that outlines the life of the Prophet Muhammad. Neither is it a book of history, science, philosophy, nor any other specific subject. Rather its primary and only concern is human beings, as individuals and as groups. Whilst reading the Quran, one comes across verses that deal with human creation, human nature, and the position of human beings amongst the rest of creation. Others verses discuss the Islamic faith and message, together with our moral, social and spiritual development. Some verses explain what motivates people and what tempts them towards evil and injustice. Still others point out what leads humans, as individuals and nations, to success and prosperity, and what leads them towards destruction. The Quran addresses all that affects people's success in this life and in the Life to Come. It highlights the approaches that were adopted by the great Prophets of Allah to bring about positive reforms in their societies. It offers guidance on the starting point, the goal, the methodology, and the broad principles that must be adhered to during efforts for societal change. In fact, it provides very comprehensive guidance on each phase of the change process. It even discusses what one should do when faced with problems and obstacles during the change process.

A Deeper Study of the Quran

An in-depth study of the Quran and *Sira* (life of Prophet Muhammad) is, therefore, essential in understanding thoroughly the methods and guidelines for introducing social reform and change. For agents of change it is fundamental to study the Quran regularly. For a better understanding, the correct method of study should be adhered to. The background and the historical and social context of the Quranic passage should be understood. Furthermore, an effort should be made to gain an understanding of the original Arabic words. This is because reading passages out of context, and not knowing the correct meaning of the Arabic terms, can sometimes lead students to a very superficial understanding, and in some instances to wrong conclusions. Also, there are some verses of the Quran that are specific to a situation, whilst others are more general. Additionally, some have very specific meanings whilst others contain more than one meaning. The way each type of verse is understood and applied to a particular problem is therefore different. This is why an understanding of the context of the passages is essential.

Application of the Quranic Guidance

A weak contact with Islam's sources of guidance (i.e. the Quran and *Sunna*) or a limited understanding of its teachings can lead Islamic workers to a state of confusion. As an example, what does one understand by an Islamic state, and what is implied by implementing Islam in society? Also, can Islam be implemented or does its system of life evolve and develop over time? Moreover, is implementing Islam limited to the application of Islamic laws only, for example, laws regarding capital punishment and inheritance? A detailed study of the Quran can help in understanding such questions regarding which so much confusion exists. The Quran clearly indicates that a society does not become Islamic merely through implementing a few of its laws. The Quran contains just over 6000 verses[2], and out of these only around 350 are related to legal issues. These deal with laws relating to marriage, divorce, inheritance, usury, gambling, loans, sales and crimes and penalties. The vast majority of Quranic verses deal with aspects of faith, worship of God, purification of character, morality, spirituality, social welfare, justice, and social relations. A large portion of the Quran also provide guidance for changing the socio-political context and efforts for introducing changes in society through stories explaining how the previous Prophets of Allah struggled to change their societies and bring people to His path.

With this in mind, the legal aspects form only a small percentage of Islam's overall system of life. Thus, by only implementing the legal aspects of Islam in society, does not necessarily indicate a full Islamic society. Other aspects such as faith, God-consciousness, good character, morality, social relations and social welfare, which form the bulk of Islam and which underpin the Islamic way of life, cannot be implemented. Rather, they have to be taught, encouraged and nurtured in a healthy social atmosphere and therefore they develop over time. In actual fact, a great deal of the Prophet Muhammad's time and efforts went into cultivating faith and good character, and nurturing moral values, creating healthy social conditions and culture, and with this foundation laid, the legal aspects were implemented quite smoothly within a very short period.

Furthermore, according to the Quran, prior to the implementation of Islamic laws, certain moral, social and economic conditions are a prerequisite. If these conditions do not exist in a society, then Islamic laws cannot be applied. This point is agreed upon by all Muslim scholars and jurists, past and present[3]. As an illustration, every individual in an Islamic society is encouraged to make efforts to earn a lawful livelihood, and begging is discouraged. However, if after exerting their best someone fails, then society, i.e. relatives, the community and also the government, is obliged to help and support them. Individuals are, thus, entitled to receiving support from relatives, friends or the government if they cannot find work or for other similar reasons. If, however, society, in particular the government, is unable to provide support to such a person, and as a result he/she is compelled to commit a crime in order to meet their basic needs, then they are not punishable according to Islamic law. On the contrary, the government is held responsible for its failure to provide the basic needs to sustain life. This is why Umar ibn al-Khattab, the second Caliph, relaxed capital punishment in special circumstances. As an example, he did not cut off the hands of those who committed theft during a famine in Medina, simply because his government could not provide for all people in that particular situation[4].

This applies to the implementation of all Islamic laws and regulations. Taking another example, Islamic laws regarding the punishment for fornication can only be enforced if a moral and God-conscious atmosphere is established, marriage is promoted and made easy, and all avenues, means and temptations that lead to such evil are removed from the social environment. In short, an Islamic government would not rush into applying its laws in society, rather it would, as a priority, work to create moral, social, economic and political conditions (i.e. change the socio-political context) that lead to a better and more dignified life for all its citizens, and which shield people from crime and immoral ways (see Chapter Seven for further discussion on this point). Thus, a comprehensive understanding of the Quran and *Sunna*, and Islamic jurisprudence is required for guiding social change and implementing Islamic laws.

> *"This religion cannot be taken except from the one who encompasses it completely."*
>
> (Bukhari)

Furthermore, Islam has set an order of priority for all things and this order must be followed. There are things that are essential (*fard* and *wajib*), others that are less essential and some that are even optional (*nafal*). Some things are clearly prohibited (*haram*), others are recommended (*mandub*), or disliked (*makruh*), or even simply permissible (*mubah*). However, even here there are exceptions to the general rule; those actions that are essential in one context may not be essential in another. For example, regarding food, the Quran states:

> *"He has forbidden to you only dead meat, blood, and the flesh of swine, and that which is slaughtered as a sacrifice for others than Allah. But if one is forced by necessity without wilful disobedience, nor transgressing due limits – then he is guiltless. For Allah is forgiving, Most Merciful."*
>
> (al-Baqara 2: 173)

In general, therefore, Islamic teachings advise that for any particular condition or problem situation, one must keep in mind the order of priority that has been set by Islam. Muadh bin Jabal, a Companion of the noble Prophet, was advised:

> *"You are going to a people of the Book. When you reach them, call them to witness that there is no god but the one Allah and Muhammad is His Messenger. And when they accept this, then tell them that Allah has enjoined on them Prayers. And when they accept this, then tell them that He has enjoined on them Zakat (poor due), which is to be taken from the rich amongst them and given to the poor."*
>
> (Bukhari)

Thus, a strong attachment with the Islamic sources of guidance is essential for introducing Islamic ideas and addressing social problems and issues. In addition, Islamic workers must attempt to understand Islam's principles and its methodology of jurisprudence (*Usul al-Fiqh*) and familiarise themselves with Islamic law and the methods for its introduction. Further, the lives and works of great Muslims in the past can help one to learn and understand how one should work for reform and change.

Work of the Earlier Prophets

Further, the Quran describes the work, approach and priorities of some of the earlier Prophets. Most of these Prophets of Allah started their work in very degenerate and corrupt societies, and their context presents different scenarios. As examples: the Prophet Moses went to Pharaoh to liberate his people, Shuayb strove to eradicate economic injustice, and the Prophet Lot dealt with social and sexual perversion. Thus, their context, strategy and approach, as contained in the Glorious Quran, should also be a source of guidance for Islamic workers. When studying their lives and missions from the details contained in the Quran, it is important to ask questions such as: how did they initiate their work? What strategies and methods did they adopt? From what areas did they encounter problems and why? How did they prepare their followers for the cause? How did they promote their system of life to their people, suddenly or gradually, etc.? Islamic workers should attempt to analyse the methodology adopted by the noble Prophets of Allah with the intention of searching for guidance on how to work in the present day and age.

To conclude, this chapter attempted to highlight the major contemporary challenges facing the Muslim community, both from within and without. Being aware of these challenges, having a clear vision, and adhering to the Quranic guidance in the change process, are all essential tools for the formulation of effective reform and change strategies.

Notes:

1. This quote appeared in Geaves, Ron, *Sectarian Influences within Islam in Britain, with References to the Concepts of 'ummah' and 'community'*, Monograph Series, Community Religions Project, University of Leeds, p. 76. It was quoted from: Hadden, Jeffery K. & Shupe, Anson, *Secularisation and Fundamentalism Reconsidered – Religion and the Political Order*, Vol III, New York: New Era Books, 1989, p.xvii. quoting from Dobbelaere, Karel, *The Secularisation of Society? Some Methodological Suggestions.*
2. Denffer, Ahmed Von, *Ulum Al-Quran. An Introduction to the Sciences of the Quran*, Leicester: The Islamic Foundation, 1983.
3. Kamali, Mohammad Hashim, *Principles of Islamic Jurisprudence*, Cambridge: The Islamic Texts Society, 1991.
4. Ibid, p.247

PART II

The Change Process: Framework and Methodology

CHAPTER VI

Framework for Social Change

Part One of this book has attempted to depict the vision of Islam for individual and social life. It also identified the major challenges facing Islamic movements in their endeavours for advancing positive values in human society. This first Chapter of Part Two begins to look at how a change based on Islam should be brought about. It presents the Islamic framework for guiding social change. This framework sets the parameters and boundaries for the change efforts, provides the values, principles and priorities, and indicates where one should begin and what is the ultimate goal of the change endeavours. The methodology, which is based on this framework, provides key ingredients and components that should form the basis of a change strategy and this is examined in the next Chapter. The relationship of the Islamic framework and methodology are shown in Figure 1.

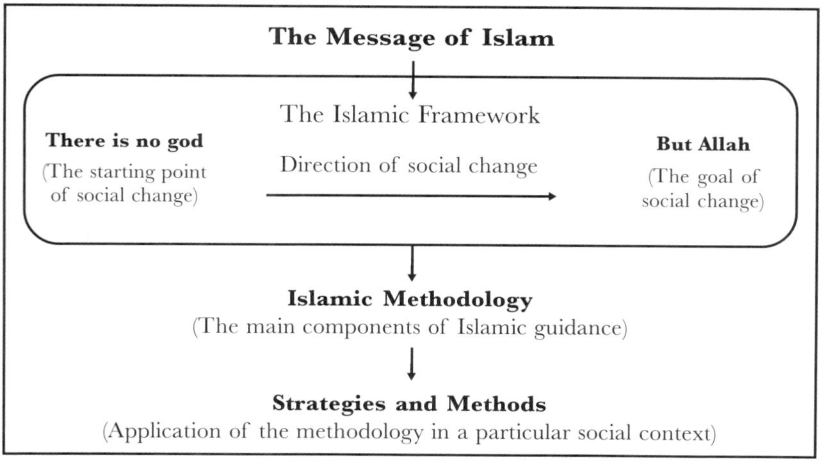

Figure 1: Diagram showing the relationship between the Islamic framework, methodology and operating strategies.

As this diagram shows, the Islamic framework for social change is directly derived from the universal Islamic message; a message brought by all the Prophets of Allah to humanity. The first part of the Islamic message[1], contained in the declaration of faith, is:

> *"Let there be no god, but (the one) God."*

Initially, one may not see the relevance of this message to social change. However, on a deeper reflection, the unique and rich guidance contained therein will become evident, and the significance of its meaning and implications for the agents of change and society realised. The discussion that follows attempts to expound the meaning of the term "Let there be no god, but God" so that its significance in guiding efforts for social change can be grasped.

The Universal Message of Islam

Although the message "Let there be no god, but God" appears to be a short and simple statement declaring the Oneness of Allah (*tawhid*), it has profound spiritual, moral, social, economic and political implications. Not only does this message form the foundation of an Islamic culture and society, it also provides a framework for guiding social, economic and political affairs. As was mentioned earlier, this is not a new message for humanity. The Quran contends that the Prophet Muhammad was not the first to pronounce this statement. All true Prophets of Allah invited their people to this same message again and again. For example, hints of this message are cited in numerous instances in the Bible as well[2], although its authentic meaning has become somewhat obscure through the passage of time.

The Islamic message hints at both the inner and outer dimensions of human life. The inner dimensions include faith, God-consciousness (*taqwa*), worship of Allah (*ibada*), devotion and humbleness (*khushu*) gratitude (*shukr*), remembrance of Allah (*dhikr*) and constant turning towards Allah and asking for His forgiveness (*tawba*). These all aid in producing a deep love of Allah, an integrated personality, and a concern for humanity. The outer dimensions, as will be detailed below, include efforts to fulfil the Will of Allah in society. Islamic guidance translates the Will of

Allah into concrete objectives that must be realised in all spheres of individual and social life. This includes efforts to establish justice, peace, co-operation between people and better social conditions. Both these inner and outer dimensions are, thus, interdependent; they support and nurture each other.

The Islamic Framework for Guiding Social Change

An analysis of the Islamic Message brings out four elements and these form the Islamic framework for guiding thought and actions for positive change:

1. *Starting Point: Let there be no (false) god*: This first element of the framework indicates that change efforts must begin by liberating people from the influence and domination of all kinds of false gods, both from within a person and from society.
2. *Goal: But God*: The second element asserts that Allah should be the goal of all endeavours; everything should be placed at His service; all desires, motives, efforts and resources should be directed in the service of Allah. In other words, the objective of Islam is to invite people to Allah and establish His Sovereignty and chosen Way for humanity in society and the world at large *(iqamat ad-Din)*. This incorporates endeavours for developing and nurturing good individuals as well as establishing a just social life based on God's revealed guidance, with the sole intention of seeking the good pleasure of Allah in this life and in the life Hereafter.
3. *Process of Change*: The final element of the Islamic framework suggests a direction, a process and a wider strategy for individual and social reform. It directs efforts towards changing a society where false gods dominate, within and without, to a society where Allah is the Sovereign.
4. *Values*: The Islamic message also contends that Allah Alone is the source of true human guidance, values and a social code. These must be understood, imbibed and adhered to in all individual and social endeavours, including efforts for social change.

Each of these elements of the Islamic framework are elucidated upon below.

The Starting Point – A Rejection of False Gods

The first part of the Islamic message is a declaration rejecting all false gods in society (let there be no god), and this defines the starting point for social change as well. What does this imply for change agents in concrete terms? Is this part of the Islamic message simply suggesting that people should reject idols and worship Allah alone, or is there a deeper meaning to it? From a general analysis of Islam and after reflecting over the meaning of the Arabic words used in the Islamic message (particularly the word *ilah* for god), we conclude that a very significant and fundamental point is being made; a universal truth is being expressed. This statement is a call to dislodge all powers that have become (false) 'gods' in society and the world since they are, as the following discussion highlights, the root cause of human problems and miseries. In order to clearly unravel the deeper implications of this statement, a grasp of the following points is required: who are these false gods, how do they arise and take hold of society and why are they the root cause of human problems? Each of these points will be considered in this section.

The False Gods

Who are the false gods that have to be rejected and from whom people have to be liberated? A general analysis of Islam leads us to conclude that the first part of the Islamic message "Let there be no god" actually presents a unique and radical meaning to the term 'god'. The Arabic word *ilah*, used for god in this book, is comprehensive in its meaning. Broadly, it refers to an object of worship, or someone (or thing) who is served and obeyed and whose help and guidance is sought[3]. From the Quran it can be deduced that the false *ilahs* or *false gods* are no other than certain people: as individuals, groups, religious leaders, kings, dynasties, dictators, etc., who assume, consciously or unconsciously, the role of 'gods' in human affairs, acquiring absolute sovereign powers. They manage, by hook or by crook, to dominate a people or exert some kind of influence over them in order to exploit them. People and communities turn to them for guidance and leadership, or out of fear, or to fulfil some kind of emotional, economic or social need. These false gods, may not, however, be directly visible, since they generally tend to screen themselves and their evil motives behind certain symbols, rituals, slogans, ideologies, cultural practices and societal structures.

Shirk – *The Root of Human Problems*

In the light of the Quran, the false gods are the root causes of human miseries. Thus, the Islamic Message suggests that the root to human anxieties and calamities is not nuclear weapons, environmental pollution and destruction, political corruption, oppression, genocide, civil wars, social inequalities, crime, drugs, the breakdown of the family and so on. These are all, in actual fact, symptoms and the Quran identifies the root of human miseries to be *shirk*. This term refers to assigning or associating the attributes of Godhead to others besides the real God. In other words, *shirk* denies Allah an Exclusive Sovereign role in human affairs. The Islamic message points out that when people reject Allah, partially or wholly, and instead submit to, follow or serve false gods and turn to them for guidance, worship and solutions to their problems, which all amounts to committing *shirk*, then the seeds of corruption, injustice and misery are sown in the social fabric.

> *"Verily, Shirk (leads to) the greatest oppression."*
>
> (Luqman 31: 13)

Islam considers *shirk* as the greatest of all sins, the highest transgression against Allah and the root of all human crises. This is because the implications of *shirk* are profound; as the following discussion will highlight, it leads to the domination of man over man, of class over class, oppression, injustice and other social crises. Islamic guidance indicates that *shirk* is a universal issue and can affect any people, in any age.

> *"And indeed We sent forth in every people a Messenger, (saying): Serve Allah only, and shun Taghoot* (i.e. all powers of rebellion against Allah)."
>
> (an-Nahl 16: 36)

However, many people, including intellectuals and philosophers, fail to recognise the root of human problems and miseries. This may perhaps be the reason why many individuals, pressure groups and political parties, generally strive to address the symptoms of human issues and problems rather than their root causes. Islam stresses that unless people turn away from false gods of their times, social evils will continue and worsen – and all efforts for social change will be fruitless. Merely striving to bring changes in our neighbourhood, communities, education, or economics, without first working to free people from the hold and influence of false gods, will not bring about a change based on justice – the evils of false gods will simply reappear in other areas of life.

Archetypal False Gods

The Quran points our attention to four major archetypal false gods that appear in human society. These are:

1. Social and political elites
2. Religious elites
3. Cultures and ideologies that are not sanctioned by God
4. Slavery to one's ego

All these are archetypal false gods, and if any one of these are allowed to root or dominate in social life, they would lead society towards misery and social disintegration. The subsequent discussion provides some examples of these archetypal false gods and explains how they arise in a society.

Social and political Elites

This archetypal false god includes evil elite groups who endeavour to dominate people and effectively assume the role of gods. Examples include Nimrod, Pharaoh, corrupt kings, dictators, the ruling class or other forms of corrupt political and social leadership. Secret organisations, political groups and alliances, and business corporations can fall into this archetypal false gods if they have evil designs and are intent upon furthering their power and influence to the detriment of others.

"Pharaoh said: 'O chiefs, no god do I know for you but myself ...'"
(al-Qasas 28: 38)

History presents many cases of political figures and elite groups who were able to dominate their people by using ingenious and cunning methods. Examples can be cited from numerous civilisations such as the early Mesopotamian, Assyrian, Greek, Roman, Indian, and Chinese. As an illustration, during the time of the Prophet Abraham, Nimrod asserted sovereign powers. He claimed to derive the authority of his sovereignty from the moon god, Nannar, on whose behalf he alleged to rule. Nimrod and some of his predecessors, with the support of the high priests, the elitist group of that time, manipulated and engineered social conditions, instituted certain rituals, customs and ceremonies, and divided people into social classes so as to dominate and consolidate all power in their hands. In fact, according to Mawdudi[4], the shrine of Nannar, the moon god, was a royal palace to which people were religiously required to bring offerings and their wealth. Some female worshippers were also obliged to go there to symbolically become Nannar's bride, but in reality to become slaves to the priests. Through such practices, the king and the priests were able to exploit and dominate the masses. This was further facilitated through dividing their society into the following classes[5]: the King having absolute powers, the Amelu, the highest class consisting of priests, state officials, etc. – the Prophet Abraham was born into this class, the Mushkenu, merchants, craftsmen and farmers, and the Ardu, slaves. The highest class dominated communities from the lower classes, usurped their property and enjoyed many special privileges.

Similarly, according to the Quran, Pharaoh also claimed sovereign powers and he and his predecessors achieved this through carefully manipulating and misguiding his own people and enslaving the Israelites, the ethnic minority of his time. The Prophet Moses came forward to challenge the sovereignty of Pharaoh and his ruling elite, and during the exchange of words that took place, Pharaoh said to him:

> *"If you take anyone other than me to be your Sovereign (god), I shall surely throw you in Prison."*
>
> (ash-Shuara 26: 29)

As a matter of fact, during the times of most Prophets, either some particular individual or an elite class of people had dominated and established themselves in the land and used their power to suppress and exploit other people, or were involved in some other kinds of social injustices. This is why many such leaders saw the Prophets of Allah as a threat to their self-interests. Some were so corrupt that they even went as far as killing the Prophets of Allah.

> *"That was because they rejected the signs of Allah and killed the Prophets wrongfully..."*
>
> (al-Baqara 2: 61)

Thus, social and political elites, when blinded in the pursuit for power and wealth, usually endeavour to engineer society and manipulate people in order to further their selfish interests, and in the process commonly lead them to many social and political miseries and crises.

> *"and they shall say, Our Lord we obeyed our leaders and our great men, and it is they who led us astray from the right path."*
>
> (al-Ahzab 33: 67)

Regarding this point, Alija Ali Izetbegovic indicates how the mass media in modern societies are employed to manipulate people into blind following:

> "The so-called mass media (press, radio and television) are in fact the means of mass manipulation. On the one side are the editorial offices of a small number of people who created the program, on the other side is a passive audience of millions...It offers ready-made solutions for all problems in life. Our time offers examples of how mass culture media (radio, film, and television, being a government monopoly) can be used for a mass delusion of the worst kind. There is no need for brutal force to rule people against their will. That can now be attained in a legal way by paralysing the people's will, by offering them cut-and-dried truths, and by preventing them from thinking and arriving at their own opinions of men and events."[6]

It is through similar means that powerful secret organisations, elite groups or those who control financial institutions and the mass media in our contemporary world, are able to shape society in ways that serve and further their own interests. For example, in order to embed consumerism in society, capitalists have atomised society and created a consumer culture through the aid of the mass media. This, in turn, has led to an increase in their profits and, hence, their power and influence. However, such changes have also been devastating for society. The community has declined, families are on the verge of disintegration, and consequently crime and corruption are on the increase.

Religious Elites

In like manner, according to the Quran, religious elites can become false gods in society if they contrive to exploit the ignorance and emotions of ordinary people. Thus, corrupt organised religious figures and institutions are included in this second group of archetypal false gods. This archetype can also include those who adopt crooked religious views, or who have invented false beliefs and unnatural practices, for example, celibacy, monasticism, etc., and who strive to impose these on their communities.

> *"They take their doctors of law (rabbis and priests) and saints (and monks) to be their Lords, instead of Allah. And (they take as their Lord) Christ, the son of Mary; yet they were commanded to submit to the one Allah: there is no Allah but He. Praise and glory be to Him. (Far is He) from having the partners they associate (with Him)."*
>
> (at-Tawba 9: 31)

Many instances can be cited where certain religious figures and institutions, who use religion for pursuing their own personal ambitions or for other wrong purposes, have played 'god'. They have led to the emotional and mental enslavement of millions of people, instituted numerous meaningless rituals, ceremonies and corrupt practices, and rooted manifold moral and social miseries. Commonly, those at the top of the religious hierarchy have considerable power and authority. In some cases, they are even invested with absolute god-like authority of making things lawful or unlawful, since people look up to them for guidance and leadership. However, history shows that at many times these positions have been abused and people have been exploited and led astray from the right path. Interestingly, Islam has no priesthood or clergy, and no religious hierarchy is recognised, so as to prevent such evils taking root in society.

> *"O believers, many of the rabbis and monks indeed devour the wealth of people wrongfully and bar from Allah's way."*
>
> (at-Tawba 9: 34)

Culture and Ideologies that are not Sanctioned by Allah

This archetypal false god implies a blind following of the popular customs, cultures and ideologies that are formed out of human reasoning and which conflict with what Allah has revealed to humanity. For example, the following contemporary ideologies and ways of society can be included in this category of archetypal false gods: secular-materialism, extravagant lifestyles, infanticide (e.g. abortion), as also nationalism, tribalism, secularism, materialism, capitalism, communism, and so on, or what the Quran refers to as a blind adherence to the way of forefathers.

> *"When it is said to them: "Follow what Allah has revealed", They say: "No! we shall follow the ways of our fathers". What, even though their fathers were void of wisdom and guidance."*
>
> (al-Baqara 2: 170)

> *"What! Have they partners with Allah (false gods) who have instituted for them some religion without sanction from Allah?"*
>
> (ash-Shura 42: 21)

In actual fact, as has already been pointed out in Chapter Four, a culture and way of life emerges from an ideology. Islam contends that by blindly accepting and submitting to any ideology, or the prevalent culture, which is not sanctioned by Allah (in other words, acceding to something which is not compatible with human nature) leads to the domination of man over man, nation over nation, and to numerous social, economic and global problems. For example, by adopting capitalism, communism, fascism and other ideologies that have been produced out of human reasoning to direct and shape collective affairs, humanity has brought upon itself numerous local, national and international problems and crises. Some examples of the corruption, imbalance and social miseries that have emerged from an adoption of such ideologies were given earlier in Chapter Four. Here it would suffice to take nationalism as an example. A blind adherence to nationalism has led to the domination of a few nations in the world over others. It has also led to many major wars, to oppression and exploitation, and is found behind efforts to enslave people, both in this century as well as in the past. Taken to extremes, nationalism encourages imperialism and fascism. Put another way, a total slavery to one's nation (particularly if it is involved in aggression and oppression) results in conflict, barbarity and disorder. Today, the powerful nations of the world are striving to accumulate world power and control the earth's resources, and in the process are causing genocide or great social and economic upheavals, poverty and racial tensions. Examples from the recent past include: the First and Second World Wars, genocide in Vietnam, Rwanda, Bosnia and Kosova, oppression in Palestine, apartheid in South Africa, the Gulf War and the Third World debt. All these have been a direct result of nationalistic interests and policies.

Various tactics are employed for furthering a nations interests or achieving its domination over weaker nations. Generally, the major obstacle in the way of nationalists are a people who are organised around a shared vision and who hold common values and beliefs (since organised people are a source of resistance). This is why a strategy to reduce a peoples' attachment to common values and religion that unites them is frequently employed. A similar strategy was employed by many Western nations during their efforts for imperialism and colonisation and this is very well articulated, in relation to the Muslim world, by Baron Carra de Vaux as quoted below:

> "That we should endeavour to split the Muslim world, to break its moral unity, using to this effect the ethnic and political divisions ... Let us, therefore, accentuate these differences, in order to increase on the one hand national sentiment and to decrease on the other that of religious community among the various Muslim races...In one word, let us segment Islam and make use, moreover, of Muslim heresies and the Sufi orders."[7]

Through the employment of such strategies, powerful nations attempt to weaken a people's unity, their solidarity and their resolve for living in freedom and maintaining control over their own lands and resources. As opposed to this, Islam denounces all regional or national loyalties that lead to the oppression and domination of any people; it opposes the motto "my nation, right or wrong", and teaches that all people are the descendants of Adam and Eve; they are equal before God, and, therefore, no one should be wronged or exploited in any way, by anyone.

> *"O people, We have created you from a male and female, and made you into tribes and nations, so that you may know each other (not that you despise each other). Surely the most honoured among you is the one who is most Godly..."*
>
> (al-Hujurat 49: 13)

Thus, cultures, ways of life and ideologies and beliefs that are not sanctioned by Allah, have the potential of becoming false gods and consequently result in social and global ruin and destruction.

Slavery to the Ego

Finally, a slavery to one's own ego is another potential *false god* highlighted in the Quran. This fourth archetypal false god implies extreme self-indulgence and slavery to selfish desires, greed, negative emotions, and slavery to one's own opinions.

> *"Have you noticed the man who has made his ego (selfish desires) as his god ..."*
>
> (al-Furqan 25: 43)

An unrestrained submission to ones own ego blinds human reason, impairs moral consciousness, and results in numerous personal and social injustices and wrongs. For example, many social problems such as drug abuse, gambling, adultery, crime, jealousy, hatred, psychological disorders, murder, corruption and so on, actually stem from an unrestrained submission to the ego and excessive self-indulgence. Moreover, a person who becomes a blind slave to his/her own opinions, views, beliefs and convictions can also create enormous inter-personal problems and even social disorder. If power and resources were also made available to such people as those who worship their ego, then this assistance would most likely give rise to other archetypal false gods mentioned above.

In conclusion, archetypal false gods, depicted above, arise and begin to dominate a people by gaining some kind of power or influence over individual life and society. Different forms of power can be held by these false gods and includes: coercive (for example, military), intellectual (for example, experts or specialisations), referent (for example, hero worship, or adducing spiritual or religious power), economic or political power. However, whatever kind of power is gained by such false gods to accomplish their objectives, they inevitably plague society with on-going tension and conflict; they create social and political hierarchies that divide and discriminate between people. Groups of people then continuously compete and engage in conflict to reach the top of these hierarchies in order to secure control of power and societal resources. Society, thus, becomes devoid of peace, human dignity and justice.

How do False Gods Arise in a Society?

We can now move on to discuss how false gods emerge, take root and begin to dominate a people. In the light of Islamic guidance, false gods arise and gain ascendancy over individuals and society when certain factors, attitudes, practices, and social conditions become rife in society. Some of these key factors are:

1. Widespread and deep-seated ignorance *(jahiliya)*, arrogance and transgression (*taghoot* – disbelief and rebellion against Allah). All these lead to a confusion in beliefs and world-view, arrogance, rebellion, moral confusion, conceit, depravity, corruption and apathy.
2. Widespread self-indulgence, ego worship, immoral temptations, and excessive individual and collective greed for power and wealth (materialism).
3. Extremism, that is, an imbalance in social attitudes and norms: for example, when a people become too cautious or lax, develop

extreme love or hate for some person, nation or material object, or when they place too much emphasis either on the spiritual or the material, and so on, at both individual and collective levels.

These factors open up many doors of opportunity for those people who have inclined themselves towards evil to gradually make their way to the helm of societal affairs. They yield the way for tyrants, totalitarian regimes, corrupt religious figures and institutions, or even for dynasties to appear that begin to dominate and exploit the masses. Below we attempt to depict a general pattern of how false gods arise in society. Specific cases, for obvious reasons, may not completely conform to this general pattern. The following three broad steps describe the general process of how false gods gain ascendancy over a people: entry, taking roots and domination.

ENTRY

The seeds of evil are sown when certain individuals, motivated by excessive greed or extremist ideas, either on their own or by aligning themselves with others actively and aggressively strive to further their interests in society. Such people, as individuals or groups, referred to as false gods, attempt to satisfy their greed and further their selfish interests through a variety of methods and stratagems, that are dependent on their intelligence, initial resources and contacts. For example, they may push forward with their agenda through engineering social conditions, gaining access to and control of societal power and resources, controlling information, creating deception, misguiding people through manipulating their emotions and sympathies, or by confusing issues and concepts, and the like. History highlights that in some cases, false gods have even attempted to make people believe that they directly possess supernatural powers, have knowledge of the Unseen, are descendants of gods, saints, or super-human beings, or that they have exclusive access to Allah. Other examples include incidents where false gods, with support from intellectuals or high priests – religious or secular, have contrived superstitious beliefs and myths, or cultivated misguided philosophies, theories, ideologies, and slogans (such as nationalism, liberation, power to the people, etc.), or even advanced certain lifestyles. At other times particular rituals, entertainments, or certain customs and festivals have been instituted by false gods so as to keep ordinary people in a state of false consciousness, their attention turned away from their machinations, or so as to simply exploit them.

> *"And in this way did the supposed gods of pagans make infanticide appear an approved act in their eyes, in order to lead them to their own destruction and confusion in their religion ..."*
>
> (al-Anam 6: 137)

Initially, false gods may refrain from asking ordinary people to support or serve their interests directly. They may begin by prompting them to accept and succumb to some particular objects, or to embrace certain concepts and practices. For example, many communities in the past have been manipulated into worshipping stone idols, super-human and legendary figures, saints, certain animals (for example, the golden calf), stars and planets, or visiting shrines and making offerings to idols. At other times, we find that certain thinkers, saints and even Prophets of Allah after their death have been idolised, or turned into gods (or sons of God), and the false gods pretend to derive their authority from these great personalities.

> *"(Allah) said (to Moses), We have tested your people in your absence. The Samiri* (who managed to make his people submit to the golden calf in the absence of the Prophet Moses*) has led them astray."*
>
> (Ta Ha 20: 85)

TAKING ROOTS

Such approaches are employed by false gods to gain power or to legitimise their authority over their people. They propagate their ideas and evil practices in a way that makes them sound quite appealing, modern, trendy, progressive and liberal. This entices many ordinary people into believing that these can actually bring them benefit and prosperity. Through the sustained injection of such concepts and practices into society, false gods manage to influence and direct a people and society. This also allows them to shape values, attitudes and life-styles and to engineer a culture that occupies the population with rituals, festivals, trivia or sensational entertainments.

DOMINATION

Gradually then, new or modified social and political processes and structures begin to take root in society. These structures are generally intended to remove opposition, prevent noble people from holding powerful positions, reduce social interaction and atomise people, and thus, enhance the power and domination of false gods. The following Quranic verse suggests how manipulation and the re-structuring of society can eliminate and prevent noble, good and pious people from positions of power.

> *"Verily, the monarchs, when they enter a land, despoil it (physically) and make the noblest of its people into the lowest."*
>
> (an-Naml 27: 34)

The false gods, though firmly entrenched at the top of the political hierarchy and being in total control by this stage, continue to pay lip service to moral values and just principles in order to keep hold of their leadership and power. However, if their tactics fail, some false gods may even go as so far as to use brute force to suppress any opposition or signs of rebellion.

To sum up, the Quran presents four major archetypical false gods and elucidates how they root themselves in societies. However, it stresses that they only succeed in their evil plans when people turn away from God's revealed guidance by becoming indifferent, lax vigilance on social evils, turn into blind followers or allow society to be divided. Thus, the message of Islam declares that whichever false god people submit to, the results will be the same: domination of man over man, enslavement, misery and ruin.

> *"And your God is One Allah. There is no god but He, Most Gracious, Most Merciful."*
>
> (al-Baqara 2: 163)

By accepting Allah and following His guidance, humanity will obtain contentment, inner peace, integration, personally and socially, and be led towards social peace and harmony, freedom, justice and prosperity. False gods use and abuse people and the resources under their control to further their selfish interests, whereas the real Allah cares, He is the Compassionate, the Merciful and the Forgiving, the All-Wise and All-Mighty. He gives and provides for all essential human needs, while false gods take and exploit. Allah is independent of His Creation, whereas false gods are very much dependent on the people they dominate and exploit.

In relation to this, Mawdudi highlights the objective of Islam by proclaiming:

> "My call is: come let us put an end to the world-wide tyranny and chaos. Let us uproot the domination of man over man and let us build a new world on the lines indicated by the Quran in which humanity should regain its proper place and people may live with honour, freedom, justice and brotherhood."[8]

This view is also supported by the words of a Companion of the Prophet Muhammad, Rabi bin Amer, who boldly said in front of Rustum, the commander of the Persian army and his courtiers:

> "(he said to Rustum) We have come to take, whoever wishes, out of the domination of men, into the servitude of Allah alone..."[9]

To conclude the above discussion, it is only when individuals and communities begin to free themselves from the influence of false gods, that a change according to Islam will be initiated. Put another way, it is only when the evil designs of false gods are made manifest that there will be a re-awakening of a population. Further, the breaking of chains and freeing one-self from the influences of the false gods will lead to a noble and more elevated state of heart and mind. It will assist in liberating ones thoughts and actions and enable one to face social injustices with great courage and resolve. It was due to a deep understanding of the Islamic message, that the Prophet Muhammad strove to cultivate the Islamic belief and world-view in his people. He and his Companions renounced every false god and made the real Allah the centre of their lives. They adhered to His guidance alone. This provided the means to draw closer to Allah and at the same time prevented them from abusing power and to dominate and exploit people like the false gods of their time.

The Goal – Establishment of God's Sovereignty

Let us now move onto exploring the goal of Islamic change. Once people set themselves free from the influence of false gods, a huge amount of energy becomes available for constructive work. Islam then channels this energy towards accomplishing its goal in society. This goal is to establish the Sovereignty of God in social life and the state. In concrete terms, this implies that efforts must be directed towards changing the socio-political environment that aids in awakening people and freeing them from the influence of false gods, nurturing morality and establishing justice in all systems of social life.

Islam stresses that Sovereignty, that is the absolute power to command, to define beliefs, laws, rights and wrongs, belongs only to Allah. It cannot be shared between different gods; cannot be distributed amongst a number of individuals or groups.

> *"He alone is the Sovereign of the Heavens and the Earth ..."*
> (az-Zukhruf 43: 84)

It can be inferred from this that the meaning of the Sovereignty of God has great social and political implications. It sets parameters for the use of power in society. It calls for the dethroning of all false gods in society – strips them of their sovereignty, so that all power is submitted to the All-Powerful God. In other words, Islam aims to build a society that is free from religious, social or political hierarchies, and in which everyone, including the policy makers, social institutions, and the rich and wealthy in society, can all be held accountable for their actions. Islam emphasises that no one can be above the law or allowed to abuse power and authority in any way. Allah Alone is the supreme authority in society. However, political sovereignty – a limited, relative sovereignty (*mulk*), or the power to enforce the law, can be vested in an Islamic government, which has to rule in accordance with Divine guidance.

Thus, a caliph, the head of the Muslim world-community, is not considered as a sovereign, a dictator, or someone with extra-special rights and privileges. Rather he is respected, but at the same time he is accountable to the people for all actions concerning his office. He has to govern and conduct societal affairs according to God's revealed guidance and adhere to the system of *shura*, i.e. consultation in all decision making with the citizens directly or with a representative body. To give an example, below is a quote from a speech delivered by the first Caliph, Abu Bakr (d. 634 CE) upon his taking office:

> "Help me if I am in the right; set me right if I am in the wrong ...Obey me as long as I obey Allah and His Prophet; If I disobey Him and His Prophet, then obey me not..."[10]

Islam emphasises that the establishment of God's Sovereignty can alone ensure justice to all people. Reflection over this statement is important. If sovereignty and the exercise of absolute power are in the hands of any particular individual or group, they will naturally use this to protect and further their interests and that of their own people, which often results in injustice and oppression. As Lord Acton put it so succinctly: *"Power tends to corrupt, and absolute power corrupts absolutely"*. In contrast, since God is the God of all people, His guidance, enshrined in the Quran, does not favour any particular people or group over others, nor is it biased in any way towards anyone. God and His guidance is free from human weaknesses. Since His Mercy extends to all His creation, He does not tolerate any form of injustice or oppression. Allah's guidance, thus, provides a moral, legal and an equitable framework to guide all decisions and social policies.

> *"Those who do not judge according to what We have revealed are the wrong-doers..."*
>
> (al-Maida 5: 44–7)

On the contrary, as present practices highlight, many dominant political and elite groups, decision makers, movers and shakers in our society, and the rich and wealthy (who have become the gods of society) are able to shape social policies and conditions in their favour. Many decisions and policies are actually politically motivated and aimed at safeguarding the interests of particular powerful groups or classes. At times, this is achieved through immoral ways such as bribery, coercion, delaying tactics, manipulation, holding onto information and other immoral methods. The general public, made powerless through social atomisation, careful manipulation of social conditions and cut-off from the corridors of power, are at their mercy. In many contemporary societies, policy makers are not very accountable and there is little concern for the less privileged. Furthermore, the dominant groups set the framework for addressing issues together with the social and political agenda in society. *"Might (or majority) is right"* is the norm and there is hardly any permanent framework or ethical basis to guide policy making in modern day secular societies. Sovereignty, in theory, belongs to the people, but in practice to a ruling elite who are not usually bound by any permanent values. Things that are considered illegal and immoral today, could become legal and proper tomorrow, and vice versa.

In conclusion then, Islam's message for humanity provides a framework for guiding efforts for social change. This is as follows: first, change is initiated when people renounce all false gods in society. This develops an independent thought, enables people to escape the deceptions of false gods, and in turn helps them to view their social conditions more objectively. Further, efforts for change are not limited to addressing the symptoms, but rather focus on the root cause of human problems and miseries. People and society must be emancipated from the domination of false gods, and in their place the Sovereignty of the True God should be established. This is the ultimate objective of Islamic endeavours so that justice can be ensured to all people.

The Process of Social Change

With the starting point and the goal of social change defined, the Islamic message also suggests a broad process for change; that is, how to move from the starting point towards the goal. Put another way, the process guides thought and actions on changing a society in which false gods have assumed absolute sovereignty, to a society where the Sovereignty of God is established. This process provides a wider strategy and guidance on addressing social evils and changing the corrupt and unjust systems of life under which people live. The details of the change process are contained in the methodology which is examined more closely in the next Chapter. At this stage, the broad process and strategy for shaping society that are suggested by the Islamic framework are discussed. These underpin the Islamic methodology.

At first sight, the Islamic framework for social change appears to be simplistic; particularly if it is applied to effect change in our hi-tech, information age. But as one probes deeper and examines the full significance of this framework, one realises that it offers deep insights and wisdom for the task of social change. The Quran states unequivocally that all Prophets of Allah, in every age, used this framework to guide their efforts for social reform and to address social issues. This implies that the framework outlined is universal; for all times and for all societies.

As mentioned previously, every world-view or ideology leads to a particular socio-political environment and creates its own particular methods and approaches to life. Those holding secular-materialistic views would approach social problems and issues from a different perspective as compared to those who hold the Islamic world-view. As an illustration, secular methods of problem solving, at the very best, only treat or try to address the symptoms. This is because a reductionist approach is employed. Problems are narrowed down and addressed in isolation of other wider issues that may be important factors in their cause. This is why solutions lack the links with elements outside the problem boundaries, and as a result are unbalanced and incomplete.

Undoubtedly human beings have limitations, physical and intellectual. We possess limited information processing capabilities. It is, therefore, impossible for us to take into consideration all the wider issues and factors affecting a particular problem situation. This is why humans require Divine guidance which employs a holistic approach. Islam addresses the root of our problems and takes into consideration all factors impinging on a problem situation. Softer factors such as faith, social structures, the dominant culture, social attitudes, economic conditions, the level of care and welfare in society, etc., are all factors that must be taken into consideration when solving human problems. However, many of these hardly come into the equation of secular approaches to problem solving. The Quran, being Divine guidance, gives comprehensive, pragmatic and balanced solutions to our social problems. Also, solutions or problem solving strategies to newly occurring problems can be derived from the basic principles and framework provided by Islam.

To illustrate the above point, it is generally agreed that crime and social evils, if not checked, would disturb the social order and peace in society. So how can crime be checked or eliminated completely? A secular approach would look at the particular crime, and find either technical or legal solutions to address it. Take house burglaries for instance. To address this problem, a secular approach installs more secure locks and alarm systems in houses, imposes a greater fine on burglars, has more police in the streets, encourages neighbourhood watch schemes and so on. However, it is found that, with every problem solving strategy the crime prevention officers come up with, the burglars manage to find even more sophisticated ways of breaking and entering. Thus, despite the fact that there are tougher penalties and more surveillance, burglaries have not been reduced. Thus, one can discern that these solutions are not in effect solutions, on the contrary they have in fact led to worse problems. According to Islam, and as is discussed below, the solution does not lie in more security cameras or police, rather the deep recesses of the heart and soul have to be affected with faith in order to change people's behaviour and attitudes towards crime and social evil.

As another example, how can racial tensions be reduced in society? Again secular responses try to contain the problem rather than solve it. These solutions have included the setting up of race relations bodies, the formulation of the race relations act to counter racial discrimination, and have established equal opportunity forums. Several millions of pounds are spent annually to form and maintain such forums and bodies, but with little result. As anticipated, such approaches have mostly failed to lead our societies towards racial harmony, and at most have only succeeded in creating some awareness of the problem and in producing statistics on the whole issue. In contrast, Islam draws our attention to the fact that racial tensions stem from one's beliefs and views on race; they cannot, therefore, be removed through legislation alone.

One further example here will help to illustrate the point being made. In America, during the 1920's, the government, on realising the harmful effects of alcohol, decided to make it illegal in the country. What method was employed? At first the government began by educating the public about the harmful effects of alcohol on social life through various means such as the media, schools and so on. When it was judged that the message had gone across, the government introduced a law prohibiting alcohol. However, the public, instead of complying, started to make and drink alcohol undercover, and it became so widespread that the government was compelled to repeal that law soon after it was enacted. Again the secular approach and solution did not work, despite expending millions of pounds in the process. Similar methods and approaches have been employed for creating an awareness about AIDS, drugs and smoking, but with little effect.

Contrast this with the approach employed by Islam. When the verse of the Quran prohibiting alcohol was revealed, people immediately gave up its drinking without any hesitation. Even those who had alcohol in their mouths spat it out as soon as they were informed of the revelation. This was accomplished without any state intervention, policing, or by any other similar means. *What was the secret?* It was simply the application of the Islamic process of social change. Unlike the American government, the noble Prophet of Allah did not start by educating people about the harmful effects of alcohol. Rather, he worked to clarify and root the Islamic world-view and strong faith amongst his followers. When people had accepted Allah as the only Sovereign from the core of their hearts and believed that success only lies in obeying Him and in submitting to His guidance, then whatever came from Allah was accepted willingly and acted upon. With this foundation laid, the Quran at first hinted that people should not offer prayers while drunk, then they were briefly educated about the harmful effects of alcohol and many of the Prophet's Companions gave up drinking alcohol at that stage. Finally, the Quranic verse containing the total prohibition of alcohol was revealed; at this stage, people on the whole stopped drinking alcohol immediately. In fact, barrels and containers that stored alcohol were broken in the streets by the people themselves.[11]

Prohibition of Alcohol: The Islamic approach

Stage 1 (verses revealed in Makka):

> *"We give you from date-palms and vines a drink from which you derive intoxicants and also pure food: indeed there is a sign in this for those who make use of their common sense."*
>
> (an-Nahl 16: 67)

Quranic commentators have stated that the above verse hints at a dislike for alcohol. A few Companions actually stopped drinking alcohol after revelation of this verse. Later on, the following verse was revealed and although it was more direct, it nevertheless did not prohibit alcohol and intoxicants in general.

> *"They ask you concerning intoxicants and gambling. Say: in them is a great harm and (some) benefit for people, but their harm is greater than their benefit."*
>
> (al-Baqara 2: 219)

Stage 2 (verse revealed in the early Madian period):

> *"O believers, approach not prayers when you are in a drunken state until you know (the meaning) of what you utter..."*
>
> (an-Nisa 4: 43)

Stage 3 (verse revealed towards the end of the Prophet's mission in 8 AH totally prohibiting all forms of intoxicants):

> *"O believers, intoxicants, gambling, (ungodly) shrines and divining devices are all abominable works of Satan: therefore, refrain from these so that you may attain success. Indeed Satan intends to sow enmity and hatred among you by means of alcohol and gambling, and to prevent you from the remembrance of Allah and from prayers. Will you not, therefore, abstain from these things."*
>
> (al-Maida 5: 90–1)

Likewise, usury, gambling, infanticide, adultery, and other social vices were abolished by a few verses of the Quran, or a few words from the noble Prophet. There was little need for policing, extensive legislation, administrative institutions, and so on. Most of the social reforms and changes in society advanced by the Prophet Muhammad were accomplished within a few years. This was because the Islamic message and faith were introduced prior to social reforms which had permeated into peoples hearts, minds and souls.

In contrast, secular-materialistic approaches have to rely on legislation, educational institutions, the media, police, and other systems of administration to enforce laws. However, the law is only able to control what is done in the public domain, and it is common knowledge that all sorts of illegal activities and social evils flourish underground, since the law cannot reach everywhere. That is why, despite the legislation social evils continue and are spreading. According to Islam, although the law cannot reach everywhere, Allah is everywhere. He is Omniscient and Omnipresent. He is even closer to us than our jugular veins. He sees, hears and knows all things. Thus, God-consciousness is the key to reducing social evils in society.

> *"It is We who created man, and We know what dark suggestions his ego makes to him: for We are nearer to him than (his) jugular vein."*
>
> (Qaf 50: 16)

One should not infer from this that laws are not important. Certainly laws and control mechanisms play an important role in establishing order in social life. Islam has also resorted to deterrent punishments to protect society from certain heinous crimes, but this is a small part of a wider strategy for social reform. In an Islamic society, laws are generally employed for guiding inter-personal conduct and as deterrents. The cultivation of faith, God-consciousness, morals, and a sense of accountability to Allah in the life Hereafter are prerequisites since they develop an inner respect for societal values and laws. Taken together, these can ensure a change from within and without. Abhorrence of crime and evil comes from within and, thus, the seed of change must be sown from within. Therefore, relying only on laws to change people and social systems may not lead to an effective overall and lasting change in society.

From the above discussion, it follows that the Islamic method and process of addressing social issues is distinct from secular ones. Societal change, according to Islam, does not commence by addressing the symptoms, or by implementing laws and regulations. On the contrary, Islam commences its work of change by nurturing faith and values, and simultaneously addresses the causes of social evil and injustice. It works to purge evil influences, concepts, customs and traditions that may be deep-seated in social affairs, since it is these that cause social evils and injustices to flourish. Simultaneously, efforts are made to create healthier social conditions founded on God's guidance (for example, through establishing a mosque, and encouraging prayers, fasting, improving personal relationships, and righteous actions, etc.). These social conditions, in turn, give rise to an atmosphere of Godliness, human fraternity, care and concern for others. It is such an atmosphere that can motivate people to excel in good works, while at the same time discouraging them from wrongs and injustices. These conditions gradually lead to social order in which Allah's Way begins to prevail in every sphere of life.

As documented by Muslim historians, the Prophetic method of social change gave rise to the finest civilisation humanity has ever seen. Islam succeeded in raising people above racial differences and enabled different communities, black and white, to live together in peace and harmony. Islam, thus, eliminated racial tensions from society and it did away with many corruptions, ills and social injustices. All this was attained without any sophisticated schemes, or by any complicated legal and political drama, just by simply applying the Islamic method to social issues and problems.

Islamic Values

Finally, the importance of adhering to Islamic values also forms part of the Islamic framework for social change. Although these are rooted in all elements of the Islamic framework, special reference to them is nonetheless required. Since Allah is the Sovereign, then all values and guidance must come from Him alone. These values are contained in the Quran. Islam asserts that social values and principles must not be sought from anywhere else – whether they be from thinkers, intellectuals, scholars, philosophers or anyone else. The Quran alone is the criterion between right and wrong, truth and falsehood, and good and evil.

> *"Ramadan is the month in which the Quran was revealed. This Book is a perfect guidance for humanity, and contains clear teachings which show the right way and are a criterion (of truth and falsehood) ..."*
>
> (al-Baqara 2: 185)

Some examples of Islamic values include: worship of Allah, truth, honesty, justice, charity, generosity, kindness and mercy, moderation, self-discipline, living a collective life, social welfare, care and respect for others, consultation, co-operation in good works, steadfastness and patience (*sabr*). Islamic values also form the basis of social and economic policies in an Islamic society. Thus, turning to Allah for guidance can save people from ethical and moral confusion, social injustices and the enslavement of others, since He only enjoins that which is good and beneficial for people.

> *"Surely Allah enjoins justice, and the doing of good and giving to kinsfolk, and He forbids all indecency, wrongs and rebellion."*
>
> (an-Nahl 16: 90)

Those who are involved in efforts for societal reform must imbibe the values and social principles contained in the Quran and mould their personal and collective lives according to them. The Quran states that if these are not adhered to, then people will deprive themselves of God's help and mercy. Thus, adherence to Islamic values and principles in all efforts is a prerequisite for successful change. Agents of change must refrain from evil, restrain their anger, and exhibit good character. Indications to this effect can be found in many parts of the Quran.

> *"Allah has promised to those among you who believe and practise righteous deeds that He will surely establish them in the land, as He established those before them ..."*
>
> (an-Nur 24: 54)

> *"successful are the believers. Those who humble themselves in prayers; who avoid vain talk, who are active in deeds of charity, ..."*
>
> (al-Muminun 23: 1–11)

To sum up, this Chapter has attempted to expound the main elements of the Islamic framework for social change. The Islamic message provides a broad framework to guide thought and efforts for social change. It sets the starting point, guides the process and helps to focus efforts on the goal of Islam, which is to establish God's Way in society. Put another way, the framework provides a vision and direction to the change efforts. The starting point prepares people and society for change. It directs people to free themselves, spiritually, emotionally and socially from the lordship of false gods. It awakens them from a false consciousness and encourages them to take charge of their own lives and future. All this helps in liberating peoples' energies for constructive work. Furthermore, by helping people to focus their minds on the goal of Islam, they are provided with a vision and enthused with a sense of mission. With these qualities nurtured, a social change based on Islam becomes unstoppable. This framework is universal, for all times, all places, and relevant for all social conditions. However, the Islamic methodology for social change has to be interpreted and applied appropriately to a particular social situation. The Islamic methodology for social change and its application is discussed in the next two Chapters.

Notes:

1. The second part of the Islamic message is '*Muhammad is God's Messenger*'. Thus, the first part provides the framework for social change, and the second part (Muhammad is God's Messenger) forms the methodology, since it was the Prophet Muhammad who showed the way of living and working for Islam.
2. For example: "You shall have no other gods to rival me. You shall not make yourself a carved image or any likeness of anything in the heaven above or on earth beneath or in the waters under the earth. You shall not bow down to them or serve them..." (Exodus 20: 3–5), and again in: "Then Jesus replied: Away with you, Satan! For scripture says: The Lord your God is the one to whom you must do homage, Him alone you must serve" (Matthew 4: 10). Both passages are quoted from *The New Jerusalem Bible, Reader's Edition*, London: Darton, Longman & Todd Ltd. 1990.

3. See Mawdudi, S. A. *Four Basic Quranic Terms*, 2nd edition, translated by Abu Asad, Lahore: Islamic Publications, 1982.
4. See Mawdudi, S.A., *The Meaning of the Quran*, Vol. 1, al-Fatihah – al-Baqara, EN: 291, also see al-Anam EN: 52, Lahore: Islamic Publications Ltd. 8th edition, 1986.
5. See Mawdudi, S.A., *The Meaning of the Quran*, Vol. 3, al-Anam EN: 52, Lahore: Islamic Publications Ltd. 7th Edition, 1985.
6. Izetbegovic, Alija Ali, *Islam Between East and West*, 3rd edition, Indianapolis: American Trust Publications, p.54, 1993.
7. By Baron Carra de Vaux, in a fortnightly journal entitled *Questions diplomatiques et coloniales 1901*, Quoted by Dr. Ataullah Siddiqui (in CSIC papers No. 3 Oct 1995, *Muslims in Dialogue with Christians, Context and Concerns*) from Buhairy, M.R., 'Colonial Scholarship and Muslim Revivalism in 1900', *Arab Studies Quarterly* 4, Nos. 1–2 1982, p.5.
8. Mawdudi, S.A., *Musalman aur Maujuda Siyasi Kashmakash*, Lahore: Islamic Publications, Part III, p.28. 1939.
9. Ibn Kathir, *Al-Bidaya wa an-Nihaya*, Beirut: Dar Ihya al-Turath al-Arabi.
10. Khan, Muhammad Habibur Rahman, *Life of Abu Bakr, First Caliph of Islam*. Lahore: Ashraf Publications, pp.55–6. 1973.
11. See for example Siddiqui, Abdul Hameed, *The Life of Muhammad*, Lahore: Islamic Publications, 1969.

CHAPTER VII

Methodology for Social Change

The Islamic framework, which was discussed in the former Chapter, sets a broad structure, and provides general principles, priorities and a direction for realising the vision of Islam in individual and social life. The methodology, on the other hand, is a system of methods and principles derived from Islamic guidance for introducing change. It translates the Islamic framework into its practical components and offers a broad strategy for social reform and change. A framework is, thus, of a universal and higher order than a methodology, and it can be used as a lens for evaluating differing methodologies. This Chapter elucidates the Islamic methodology for guiding social change.

The Prophetic Methodology for Social Change

"Verily, in the Prophet of Allah you have a perfect example to follow ..."
(al-Ahzab 33: 21)

The most perfect model for Muslims is the Prophet Muhammad. Not only was he a perfect model in character and conduct, but he also presented before humanity a perfect model for introducing individual and social change. A deep study of the life (*sira*) of the Prophet Muhammad is, therefore, crucial for those who aspire to advance a change based on Islam. Below, the salient points of the Prophetic methodology are presented.

As documented by Muslim scholars[1], the whole world at the time of the Prophet Muhammad, around the 6th century CE, was steeped in moral confusion, ignorance and corruption. The superpowers of the time, the Romans and the Persians, oppressed and enslaved people under their rule. The condition of human beings was, in many regions of the earth, worse than animals; they were even sold and purchased like cattle. It was common to find the strong oppressing the weak and the rich exploiting the poor. In Arabia, some people even buried their baby daughters alive. Immorality, fornication, drunkenness, crime and other social vices were deeply entrenched in social norms and practices, even in religious institutions. Many people could not make sense of life, and on the whole society was devoid of law and order and lacked a sense of purpose and direction.

Amongst all this confusion and immorality, the Prophet Muhammad was sent by Allah to address the issues of his time and to transform such a state of affairs. With help and guidance from Allah, he brought about a great revolution; a revolution in ideas, thought, conduct, practices, systems of life and culture in his society and the world. Within a very short period (610–32 CE), a mighty change in all aspects of human life was introduced. It is true that many leaders have brought about numerous changes in their societies. However, all these are very limited, both in breadth and depth, when compared to what the Prophet Muhammad accomplished. Some leaders have succeeded in introducing political changes only. Others have managed to effect small changes in economics, and still others have influenced minor changes in social norms and practices. But the change advanced by God's final messenger in his society and world, was the greatest of all. He managed to change peoples' world-view, beliefs and perceptions. He changed the state of their hearts and minds; their attitudes and conduct. He revolutionised family and community life and introduced radical, but equitable, social reforms and changes in social welfare, and in political, legal and economic matters. A new person and a new culture gradually evolved from these changes. The following are two Western writers' views on the achievements of the Prophet Muhammad:

> "Philosopher, orator, apostle, legislator, warrior, conqueror of ideas, restorer of rational dogmas, of a cult without images, the founder of twenty terrestrial empires and of one spiritual empire, that is Muhammad. As regards all standards by which

human greatness may be measured, we may well ask, is there any man greater than he?" (Larmartine, 1854)[2]

"My choice of Muhammad to lead the list of the world's most influential persons may surprise some leaders and may be questioned by others, but he was the only man in history who was supremely successful on both the religious and secular levels..." (Hart, 1978)[3]

From the *sira* of the Holy Prophet it is quite evident that under the guidance of Allah, he initiated his work with a clear mission of changing man and society. He did not just react to the problems of his society. His work was also carefully planned and followed a methodological approach. Moreover, his vision at the very outset was global. However, he acted within the context of his society and with great wisdom. His approach, style and language were all appropriate and relevant to the people he addressed. At each stage in his efforts for a just and cohesive society, he gave very careful consideration to the future implications of his actions.

The change efforts of the noble Prophet followed a certain sequence. In very broad terms this was as follows:

1. *Core Group Development*: The Prophet Muhammad's initial focus was on clarifying the Islamic vision and mission, developing a strong, God-conscious, moral, dynamic and disciplined core group which would shoulder the burden of the change efforts. This was also important because pious, compassionate and upright people are essential for a good society. He, therefore, directed his followers towards their inner change; to get closer to Allah, strengthen their faith, purify their hearts from greed and selfishness, nurture love of Allah and His noble Prophet, produce mercy and softness in their hearts, a spirit of kindness and care, good character and patience. Furthermore, they were assisted in strengthening their inter-personal relations, so that they could gel into a cohesive group. To facilitate this process, the noble Prophet encouraged his Companions to meet often to study the Quran together and discuss the issues affecting their society, offer prayers, engage in constant

remembrance of Allah, and help the poor and needy. In referring to the Prophet during the early days of his mission, Allah says in the Quran:

> *"O you who are wrapped up in a mantle, stand (to pray) by night ... and recite the Quran...Soon shall We send down to you a weighty message."*
>
> (al-Muzzammil 73: 3–4)

In addition, these pious Companions were constantly encouraged to develop their knowledge, talents and skills in order to meet the challenges from the corrupt powers of their time and to bring about societal changes based on Islamic ideals.

2. *Open Invitation to Islam* (Dawa) *and the Development of Strategic Relationships:* During the formative years, the task of the Prophet was to invite and prepare his people for a change based on Islam. To achieve this, he invited them to a total and unreserved obedience to Allah, their Lord and Master, a lack of which was in reality the core problem facing his society and world. If Allah was not accepted as the Sovereign, then His Guidance would not be followed, and so attempts to reform and improve social conditions would not succeed. The noble Prophet, therefore, strove to awaken and liberate his people from misguided ideas, beliefs and notions about life. He strove against immorality, arrogance, extravagant life-styles, disgusting habits, corrupt practices and general disorder. He actively shared Islam's message and teachings with his people, individually and in groups. He approached his people at their homes and in public places. He organised meetings with tribal leaders to discuss the issues in society that were causing misery and injustice, so that they may see Islam's relevance and importance. In all his efforts he employed wisdom, persuasion and exhortation.

> *"Call to the Way of Your Lord with Wisdom and fair exhortation..."*
>
> (an-Nahl 16: 125)

Through continuous interaction and dialogue, many people were compelled to question their long-held erroneous beliefs, the depraved ways of their forefathers and the unjust ways in which their society was structured and functioning. Progressively, people began to rally around his message and work. Those who responded to his invitation were connected together and organised into a social movement, whose leader was the Prophet himself. Through the work of this movement they were facilitated in their self-development, spiritual, moral and intellectual. Their level of God-consciousness was raised and they cultivated closer and better relations amongst themselves. As the momentum increased, the people in his society became divided into a number of groups as follows:

i. Those who responded to the Prophet's invitation out of conviction; these included his close Companions – the core activists. These people were totally committed to Islam in every way; intellectually, emotionally, morally and politically.
ii. Those who, though being sincere, joined for emotional reasons rather than from conviction. These people can be classified as fellow-travellers or those who sympathised with Islam from a distance. Their reasons for affiliating with the Prophet of Allah varied considerably; for example, out of tribal loyalty, for seeking a meaning in life, for belonging to a better group of people, or even having a hope that if Islam succeeds, it will bring them some benefit as well.
iii. There was also a fringe of cynical opportunists and hypocrites who either joined the Prophet for malicious reasons (hypocrites), or in the hope of gaining some tangible benefits (opportunists), or who were simply gambling on the outcome of the Prophet's efforts (free-riders).
iv. The silent majority who could not make up their minds which way to go.
v. The Prophet's clear opponents and enemies.

3. *Consolidation and Community Development*: As the number of people turning to Islam increased, the noble Prophet of Allah began to concentrate on identifying a power base in order

to consolidate his followers, improve the social environment, establish a model community, enjoin good (*maruf*), forbid wrongful practices, and work to liberate people from oppression. A base was eventually found in Medina, to which the Muslims from Makka emigrated, and where a cohesive Muslim community was established.

4. *Establishment of Islam*: In Medina, once his followers were consolidated and had imbibed Islamic values and principles, the focus of attention turned towards rooting Islam in all spheres of life. This included the gradual establishment of God's worship, *salat*, *zakat*, *sawm*, *hajj*, etc., the development of people and community life, the creation of a Godly and moral culture and the introduction of Islamic laws, rules and processes in all areas of individual and social life.

5. *Global Mission*: From Medina, which had by that time become a model city-state based on Islam, a programme for sharing Islam with humanity at large was initiated. Rulers from neighbouring lands were invited to Islam and efforts were made to play a constructive role in world affairs.

Thus, the Prophet Muhammad initiated his work by calling people to free themselves from the false gods of their times and other harmful influences. He invited them to worship and submit to the One and Only God and assisted in moulding their lives according to His revealed guidance. Those who responded to this call were supported in changing, improving and developing themselves so that they could become better and responsible people and effective witnesses of Islam. As more and more people joined the Islamic movement, it began to grow and take root in social life. More people meant more skills and resources and, hence, more power and influence for Islam. This enabled Muslims to take more effective action for introducing Islamic values and systems. Actions were planned and executed for engaging with corrupt societal powers in order to eradicate social evils and for promoting good in society. Through this process, the Islamic movement emerged as an ideological, moral and political force. God's Way for humanity eventually prevailed over the whole of society. Islamic laws, which were logically revealed towards the end of the Prophet's mission in Medina, were implemented gradually over a period of time, with great wisdom and care and Islam became the established system of life.

Throughout his mission, the Prophet Muhammad did not take any hasty action nor did he work for quick fixes. Furthermore, he never sought confrontation since his aim was to remove evil and injustice from society and not to take revenge on his enemies or to punish the wicked. On the contrary, he wanted the betterment of all human beings, even of his most ardent opponents. In short, the Prophet Muhammad wanted all people to share the blessings which Islam offered. He came as a mercy to humanity.

"And We did not send you but as a mercy to all the worlds."

(al-Anbiya 21: 107)

However, the Islamic change was not achieved smoothly. There were problems and difficulties. The Prophet Muhammad was confronted and persecuted by his own people. He and his Companions faced abuse, ridicule, social boycotts and were even driven out of their home city, Makka, and compelled to migrate to Medina, leaving behind all or most of their belongings. Yes, tremendous sacrifices of money, property, jobs, of near and dear ones, and even lives were made in the process of change. Faith, God-consciousness, moral character, brotherhood and sisterhood, attachment to God's revealed guidance, patience and fortitude (*sabr*), and a spirit to win God's pleasure, were some of the qualities that carried them through all the hardships and sufferings they had to endure. By virtue of all this, they were, and will continue to be, a great source of inspiration for Muslims in every age.

Incidentally, the Prophet Muhammad could have gained power in his society by starting a class struggle (the poor against the rich), or by rallying people for Arab unity, or even for moral reform. However, he did not adopt any of these approaches, since these go against the Islamic framework for social change. If he had, then, undoubtedly, he would have failed to transform the social environment where justice prevailed, or his changes would have been very limited and short lived. For example, Arab unity would not have eliminated oppression, but on the contrary, would have cut out a great part of humanity from the blessings of Islam. Likewise, a class struggle would have replaced one set of people by another, and evils would have continued. Similarly, teaching and educating people about morality, without nurturing Islamic faith and Islamic thought, would not have made people moral since morals and good practices are built upon and emanate from a sound and deep faith.

Core Ingredients of the Change Process

> *"O Prophet, truly We have sent you as a Witness (shahid), a bearer of Glad Tidings (bashir), and a Warner (nazir). And as one who invites (Daiya) to Allah by His leave, and as a radiant lamp (Sirajun Munir)."*
>
> (al-Ahzab 33: 45–6)

The five aspects of the Prophet's work mentioned in this Quranic verse can be considered as the core ingredients of the Prophetic methodology for social change. Their implicit meaning is explored below.

A Witness (Shahid)

The word 'witness' refers to a person who is an embodiment of something. In its broadest Quranic sense, it refers to someone who carries a message, understands it, lives by it, is committed to sharing it with others and is also willing to give his/her life for that message. The Prophet Muhammad was a witness of Islam in this sense; he was an embodiment of truth and piety, mercy and compassion, and was described by one of his Companions as "having a character of the Quran". This suggests that the teachings contained in the Quran were lived by the Holy Prophet and were manifest in all his actions and dealings. Indeed, he lived by the Quran. He believed and practised what he preached and paid a great deal of attention and effort towards shaping the collective life of his followers according to God's revealed guidance. The early Muslims, thus, became a model community for humanity; exemplary witnesses of Islam.

It follows that, in accordance with the Islamic guidance, it is crucial for the agents of change to reflect Islamic values and teachings in their personal and collective life. Without this, a change in the external social environment based on Islam cannot be accomplished. It is for this reason that the Muslim community is instructed in the Quran to become witnesses of Islam before humanity. Mere talk, slogans, public gatherings and the distribution of literature are, on their own, not enough. Society must be shown the blessings of Islam through practical example.

> *"And, thus, We have made you a community of the middle way, so that you may be witnesses before humanity ..."*
>
> (al-Baqara 2: 143)

A Bearer of Glad Tidings (Bashir)

This term implies that the Prophet Muhammad, not only lived by Islam himself but he actively interacted with his people and articulated the "Glad Tidings". In other words, he shared and elucidated the great blessings and benefits which they will receive in this world and in the life Hereafter (*Akhira*), if they sincerely accept Islam and live by it. This further aided in clarifying the Islamic message and articulating Islam's vision.

The attitude of the noble Prophet was not that of denunciation. On the contrary, he tried to inspire his people by giving them a new hope and a vision of a better and just world which could be built through Islam. Giving Glad Tidings is, therefore, an intrinsic element in the process of change. It can greatly assist in uplifting people and aid in increasing their understanding of the kind of social life that will evolve from the Islamic message.

> *"And give glad tidings to those who believe and work righteousness, for them will be gardens through which rivers flow..."*
>
> (al-Baqara 2: 25)

> "*By Allah, He will complete this mission until a rider will travel from Sana to Hadrmawt* (both are places in Yemen) *and will have no fear but of Allah, and no worry but about a wolf that might harm his cattle – but you make haste.*"
>
> (Bukhari)

A Warner (Nazir)

Similarly, giving the warning, i.e. awakening people from false consciousness, or alerting them to the consequences of evil ways, was also an important ingredient of the Prophetic methodology. The warning, like the Glad Tidings, is not only limited to this life but includes that of the Hell fire in the Hereafter.

> "*Corruption has appeared on land and sea, by the actions of people. That Allah may give them a taste of some of their deeds: in order that they may turn back (from evil).*"
>
> (ar-Rum 30: 41)

> "*Has not the story reached them of those before them. The people of Noah, Ad, and Thamud; the people of Abraham, the men of Midian, and the cities overthrown. To them came their messengers with clear signs. It is not Allah who wrongs them, but they wrong their own souls.*"
>
> (at-Tawba 9: 70)

Communicating the warning exhorts people to reflect deeply over the direction their society is taking, and the long-term consequences of the same if they do not join in the efforts for reform and improvement. It directs a people to become more conscious of their social condition, and as a result, to do something to improve the state of affairs. Warning, thus, admonishes them to weigh up the options; either the way of good which will bring its blessings, or the way of evil, which may appear attractive on the surface, but in the long-term will lead to their own ruin and social disintegration. Hence the 'warning' assists in awakening a people to the realities of life and it, thus, plays an essential role in the process for improving social life.

One who Invites to Allah (Daiya)

In addition to giving hope of a better world and warning people of the consequences of not improving their conduct, the Holy Prophet also actively worked to invite his people towards Allah and His revealed guidance; to accept Allah as the Sovereign, the Law giver, and to follow His guidance in all affairs of life. He invited them towards God's Way; towards what is good, moral and beneficial. These efforts assisted in recruiting people into his movement and winning support from the general masses for Islam. This enabled the Prophet's movement to grow, expand its influence and, thus, increase it's capacity and power for reforming society.

A Radiant Lamp (Sirajun Munir)

Those who are involved in inviting others to Islam and reforming society would naturally encounter many issues and problems. These cannot be ignored or put aside, rather solutions need to be offered to make the message relevant to society. "A radiant lamp", thus, implies that the solutions offered by the Prophet, which were derived from God's revealed guidance, shone so brilliantly (like a radiant lamp) that all other solutions appeared dim and obscure before them. Put another way, his solutions to social problems were so appealing, effective and pragmatic, that all other solutions appeared inadequate and shallow. Issues relating to marriage and family life, business and commerce, education, health, employment, administering justice, and so on, were all addressed by the noble Prophet of Allah, and effective and pragmatic solutions implemented. In like manner, strategies were formulated and successfully implemented for eradicating social evils such as usury, gambling, infanticide, adultery, crime and corruption.

It can be inferred from this that change agents should not remain indifferent to social issues. In today's context, think tanks, research groups and specialised institutions can be set up that are devoted to making Islamic guidance applicable and relevant to contemporary society and the world at large, and for formulating effective social and economic policies in the light of the Quran and *Sunna*.

Islamic Methodology

From what has been discussed above, it is possible to identify the following major components that arise from the Prophetic methodology for social change:

1. *An Organised Movement*: Those who respond to Islam are connected and absorbed into an organised, disciplined, God-conscious and dynamic social movement to effect change in social life *(jama'a)*. An Islamic movement provides a social environment, prepares and involves people, helps them to adjust their behaviour, attitude and life style according to God's guidance, and also encourages them towards continuous self-development (*tarbiya*).
2. *Invitation to God's Way*: Inviting individuals and communities to the Islamic message and value-system (*dawa*). This includes the giving of Glad Tidings and warnings as has already been discussed above.
3. *Effort and Struggle*: Planning and engaging in actions against oppression and social injustices, for enjoining good and forbidding wrong, and towards influencing positive change at all levels of society and the state *(jihad)*.
4. *Establishment of God's Way*: Gradual introduction of change, reforms and improvements in social life, as well as in social structures and institutions, so that a just social life based on God's revealed guidance can be established *(iqamat ad-Din)*.

These components, which are developed further below, are found to be the most apparent, significant and integral part of the Prophet Muhammad's approach and way through which he was able to transform his people and society. The Quran also elucidates these components in many places in different ways.

An Islamic Social Movement (*Jama'a*)

"And hold on strongly, all of you together, to the rope of Allah, and be not divided amongst yourselves…"

(Ali-Imran 3: 103)

Building an organised, God-conscious, cohesive and disciplined movement was a major component of the work of all the Prophets of Allah. This is because the benefits of collective living through an organised movement are numerous. In particular, a movement:

1. Is an effective vehicle for social change.
2. Binds people around a common faith and shared vision for society.
3. Provides cultural values and an Islamic atmosphere, i.e. an alternative culture. This offers protection from the onslaught of any dominant immoral and corrupt culture that may exist in society.
4. Pools talents, resources and efforts for promoting good and checking wrong in society. It increases the social and political capacity of a movement and enables effective action for building a just and moral society.
5. Provides the continuing spiritual, moral, intellectual and social development of its members, so as to support them in becoming competent citizens and leaders of society (*tarbiya*)
6. Enables a model of the kind of change desired in society to be produced.

A movement brings people into direct contact with societal issues and challenges. This can greatly aid in the intellectual and social development of its members. Moreover, a movement sets an infrastructure for co-ordinating efforts, and for social support and welfare. Chapter Nine further elucidates the important characteristics of an Islamic movement, and Chapter Ten offers a framework for the development of the change agents.

A Call to the Message of Islam (*Dawa*)

Dawa is an essential component of the Islamic methodology and it simply means "to invite". It is an important component because without being actively engaged in calling people to the Islamic message and way of life, social reforms and changes based on Islam cannot be accomplished. Indeed *dawa* was the most significant part of the methodology of all the Prophets of Allah. In fact, the very word "Messenger" implies someone who delivers a message.

"And who is better in speech than the one who calls to Allah, works righteousness, and says: I am of those who submit to Allah."

(Fussilat 41: 33)

Dawa brings people into the fold of Islam. It enables a common vision for the future to be developed. Moreover, it helps in removing misconceptions, builds respect and tolerance for Islam and Muslims, wins support and finds allies for the change efforts. The broad aims of *dawa* are:

1. *To awaken* a people from false consciousness and *liberate* them from the influences of false gods and wrong ways. This enables them to take charge of their own lives and future.
2. *To share* Allah's message and moral values and *to invite* humanity to follow His Way.
3. *To identify* allies and win general support for the Islamic cause.
4. *To recruit* people into a movement for social change (i.e. to strengthen efforts for social change).
5. *To reform* the wider population by sharing Islamic beliefs, values, morals and rules of conduct.

Dawa, therefore, is a comprehensive concept. It directs attention and energies towards advancing Islamic principles and the Islamic moral code in society. Any mistaken ideas and notions about life and the universe have to be subjected to sustained Islamic views through effective communication and interaction. Such interactions by the way, are not about preaching or converting as is commonly understood. Neither do they suggest debating, arguing, quarrelling, finding fault, looking down, annoying or showing a sense of superiority over others. On the contrary, the purpose of sharing the message of Islam and offering a critique of wrong notions is to awaken people to the realities of life, to challenge their preconceived ideas and beliefs, to agitate their thoughts and attitudes and to support them in seeing the world and social issues from an Islamic perspective. Thus, the aim of *dawa* is to counteract the harmful social conditioning which a people may be under-going, to invite them into the fold of God's Way, and to help them discover their true purpose in life and the multiple dimensions of their existence. With continuous efforts in this direction, individuals may hopefully be guided by Allah and respond to the Islamic call.

> *"Indeed, in the creation of the heavens and the earth, and in the alteration of night and day, there are signs (in this) for people of understanding."*
>
> (Ali-Imran 3: 190)

> *"And indeed, in the cattle there is a lesson for you. We give you drink of that which is in their bellies, from between excretions and blood, pure milk, palatable to the drinkers."*
>
> (an-Nahl 16: 66)

There are many such verses as these in the Quran that challenge and agitate people to think deeper about how they live and about the universe around them, so that perchance they may understand the message of Allah. Individuals are invited, through powerful argument, to reflect deeper about the meaning and purpose of life and to critically examine their social environment.

The Islamic sources provide some general guidance on how one should interact with society and invite people to the Islamic message. Some of the salient points are:

1. The Islamic message should be made relevant to the particular society in which one is working, just as it was made relevant by all the Prophets to their own people.
2. It has to be presented using a language and terminology that is understood by the people being addressed, in a logical, reasonable, convincing and friendly way.
3. It cannot be thrust onto people, rather communication and social interaction at a deeper level needs to be established.

In short, people should be invited with wisdom and fair exhortation as indicated by the following verses of the Quran:

> *"Call to the Way of your Lord with wisdom and fair exhortation; and reason with them in ways that are best and most gracious..."*
>
> (an-Nahl 16: 125)

> *"Go both of you* (Moses and Aaron) *to Pharaoh, for he has indeed transgressed all bounds; but speak to him mildly; perchance he may take warning or fear (Allah)."*
>
> (Ta Ha 20: 43–4)

> *"And We sent not a Prophet except (to share the message) in the language of his (own) people to make (things) clear to them."*
>
> (Ibrahim 14: 4)

Wisdom implies that one should be mindful of the sensitivities of the people being addressed, have an understanding of their backgrounds, beliefs and ideas, and employ the most appropriate and effective methods and channels of communication. It is evident that all noble Prophets of Allah employed a variety of methods for sharing Allah's message, but with wisdom. As an example, the Prophet Noah cried out to Allah and said:

> *"so I called them aloud (openly), further I spoke to them in public and I also appealed to them secretly in private."*
>
> (Nuh 71: 8–9)

In fact, the Prophets of Allah made use of all the means available to them for amplifying their message in society and, hence, attempted to reach out to a wider audience. As an illustration, in order to share his message, the Prophet Muhammad met people on a one-to-one basis, visited them in their homes and made contact with them at public places, for example, at trade fairs and social functions. He also organised special meetings and dinners to share his message, he even climbed on top of a hill in Makka to call the people to Islam; this was the traditional method used for warning people about some mishap or inviting them to something, and further he wrote letters to neighbouring kings and emperors inviting them to Islam. He, thus, employed a variety of tools and methods for delivering and sharing his message.

In the present day context, the new information and communications technologies (ICTs) and the mass media can be employed as tools for advancing the Islamic message in society. However, some of the techniques and manners employed by the media for packaging and promoting consumer products may not necessarily be suitable for promoting Islam. This is because such techniques are designed in general to appeal to baser, physical human desires and emotions, for example, hunger, thirst clothing and sex. On the contrary, methods for the dissemination of an ideology need to appeal to the higher self – the intellectual, spiritual and more noble and positive human feelings. Thus, novel styles, manners and techniques must be developed so that views based on Islam can be presented effectively and have an impact. There is, therefore, ample room for innovation and creativity in this area.

Another important point in relation to *dawa* concerns people in powerful positions. Though the Holy Prophets of Allah approached all people with their invitation, they paid special attention to leaders, intellectuals, powerful and influential people. This was because people holding power and influence set the direction of society, good or bad, and if they can be reformed or won over as allies, they can be instrumental for change. It is also common for people to follow and be loyal to their leaders. Moreover, such people are usually resourceful, possess intelligence, are politically aware and understand social affairs. As an illustration, the Prophet Muhammad prayed to Allah to guide either Umar ibn al-Khattab or Abu Jahl (Amr ibn Hisham) to Islam because both of these personalities had some following, or certain leadership qualities and acumen. Moreover, Abu Bakr, Uthman, Umar, Musab bin Umayr, and Khadija were all well known and influential personalities, who came into the fold of Islam during the very early years of the Prophet's mission.

Furthermore, for an ideology to diffuse through society, it is not enough to address the general public alone. Those who possess ideological power, i.e. have power and control over ideas and beliefs, must also be approached. However, gaining access to such people is difficult due to the social barriers that usually exist in a society founded upon secular-materialism. In fact, such a society is generally engineered in a way that leads to the segregation of people into social classes. This enables the ruling elite to screen themselves and hold onto their power and influence. These barriers also obstruct the dissemination of alternative ideas and views through society, since social interaction between people at the various levels of the social hierarchy are impeded. This is why, in many societies, it is not common to find the lower, middle and upper classes freely intermingling and interacting with each other on a constant basis to discuss and exchange ideas. The upper classes and those holding power are able to screen themselves in exclusive areas, mansions, separate clubs, enjoying private health facilities, private education, and so on. These prevent ordinary people from gaining access to them. Thus, in order to disseminate Islamic ideas, the building of social and political networks is necessary and these must be established across the social and political divides so that all people can be reached with the message of Islam.

Striving for Social Change (*Jihad*)

This is the third core component of the Islamic methodology. The Arabic word *jihad* means to strive ones utmost for an objective. In Islamic terminology, *jihad* refers to well thought-out, strategic and organised actions, guided by Islamic values and principles, taken by an Islamic movement to enjoin good (*maruf*), forbid wrong practices (*munkar*) and to remove obstacles in the way of advancing positive social change. These actions, dependant on the context and circumstances, can be either intellectual, social, political or military. In other words, *jihad* engages a movement directly with the main stream of society and world affairs. This enables it to face the emerging challenges and to influence their direction for achieving an Islamic change. All possible means within the limits set by Islam can be employed for this purpose. In short, *jihad* aims at:

1. Striving against the evils within oneself.
2. Intellectually challenging ideologies, beliefs and ways of life that conflict with God's Way.
3. Challenging and engaging with societal powers for eradicating social evils, immoral ways, and wrong practices.
4. Striving to liberate people from oppression and injustice.
5. Influencing positive social, economic and political change in society according to Islamic ideals.

Like *dawa*, *jihad* is also a duty upon Muslims. This duty cannot be ignored or evaded. All the noble Prophets of Allah strove against corrupt powers and unjust practices, and the Muslims are commanded to do the same. Simply sitting in mosques, meditating, praising God and praying all day long without any practical efforts and struggle, cannot lead to much positive change in social conditions.

> *"And strive (jihad) in Allah's way as you ought to strive..."*
>
> (al-Hajj 22: 78)

> *"Believers are those who (truly) believe in Allah and His Messenger, then doubt not, but who strive with their possessions and their selves in the way of Allah; it is they who are the truthful ones."*
>
> (al-Hujurat 49: 15)

Also, significant change cannot be effected solely through preaching and delivering sermons. These have a very limited and temporary effect on an audience and societal powers. The influences of society, or the dominant culture, are so huge that they very quickly wash away any effects produced by the preaching. Thus, change agents additionally require a clear practical agenda for change, backed up by sincere devotion, firm resolve and commitment, a spirit of sacrifice, and an investment of time, energy, and resources. Further, neither the love of near and dear ones, nor the comforts of life should blur the vision, reduce the enthusiasm or hinder a movement from striving in the way of Allah.

> *"And if it be your fathers, sons, brothers, partners, your kindred, or the wealth that you have acquired, or the commerce in which you fear a decline, or the dwellings in which you delight, if all these are dearer to you than Allah, His Messenger, or the striving in His Way – then wait till Allah brings about His decision: and Allah does not guide the rebellious."*
>
> (at-Tawba 9: 24)

> *"Surely you will be tested with fear, or hunger, loss of property, or with loss of lives or fruits (of your toil); but give good news to those who patiently persevere."*
>
> (al-Baqara 2: 155)

Indeed, an Islamic movement exists for no other purpose. In fact, a movement can lose sight of its purpose and vision and get entangled in routine activities, side issues or ritualistic work, if it does not involve itself in *jihad*.

Examples of strategic actions which the Prophet Muhammad undertook include: standing on Mount Safa to call people to Islam, meeting with tribal chiefs and leaders to share his message, migration to Medina (*hijra*), Battles of Badr (624 CE), Uhud (625 CE) and others, the Peace Treaty at Hudaybiyya (628 CE) and the conquest of Makka (630 CE). These and many more were actions aimed at furthering his cause. They were not routine activities, undertaken for the sake of them, but were rather well thought-out and strategic. The kind of actions that a movement can engage in will naturally vary according to the social and political circumstances. For instance, if a people are oppressed by their governments, then armed struggle cannot be ruled out. Conversely, in peaceful conditions, actions can incorporate communication, dialogue and exerting social and political pressure. An Islamic movement must, therefore, assess the social and political circumstances and plan actions to influence change accordingly. (See Chapter Seven for a discussion on armed struggle).

In the light of Islamic guidance, actions for positive change should lead to a greater good and not to a worsening of the situation. This is why the Prophet Muhammad (peace and blessings be upon him) did not take any hasty actions or work for quick fixes that might have led to more harm than good, or which would have caused unnecessary social disruption. If taking certain actions, no matter how crucial or effective they may be considered, leads to panic and confusion, or creates social upheavals that may give rise to more evil, then they must be avoided and patience exercised until conditions change. This is because Islam aims to bring about peace and order and not chaos; its aim is to reform, improve and develop a society, to remove wrongs and corruption rather than punish the wicked or create disorder on earth.

Establishment of a Just Society (*Iqamat ad-Din*)

The establishment of a society based on God's revealed guidance is the final major component of the Islamic methodology. The Prophet Muhammad actually succeeded in establishing a society based on

God's guidance. Islamic values and principles were instituted in all spheres and systems of life during his life-time. An Islamic society and state was first established in Medina, then later in other places that became part of Muslim land.

> *"The same way of life He has established for you as that which He enjoined on Noah – that which We have sent by inspiration to you – And that which We enjoined on Abraham, Moses, and Jesus: namely that you establish the way of life, and make no divisions therein ..."*
>
> (ash-Shura 42: 13)

Once an Islamic movement wins majority support it must direct its attention towards addressing the affairs of society and formulate effective solutions to social problems in the light of the Islamic guidance. This stage of the process encompasses the enjoining of moral and equitable practices, establishing good traditions, and fair social and economic policies in society for the benefit of all citizens. The following discussion highlights some of the major issues that need to be addressed in order to establish Islam in social life:

Individual and Social Development

This is the most important issue. In part, personal and collective development can be facilitated through the establishment of the Islamic acts of worship (for example, *salat* and *zakat*) in society. These are powerful means for creating an inner change, in nurturing God-consciousness and moral development, and also in connecting people together and improving social relationships. In addition, healthier social environments and conditions must be cultivated so as to foster a caring attitude, good and responsible conduct, and a respect for the law. From Islamic guidance, this can be achieved through building an integrated family life, a cohesive community, coupled with the establishment of Islamic traditions and social institutions. Proper use of the media, encouraging the development of role models and creating an atmosphere of mutual co-operation and respect for human dignity can all contribute in this process. These provide the Islamic values, culture and moral standards, all of which are essential for individual development.

Economic Development

To alleviate poverty and to ensure a fair distribution of wealth, Islamic economic principles must be rooted in society. Thought will need to be devoted to issues such as employment, industry, agriculture and social services, in the light of Islamic guidance, as these underpin the economic growth of a society. The expansion and growth of useful products and natural produce need to be ensured, together with establishing a system to collect and distribute *zakat* (welfare contribution). Islam lays down guidelines for the equitable distribution of wealth and resources, and for the provision of social security, allowances and pensions for the needy, unemployed and elderly. Public institutions that provide healthcare, education, security, transport, and so on, also need to be re-examined in the light of Islamic guidance for improvements, effectiveness, efficiency and fairness.[4]

Furthermore, economic values and good practices such as fairness, honesty, trustworthiness, adherence to contractual agreements, giving accurate measurements and weights, and ensuring fair recruitment practices and treatment for employees and workers need to be rooted in all economic activities. Also economic evils such as usury, hoarding, and unlawful trade such as black-marketing, false advertising, misrepresentation, wastage and the destruction of surplus produce, need to be checked, and economic conditions created and mechanisms developed that will ensure their prevention.[5]

Checking corruption and social evils

In addition to building effective social systems, socially harmful and immoral activities need to be checked. These include gambling, drug abuse, adultery and fornication, murder, theft and robbery, corruption and exploitation, and all forms of discrimination. Not only do these evils need to be eradicated, but also all the means that lead to them need to be blocked. Again, in addition to legislation, strong faith, developing God-consciousness and conducive social and economic conditions can all facilitate this process.

Instituting the Islamic Political framework

Last, but not least, political issues require attention, since without a fair and effective political system the above concerns cannot be addressed effectively. The Islamic systems of *shura* (consultation with the citizens or their representatives), well-thought out checks, balances, and procedures for the accountability of all those holding public office need to be formulated and implemented. Furthermore, political hierarchies and processes that give rise to injustice or assist in the domination of certain people or groups have to be examined in the light of God's revealed guidance, and changed or modified accordingly. Also, the existing legislative, executive and judiciary[6] processes have to be examined and shaped according to Islamic guidelines to ensure the effective administration and smooth implementation of Islamic guidelines, system of worship, laws and policies.

The above discussion shows that the role of a government is not merely limited to economics, that is securing economic development, material prosperity and raising the standard of living, or to maintaining internal order. In addition, it must work, of necessity, to nurture better and more responsible people, build a moral society, ensure social justice to all people and guarantee society's long-term viability. Finally, to ensure that changes are introduced and managed competently and implemented smoothly, with as little disruption to social life as possible, the Islamic methodology enjoins that they should be advanced gradually. The importance of this is addressed below.

Gradual Change

Changing people is not a simple task. Individuals become set in their beliefs and attitudes, and dominant practices, customs and traditions become part of their life. To change these will require hard work and a great deal of patience. Therefore, keeping human nature in mind, all the noble Prophets of Allah worked according to the set priorities of Islam and introduced change gradually so that it could become firm in people's hearts and minds. As a priority, they strove to awaken and warn their people by drawing attention to wrongs and injustices that were rooted in social life. They invited them to God's way by appealing to them in a logical and convincing way. For example, the Quran passionately petitions:

> *"And when the baby girl will be asked for what reason she was buried alive."*
>
> (at-Takwir 81: 8–9)

Once people begin to respond to Islamic values and ideas, the door to change is opened. However, even at this stage, change should be manoeuvred in slowly. If it rushes in, it could have a negative impact on the person or society that is being changed. Aisha the wife of the noble Prophet, explains the importance of keeping the priority set and introducing change gradually in the following *hadith*:

> *"Aisha said* (about the Quran), *the first thing to be revealed was a chapter (sura) which mentioned paradise and hell* (i.e. matters of faith). *When people embraced Islam, the verses regarding legal and illegal things were revealed. If the first thing to be revealed was 'Don't drink alcohol' people would have never given it up, and if 'don't have illicit sex' was revealed, they would have never given up adultery and fornication."*
>
> (Bukhari)

There are other sayings of the Prophet Muhammad to this effect. Two are given below:

> *"The religion of Islam is a lenient one – so go into it with ease and patience. No one who attempts to storm his way into it will come out victorious."*
>
> (Bukhari)

On another occasion, Muadh bin Jabal, a Companion of the noble Prophet, was advised:

> *"You are going to a people of the Book. When you reach them, call them to witness that there is no god but the one God and Muhammad is His Messenger. And when they accept this, then tell them that God has enjoined on them Prayers. And when they accept this, then tell them that He has enjoined on them Zakat (poor due), which is to be taken from the rich amongst them and given to the poor."*
>
> (Bukhari)

The more abruptly a change is introduced, the more short-lived it generally turns out to be. As a priority, people must be given time to understand the proposed changes and to remould their lives according to them. Time must be allowed to dispel fears, to adjust life-styles, to learn new practices and to adapt to change. Self-discipline and understanding of Islam takes time. Making haste in changing societies can backfire and perhaps result in greater social disorder, and may well invite unnecessary resistance and opposition.

> *"Whoever of you sees an evil act, let him change it with his hand; and if he is not able to do so, then with his tongue, and if he is not able to do so, then with his heart and that is the weakest of faith."*
>
> (Muslim)

The above saying hints at the various stages of the change process and offers a priority order for action. It highlights pragmatism, the importance of patience and gradual change. The term "changing by hand" is implied by scholars as possessing political power – the arm of the law, the ability to effect change; the power to enjoin good (*maruf*) and forbid wrong (*munkar*). Without gaining political power, an Islamic movement cannot really implement its change ideas in society. Until this stage is attained, it is advised to restrain itself from any action that disturbs social peace, and instead to limit efforts to inviting, appealing and exerting political pressure.

The following examples[7] demonstrate how gradual the introduction of Islamic laws in society were during the time of the Prophet Muhammad. Though alcohol was disliked even during the Makkan period, it was not abolished until 8 AH (after the migration to Medina). Similarly, the evils of usury (*riba*) were stressed in Makka, yet it was not practically prohibited until 9 AH after the new social and political order was established. Inheritance laws were enforced in 3 AH, and the rules and regulations pertaining to marriage and divorce implemented in 7 AH. Further, the criminal code was implemented over many years, and only finalised around 8 AH. Thus, change agents need to work and prepare the ground for change as a priority; in other words, create social conditions to facilitate the change process.

Time-frame for Introducing Social Change

Finally, misconceptions regarding the time frame to achieve reforms in a society need to be removed. Some activists make emotional statements such as introducing Islam within 24 hours of obtaining power. This is not only very impractical, but also shows how superficial people can be in their understanding of the complexities and dynamics of the process of social change. Obtaining power alone is no easy task, but expecting the whole of society (individuals, families, communities, trade and commerce, education, legal and political processes, etc.) to adjust and comply to the changes overnight, is both bizarre and humanly impossible.

> *"Therefore patiently persevere, as did (all) the Messengers of clear purpose; and be not in a haste about the (corrupt)."*
>
> (al-Ahqaf 46: 35)

In actual fact, the time frame for change will vary from place to place, people to people, and from age to age, and is dependent on many other factors and parameters. For example, it could depend on how powerful and organised is the opposition to change, and how deeply entrenched is disbelief, evil, corruption and injustice in society. The stronger and deeper the roots of evil, the longer it could take. Moreover it depends on how committed and organised a social movement is for effecting change. It also depends on how well thought out the strategy for change is and what resources are available to a social movement. Besides these factors, the most important one is that it depends on the Mercy and help of Allah.

> *"And our duty is only to convey plainly (the message)."*
>
> (Ya Sin 36: 17)

There were many Prophets of Allah who did not succeed in changing their societies at all. Some only managed to win over a few people to their message. For example, the Prophet Noah spent over 900 years in inviting his people to Allah's Way. In contrast, the Prophet Muhammad succeeded in establishing Islam within 23 years. What Islamic workers need to bear in mind is not the time frame or the final result, but rather success in the life Hereafter, which is the ultimate goal of all endeavours. Success in this world is a subjective concept and, thus, difficult to pinpoint. A defeated and crushed movement may leave lasting effects on the values, ideas, polity or social life in general, or may even by its defeat, prepare the way for its ideas to be rooted in society at a later time.

Thus, Islam emphasises that all change is in the hands of God. He gives power and honour to whom He wills. Individuals will be questioned on the day of Judgement for how much sincere effort and sacrifice they made towards this goal and not whether they actually succeeded in bringing about social and political reforms.

> *"say: O Allah Lord of power: You give power to whom You please, and You take away power from whom You please. You endow with honour whom You please, and You bring low whom You please. In Your hand is all good, Verily, You have power over all things."*
>
> (Ali-Imran 3: 26)

To sum up, the Islamic methodology provides further, more detailed guidance on social change. The key components of the Islamic methodology are: *dawa, jama'a, tarbiya, jihad,* and *iqamat ad-Din*. It stresses that an organised social movement is necessary. This movement must plan and execute *dawa* (calling to God's message) and *jihad* (striving) actions. *Dawa* helps in liberating individuals from wrong influences and prepares them spiritually, emotionally and intellectually for a change according to Islam. *Jihad* assists in liberating people from injustices and oppression, and in enjoining good, forbidding wrong and influencing positive change in the socio-political environment. Efforts from both these components of the Islamic methodology leads a society towards the establishment of God's Sovereignty – the goal of social change.

It can be concluded that the Prophet's approach was based on wisdom and constant effort. Positive social changes were advanced gradually so that they could be embedded in people's hearts, minds, characters and also across all aspects of social life. In addition, his efforts included the promotion of good and creating healthy social conditions. To make the changes permanent, the Prophet of Allah established practices, traditions, institutions and created a Godly, vibrant and healthy culture and implemented Islam's principles and laws in the new society.

Some important issues regarding how the Islamic methodology should be applied in a given social context are discussed in the next Chapter.

Notes:

1. Nadwi, Abul Hasan Ali, *Islam and the World*, Kuwait: International Islamic Federation of Student Organisations, 1977.
2. Lamartine, *Histore de la Turquie*, Paris, 1854, Vol. II, p.277.
3. Hart, Michael H., *The 100: A Ranking of the Most Influential Persons in History*, New York, 1978.
4. Ahmad, Khurshid, 'Economic Development in an Islamic Framework', *in Islamic Perspectives: Studies in Honour of Sayyid Abul A'la Mawdudi*, Leicester: The Islamic Foundation, 1979, pp. 223–40.
5. Ibid.
6. The meaning of these terms are given by Al-Rashid as follows: legislative (to interpret, elaborate, expand and apply Islamic guidelines in all affairs affecting social life), executive (to implement policies which have been formulated after a process of consultation) and the judiciary (to adjudicate between citizens, and between citizens and government), in Al-Rashid, Mahmood, 'Faruqi's Conception of the Islamic State', in *Al-Mizan: The Balance*, Vol.1, No. 2, pp. 23–30, 1995.
7. Mawdudi, S.A., *The Islamic Law and Constitution*, translated by Khurshid Ahmad, Lahore: Islamic Publications Ltd., 4th Edition, 1969.

CHAPTER VIII

Application of the Methodology

Inviting people to the message of Islam (*dawa*), organising them into a social movement (*jama'a*), encouraging and supporting self-development (*tarbiya*), striving collectively against social evils and injustices (*jihad*), and establishing a God-conscious, moral and just society (*iqamat ad-Din*), as discussed in the previous Chapter, form the major components of the Islamic methodology for social change. Although these components provide sufficient guidance for the change efforts, their application in a given social context requires some thought. As the saying goes: *"a little knowledge is a dangerous thing"*. A superficial understanding of the methodology can lead to its ineffective application. It can also produce intolerance and extremism amongst Islamic workers. In this Chapter, the application of the Islamic methodology for a given social context is considered and some guidelines for good practice are offered.

The Social Context

To apply any methodology in practice, it has to be interpreted and implemented prudently for a given context. This is what wisdom implies. Methodologies cannot be applied in a vacuum or in the same way in all social contexts. Also, a rigid adherence to certain ways for applying the methodology, regardless of the social context, may lead to failure and even invite unnecessary opposition and resistance. Wisdom, pragmatism and flexibility are crucial for applying the Islamic methodology successfully.

From the Quran it is evident that all the noble Prophets of Allah adhered to the Islamic framework and methodology for guiding their thoughts and actions. However, the translation of the components of the methodology into practical strategies and methods was different for different social contexts. Since the Quran is a Book of guidance from Allah, containing a universal message, for all times and places, it provides a methodology which comprises of general guidelines and principles only, which must be adhered to in all efforts for social change. However, no detailed plan of work, or a series of steps that must be followed are provided by the Quran or the Sunna, since these have to be worked out by Islamic movements for their own particular social circumstances.

The Quran indicates that some Prophets carried on the work where previous Prophets had left off, whilst others came to reform people who had confused the message of Allah. Still others had to start their work from scratch because their people had completely lost the message of Allah and had become totally subservient to false gods. In each case, the message was the same. However, the components of the methodology were operationalised in different ways, in a manner that was deemed the most appropriate and effective. The relevance and significance of the Islamic message was emphasised by drawing people's attention to the particular malice of their age. In other words, through powerful and logical arguments, the attention of individuals and communities was drawn towards examining the cause of their particular problems in the light of the Islamic message. Moreover, the noble Prophets employed strategies, language, methods and means that were suitable and appropriate for their specific social environment. As an illustration, Abraham, Lot (Abraham's nephew), Ishmael and Isaac (Abraham's sons), were all Prophets of Allah in the same period of history. Each was sent to a different people in a different place, and as Quranic evidence indicates, each addressed issues and social evils that were prevalent in their area and worked in different ways that were best suited to their social contexts. Although their message and aim was the same, the strategies adopted by each varied considerably. Thus, the social context should determine the approach and strategy for shaping a better society.

As a further example, the Prophet Joseph had no hesitation in taking a very prominent and powerful position in Pharaoh's government[1]. In keeping his position (in a non-Muslim majority society) he did not, however, let go of his principles, and he also performed his duties sincerely, diligently and competently. His efforts for inviting people to support social reform also continued. With regard to this point, Rachid Ghannouchi, a thinker and leader of the Islamic movement from Tunisia, writes:

> "Realism and flexibility are among the most important features of the Islamic methodology...Society is dynamic, and a religion which came to improve the life of man has to have the flexibility to respond to changing circumstances... Within this (Islamic) framework, the fundamentals and general principles are preserved whilst the details can be changed, updated or deduced to face new realities. The general rule in Islam is that all actions are permissible unless specifically prohibited...The Quran mentions the story of (Prophet) Joseph who, when given the opportunity, took charge of the most important office in the Pharaoh's government. He believed that it was his duty to rescue nations that were threatened by famine and drought. He did not wait for the Egyptians to renounce paganism and embrace his Unitarian religion. Through his effective participation in administering the affairs of the people he performed his responsibility of calling for Islam and encouraging people to reform their lives..."[2]

Thus, on examining the approach of the Prophets of Allah, and of Muslim reformers in history, one can conclude that they did not apply the Islamic methodology rigidly. On the contrary, they studied the social conditions of their time and used the methodology to guide their thinking, planning and actions. The Quran details the work of 25 great Prophets and Messengers of Allah, and interestingly, it is clear from the various Quranic passages, that each applied the methodology in different ways that were appropriate to their time and people. Thus, the application of the Islamic methodology will vary relative to the time, and to the social and political conditions of society.

Undoubtedly, Muslims can learn and benefit a great deal from the experiences and methods employed by the early Islamic workers and leaders, and from any other good and useful sources for that matter, but they cannot allow themselves to be confined by their approaches. It is obvious that no two situations in time and space are exactly the same. For example, it cannot be said that today Muslims are strictly in a similar situation to that of the Prophet Muhammad, either in Makka or Medina, although some parallels can be drawn. Undoubtedly, history has moved on, places and circumstances have changed, experiences have grown, and technology has been enhanced. Similarly, life styles, languages and cultures have altered and social, economic and political changes have taken place. Society is always in a dynamic state, and, thus, people cannot do things in exactly the same way as the Muslims did in the past.

Thus, an Islamic movement needs to exercise flexibility and pragmatism, without being unprincipled and opportunistic. Change agents must not only be clear as to where they are heading, but also to be fully conversant with the current state of their society. A change to the desired social conditions will not necessarily happen in one simple step, or over a short period. Many steps may need to be taken in order to reach the desired goal. Many bridges have to be built and crossed before the land flowing with milk and honey can be reached. Pragmatists, therefore, live in the present, and they use, and build upon, past experiences to create the future. They translate the successful ideas and experiences of the past into a language of today, in order to share their vision and dream for the future.

Preparing People for Change

The main emphasis of the Islamic methodology is to ensure a smooth positive change without causing much disruption to social life (*fasad*). This implies gaining public consent for the change ideas; preparing people and society prior to the introduction of social changes. Any change that is forced through, imposed or introduced abruptly will naturally lead to problems and social disruptions. This is why the Quran teaches that there should be no compulsion in Islam[3]. Put another way, no one can be compelled into accepting any belief or system of life. It is for this reason that non-Muslims living as a minority in an Islamic society (*Dhimmi*) are recognised and protected by law, given respect, allowed to practice their religion and address any disputes or problems according to their own Scriptures[4]. The Prophet Muhammad adhered to this guidance and, thus, did not seek to impose his ideas on people or employ other similar methods.

Further, he did not strive to change social life through the enforcement of law (*sharia*) only.

An effective Islamic change requires the cultivation of faith, God-consciousness, morals, correct attitudes and patience, and its systems of society evolve from these seeds, and not the other way round. As a general principle, a legal, political or an economic system must be compatible with the social life which it is seeking to regulate and direct, otherwise it will inevitably be rejected by it. For example, it would be extremely difficult to impose a communist political system on a capitalist society and vice-versa. This is also true of the physical world and of our own bodies as well. If an organ is transplanted into a human body and that organ is not compatible with it, the body will ultimately reject it. Similarly, if a system of life is imposed upon a social organisation which is alien to it, it will not be able to embed itself in the social fabric and will eventually be rejected.

Finally, in addition to preparing people and society, gaining the support of key societal leaders and power brokers is also essential for introducing social change smoothly and successfully. Without such support, advancing positive change will be difficult. As an example, it is documented in Muslim history that Umar bin Abdul Aziz (d. 719 CE, also known as Umar the Second) was a great leader and a very pious person. He saw corruption in his society and he endeavoured to eradicate it. However, though he had political authority and had at his back a group of people trained by the Companions of the Prophet, he was not completely successful in his efforts to reform the Umayyad State, simply because many of the key officials and power brokers did not support the change efforts nor were they ready to accept the reforms being introduced. Though he strove hard and managed to eradicate many forms of corruption and malpractices, some key people around him were against his reforms. Eventually, Umar bin Abdul Aziz was poisoned by his own servant. The lesson is: a leader cannot be very effective on his own without the support of other people holding power and influence. If people are not ready for change, then no matter how capable a leader may be, efforts for reform and change will not bear much fruit.

The point being stressed is that by solely exerting efforts for political change, or driving change from the top-down, will not necessarily bring about a better society. In addition, people need to be prepared and the overwhelming support of key power holders gained. Without this multi-pronged approach, little positive change can be produced in society.

What about change through armed struggle? From an analysis of the Quran one can conclude that the true Prophets of Allah had a long-term perspective of the success of their work. This is why they did not exhibit impatience at any time during the course of their mission. Furthermore, they were not motivated by greed or hatred, nor did they desire to take revenge on their enemies, or punish the wicked and create social disorder. On the contrary, their mission was to fight against social diseases so that people could live in peace and dignity. To accomplish this noble task, they employed peaceful methods wherever possible to reform their people. However, they did not hesitate to use force if the opposition was bent upon hindering them from their work (i.e. denying the right for sharing and propagating Islam) or if they resorted to organised hostilities. Force was, however, used with due care and thought, and only if all other options were exhausted, and also if they had enough power for the purpose. It is evident that they did not incite one group of people against another, disrupt social peace or start any terrorist activities. Rather, they approached everyone, their opponents, the rich and the poor, black and white, in short, all men and women in their society, calling them to God's way through peaceful means. The Prophet Muhammad himself pursued a peaceful approach as far as possible to change his social environment. He never pressed his Companions into situations that would result in their total annihilation. For instance, when he commenced his work, and there were only a few Muslims in society, he did not call for an armed struggle or provoke anyone into a conflict. In fact, God commanded the Muslims to restrain from fighting even in self-defence at this early stage of their mission.

> *"Have you not turned your vision to those who were told to hold back their hands (from fight), but to establish regular prayer and spend in regular charity ..."*
>
> (an-Nisa 4: 77)

Had a reactionary approach been adopted it would have been suicidal. On the contrary, as more and more people began to join his faith and movement, the Prophet started to look for a base to establish a model Islamic community. Through these efforts he desired to demonstrate to his people the kind of changes he was endeavouring to introduce. To accomplish this, he approached the leaders of his community, tribal chiefs and influential people in and around Arabia. When he eventually succeeded in winning the people of Medina (622 CE) to his call, he and his followers migrated there and there they laid the foundations of an Islamic society.

This society was established without a single war. Subsequently, as the Prophet now had a base, he was able to defend his community from any aggression, and it was at this stage that they were allowed by God to defend themselves against any offensive attacks. Here it is worth noting, that on his entry into Medina, the Prophet made a very comprehensive peace Treaty with the Jewish tribes living there, so that the two communities could live in peace, side-by-side, in a multi-faith society.

> *"But if they incline to peace, you also incline to it, and put your trust in Allah. Verily He is the All-Hearer, the All-Knower."*
>
> (al-Anfal 8: 62)

Further, the peace Treaty made at Hudaybiyya (628 CE) with his arch enemies turned out to be a great turning point in Islam's favour. As a result of this Treaty, Muslims were permitted to move about in peace throughout Arabia and this provided a great opportunity for sharing the message of Islam with all tribes and peoples. As a consequence, within a two year period, more people came into the fold of Islam as compared with the previous years of the Prophet's mission. This led to Islam capturing the attention of the people in Makka. Thus, interestingly enough, Islam's ascendancy in Makka (630 CE) also took place without war. In other words, both holy cities of the Muslims, namely Makka and Medina, became Islamic cities without any war.

In short, Islam aims to introduce its change by employing peaceful methods and with the least disruption to social life as is practically possible. However, the use of force sometimes becomes necessary, and even obligatory. In situations where people are oppressed or persecuted, and if Muslims are able to liberate them from such miserable conditions, then Islam allows the use of force.

> *"And why should you not fight in the Way of Allah, when those who being weak are ill-treated (and oppressed) – men, women and children, whose cry is: O our Lord, rescue us from this place, whose people are oppressors..."*
>
> (an-Nisa 4: 75)

In situations where the state denies the right to propagate Islam, again the use of force is permitted. However, in such a case, persuasion, and other means must be tried first to avert war. Going to war without sufficient power and preparation would be suicidal and not achieve any purpose.

> *"And fight in the way of Allah with those who fight you, but transgress not the limits. Truly, Allah likes not the transgressors."*
>
> (al-Baqara 2: 190)

> *"Never desire fighting but pray to Allah for peace and security. And when you have to fight the enemy, fight with steadfastness and know that Paradise lies under the shadow of the swords"*
>
> (Riyadh-us-Salihin)

> *"O Believers, take your precautions, and either go forth in groups, or go forth all together."*
>
> (an-Nisa 4: 71)

Emergent and Dynamic Processes

As was discussed in Chapter One, the introduction and advancement of social change is not a simple, step by step linear process. Rather it is complex; a multi-dimensional and iterative process. Just as an Islamic movement strives to influence and produce change in the social environment, the processes of the larger society, in which the movement is operative, are also influencing the priorities, strategies, internal processes, momentum and speed of the movement itself. Change is, therefore, a dynamic process, and issues and challenges are emergent. Change agents, therefore, need to constantly sense and analyse the feedback signals from the external environment in order to steer a movement along the most effective course towards achieving its objectives. The application of the Islamic methodology has to take this dynamic situation into consideration.

This implies that the four major components of the Islamic methodology do not necessarily have to follow each other in a linear way, or be acted upon simultaneously. An order of priority must be considered according to the social context. For example, during the early period of the Prophet's mission, in Makka, since people were being prepared for the change ideas, the implementation of Islamic systems and laws (*Sharia*) was not even raised. At that stage, efforts were being focused on *dawa*, *tarbiya* and to some extent on building a group life, *jama'a*, since these are prerequisites for the other components. However, later on, in Medina, where the majority of people had accepted Islam, efforts incorporated *jihad* and the work for establishing Islamic systems, but efforts for *dawa* also continued in parallel.

Operational Strategies and Methods

The components of the Islamic methodology provide a broad framework for guiding the process of strategy formulation. As an illustration, let us contemplate over *dawa*. How, in practice, should a movement engage in calling people to Islam? What are the most effective and appropriate methods and means that can be employed? What section of people should efforts initially concentrate upon? How should the message be made relevant to the people being addressed? What technologies and methods are available for amplifying the message? What attitudes towards Islam are dominant in that particular social context which may hinder efforts for *dawa*? Answers to these and related questions will naturally vary between different social contexts and, thus, must be clarified and the actions determined. As an example, in one context, where a society allows freedom of expression, the work of communicating the Islamic message may be performed openly. However, in another context, where people may not be allowed to share their thoughts and beliefs, it may have to be carried out by using other methods of communication. In the present

Western context for instance, suitable methods for *dawa* may include one-to-one dialogue and discussions, public programmes and campaigns, the distribution of written material, use of the Internet and mass media, meetings with academics, politicians, and other influential people in society.

In a like manner, the way a social movement, *jama'a*, is built, its structure and way of working will vary in different social situations. However, whatever the situation may be, principles of leadership, accountability, consultation and justice are universal and, hence, have to be observed. Thus, suitably clear rules and procedures for collective work have to be formulated in the light of Islamic guidance. Likewise, detailed strategies, methods and means for the other remaining components of the methodology have to be formulated by the Islamic movement for their own situation.

Finally, strategies, methods and techniques are operational in nature. They are not sacred and people can differ in their use of the same. Hence, members of a movement must be allowed to express their opinions and views freely regarding operational strategies and methods. In fact, to avoid discontentment within the ranks of a movement, proper discussions should take place so that all the pros and cons, together with any social and resource implications, are considered and thrashed out before finalising the details of a programme of action. Strategies should also be regularly evaluated and reviewed in the light of new experiences and knowledge.

Dealing with Resistance

Naturally, effective action will generate some form of tension, opposition and resistance. So how does a movement deal with such situations? Here the practice of the Prophet Muhammad becomes an excellent guide. Though the Prophet of Allah worked with great care and wisdom, nevertheless he still faced many hardships, persecutions, difficulties and a considerable amount of opposition and resistance in his efforts for change. The leaders of his people understood the message of Islam very clearly, however, they opposed him with vigour since they sensed a threat to their lordship and position in the social hierarchy. They realised well that Islam, if it prevailed, would not allow the continuation of corrupt practices.

Initially, the leadership of the Prophet's society tried to ignore him, hoping that he would sooner or later give up his work. They, however, greatly misjudged him and underestimated his determination, resolve and conviction. The Prophet continued meeting people and his message began to reach every corner of Arabia. As more and more people started to become curious about this new phenomenon, the Prophet's opponents began to react arrogantly by mocking his message and teachings, calling him a madman, a person who had been bewitched, ridiculing him and his Companions, belittling his work, etc. Despite all this, the noble Prophet of Allah showed a great deal of patience (*sabr*) and carried on calling his people to give up the worship of false gods and to submit to the one God. Through continuous efforts he gradually began to attract some powerful personalities, for example, Umar and Hamza, into the fold of Islam. This led to more problems for the Muslims. The resistance increased. The leaders became more organised and intensified their opposition. In addition, they intimidated some of the Prophet's followers. Others were persecuted and tortured, particularly the weaker ones, who were either slaves or had little tribal backing. The Prophet and his Companions, however, remained steadfast and endured all these persecutions with patience (*sabr*).

When these tactics did not work, his enemies started to think of other ways to hinder the Prophet from continuing his work of social change. They tried to bribe him, even offering him the leadership of the city if he gave up calling people to the new message. But the Prophet turned down all their offers and continued with his efforts and striving. His opponents greatly misjudged him. They were deluded into believing that he was working for his own domination and personal power. Thus, when attempts to bribe him failed, they intensified their persecutions and finally planned to murder the Prophet. God however saved him from their evil plot, and directed him to migrate to Medina, a city some 300 miles north of Makka, where he had some considerable following by that time. Yet even in Medina, the opposition, which by this stage was beginning to fear the Prophet's domination over Arabia, became more organised and intensified their resistance and hostilities.

This resulted in a number of wars between the Muslim community and their opponents. Ultimately, however, their resistance was broken and the Prophet succeeded in influencing and winning over the whole of Arabia to the message of Allah.

With this brief overview, let us pause and ask: why did certain people and groups resist his change? Scholars give numerous reasons for this including the following:

1. A fear of losing their leadership and influence. Most of the resistance came from the leaders and chiefs who had vested interests and felt that these were threatened. They feared that their machinations would be exposed to the public whom they dominated and exploited. Resistance from many of the leading hypocrites was also similarly attributable.
2. Partisanship or nationalistic feelings. Some felt that their superiority over other tribes would be crushed since all people would be equally treated, and they found this extremely difficult to digest.
3. A few based their resistance on a fear of losing their cultural norms and traditions.
4. Others were apprehensive of the disruption the new change would bring to their lifestyles.
5. Another reason for resistance was that a way of life based on a moral code would hinder immoral ways which some corrupt people were so used to.
6. Jealousy was also another factor. Some envied the Prophet, and others did not accept him simply because he was not from their own clan, tribe, nation or race.
7. Resistance was also the result of deep-rooted ignorance and a genuine lack of comprehension of the mission of Islam amongst some people.

It is a general fact that change creates some form of resistance. Islamic workers should expect some resistance to emerge at different stages of a change process. No doubt, a lot of tension was caused due to the Prophet's revolutionary message, and it is generally difficult to put aside old ideas and practices so that new ones can be learned and experienced. Many people fear the unknown, particularly a social change, and hence can sometimes show aggression towards new ideas and practices.

How did the Prophet of Allah deal with the resistance that he faced? It is apparent from his life that he used a non-confrontational approach as far as possible. To handle resistance, he employed many methods and stratagems which were suited to the kind of resistance offered. For example, he was abused, ridiculed, called a madman, rubbish and filth was thrown at him, and many of his Companions were persecuted and tortured. However, in this hostile situation he instructed his Companions to observe patience and be steadfast (*sabr*). Moreover, the Quran specifically prohibited Muslims from retaliating with the use of bad language or sarcasm, and even precluded them from insulting the idols and gods which people worshipped. The observance of such instructions helps towards opening up peoples' hearts to the message of Islam and prevents the placement of unnecessary barriers to communication. Thus, the Prophet never over-reacted to resistance on its discovery, and was always sensitive to peoples' feelings and views. He sometimes simply ignored the resistance, at other times he used wisdom and tact. For verbal abuse, he repelled it with good words or actions. As an example, he visited Taif, a city some 30 miles from Makka, to share his message. There, however, he was ridiculed and physically assaulted. Youth were ordered to stone him, and this resulted in severe physical injuries with blood pouring from parts of his body. Even with such cruel treatment, he prayed to Allah for their guidance. The Quran offers the following instructions.

> *"Nor can goodness and evil be equal. Repel evil with what is better..."*
> (Fussilat 41: 34)

At times the noble Prophet organised meetings with his opponents to clarify his message and stance. More effective though, was the purity of his character, he being merciful, forgiving, kind, generous, trustworthy and truthful which greatly helped in facing and combating resistance. However, when the opposition became determined to eliminate him and his followers, and resorted to organised violence, the Prophet had no alternative but to meet their aggression with similarly organised force. His general attitude though was of forgiveness and to overlook minor forms of resistance. For example, when the

Prophet Muhammad marched successfully into Makka, during the last phases of his mission, he was merciful to everyone, even his arch enemies. He forgave even those who had led persecutions and wars against him and his Companions, and only those who resisted and raised their swords against him were fought. Thus, it was deep faith and trust in Allah alone, clarity of vision and purpose, and a strong grounding on morality that assisted the noble Prophet and his Companions to face resistance and strive with perseverance. The Prophet of Allah prepared his Companions well for hard and difficult times. They did not become impatient at any stage of the struggle, or show a lack of will to face any resistance. In sum, individual opposition and resistance was overlooked or dealt with patiently. However, organised oppression and resistance were met in an organised way.

> *"O Believers, seek help (of Allah) through Prayer and perseverance. Verily Allah is with those who persevere."*
>
> (al-Baqara 2: 153)

An Overview of Contemporary Popular Methodologies

Finally, it is appropriate here to mention some of the popular approaches that are adopted by Muslim groups for advancing change. This will assist in understanding the current misconceptions and confusion that exist among a few regarding the methodology and its application in Western societies. The intention of this discourse is neither to examine in any detail nor to critically assess any of these approaches, since this would require a separate book. Rather, the aim is to present a brief overview of the main approaches in order to help readers to compare and contrast these for themselves, and evaluate them using the Islamic framework and methodology discussed in this book.

Each approach that is being pursued, or the way the Islamic methodology is understood and applied, is based upon, and derived from, a particular group's understanding of the objectives of Islam and the underlying reasons for the present predicament of the Muslim world-community (*Umma*). For example, one group concludes that the Muslim community's malaise is due to the loss of political power, and as a direct consequence, their priority and work focuses on actions that enable them to regain that power. In a similar way, another group firmly believes that the problems of the Muslim *Umma* exist due to intellectual stagnation, whilst another asserts that they are the result of loss of missionary spirit. Yet still another group advocates that the present predicament is due to incorrect faith (*aqida*), the poor practice of Islamic rituals, or lack of spirituality, and so on. These and many more conclusions exist, and each determines the particular approach that has been chosen for influencing people and society. Some emphasise a return to traditional Muslim life-styles and methods, others are more spiritually inclined, whilst still others are more rationalist and intellectual in their reasoning, method and approach. Thus, the various approaches are either formed out of a particular understanding of the objectives of Islam, or they differ in emphasis or priorities only.

The popular methodologies and approaches that are being pursued for social change by Muslim groups and organisations are summarised below.

Acquisition of Political Power

One approach argues that Muslims should strive to acquire political power, and more specifically to institute a caliph (head of an Islamic state). Proponents of this approach stress that this should be the focal point of endeavours and a top priority, rather than the work for reforming individuals. The caliph, having power and support from the Muslims, would then be able to reform individuals and society by establishing Islamic laws. The efforts of these groups are, thus, focused on mobilising the Muslims for gaining political power. A political awareness is created through their leaflets, circles and public gatherings. Those who were responsible for dismantling the Islamic political system in 1924 are cursed and efforts are made to make public their evil ways. Dictators, kings and leaders in the Muslim world are also condemned since they are not working to implement Islamic laws in their countries. They are considered the puppets of Western governments. However, this approach pays little attention to inner development; to Islamic social code and acts of worship, how Muslims should live and behave, and to morals and manners. It also ignors the contemporary socio-political context of change and thereby advocates a political change through applying force.

Revival of Islamic Rituals

A contrasting approach is that Muslims should work to revive faith, rituals and Islamic traditions as their priority. Proponents of this view move from place to place, and from country to country, inviting people to these aspects. They present stories of the Companions and righteous people and try to motivate people to worship by talking about Paradise and Hell. However, the social, economic and political aspects are not given much importance. In fact talking about politics, and socio-political affairs in general, is considered worldly (*dunya*) and, this according to them, has nothing to do with *din* (Islam). Striving against injustice and changing corrupt social systems are outside their agenda. More emphasis is placed on *dhikr* (remembrance of Allah), on the finer details of *wudu* and *ghusal* (ablution and bathing), methods of prayer and fasting, the types of clothing to wear, and so on.

Correction of Faith and Improvement of Islamic Practices

One group emphasises that Muslims should, as a priority, work for improving and reforming individuals by correcting their Islamic creed (*aqida*), and improving their worship and Islamic practices. Through this process, they assert, Allah will inevitably help them against corrupt people and lead them to gaining political power through which social reforms can be made possible. They call people to live the pure and simple Islam that was practised by the early Muslims, in particular the kind of life established by the Prophet of Allah in Makka and Medina. The cultural richness and intellectual developments of Muslim societies during the medieval and latter-day periods are rejected since they are considered as innovations (*bida*). Dressing like the Prophet, stressing a particular length for a beard, offering prayers according to particular opinions, following the sayings of the Prophet from particular *ahadith* collections only, and other similar things are also emphasised.

Spiritual Revival

The way of the Sufis is yet another approach. Undoubtedly, the Sufis have played an important role in the revival of the spiritual aspects of personal life. They hold *dhikr* (remembrance of God) circles, emphasise the inner dimensions of worship, and encourage reflection and meditation. However, some criticise certain Sufi groups for distorting true Islamic spirituality, mingling it with concepts from other religions, separating it from social actions, and hence producing pseudo-spiritualism. Some are also sceptical about whether they have managed to effect any social change in Muslim communities, since changing social life is not a priority on their agenda.

Islamisation of Knowledge

Another approach stresses the Islamisation of knowledge as a priority. They propagate the intellectual revival and development of the Muslim world-community. They believe that ideas are very powerful and efforts should, therefore, be made to influence academics and intellectuals in all knowledge disciplines. Through these efforts, Muslims will be able to regain their intellectual position in the world and, hence, lead humanity towards the right direction.

Striving for a Just Social Order

Finally, a view that is well established and has support from many scholars of repute, for example, Mawdudi, Hasan Al-Banna, and Sayyid Qutb, is that the way forward for Muslims is to revive within themselves faith and the sense of purpose and mission for which they have been raised as a world-community. This view argues that the present day predicaments and problems that the Muslims face are due to a loss of vision and the neglecting of the Islamic mission. Muslims should, therefore, work to build an effective and strong social organisation based on Islam's principles of leadership and consultation. This social organisation should strive to revive and develop Islamic faith and character. At the same time, it should strive to share its world-view and way of life with society at large, in a way that makes Islam relevant to the contemporary world. It should also work to advance changes in society according to Islam's guidance in order to realise its vision. This view also argues for working with wisdom, exercising patience, and avoiding all extremist methods that may lead to unnecessary tension and conflict.

Its programme of work includes: to awaken a people from false consciousness and inviting them to Islam, to reconstruct family and social life and reform government according to Islamic ideals, to liberate Muslim nations from all kinds of imperialism, colonisation, and secular-materialistic influences, to build wider co-operation and solidarity between Muslims nations, and to initiate a programme for sharing Islam with humanity and to play a constructive role in world affairs.

These are some of the major approaches adopted today to guide thinking and action for social change. If all these approaches are evaluated through the lens of the Islamic framework for social change, it can be ascertained that some contain certain weaknesses and drawbacks. These are as follows:

1. Some efforts are limited, they focus on reviving or establishing a few aspects of Islam only rather than the whole. Some of these groups concentrate on minor details and practices, about which differing opinions exist anyway, rather than establishing the fundamentals of the Islamic faith, its principles and teachings in social life. In other words, socio-political actions are entirely ignored.
2. Amongst a few groups, the order of priority is confused and, therefore, a pragmatic and wise application of the methodology is lacking. For example, there is less emphasis on calling people to Islam and more on implementing Islamic laws in society, even though a society may not be ready for these. Some other groups only attend to the symptoms and not the root problems faced by our societies; that is they do not begin at the starting point indicated by the framework or work for the goal of Islam, they rather concentrate on reviving a few rituals or traditions.
3. Finally, a few other groups only deal with Muslim issues and concerns rather than seeking to affect society as a whole. Alternatively, they limit themselves to a particular people, class or language, to the exclusion of other Muslims.

On close evaluation, one can conclude that some of the above methodologies are actually reactionary, extremist, inward looking, focus on the symptoms, or have confused Islamic priorities. A few also completely fall outside the Islamic framework for social change and, hence, would not lead to a change that is desired by Islam. Although, circumstances greatly influence the approach and methods employed, change agents must be critical and not blindly imitate any method which they may come across.

In addition to the above methodologies, a few specific methods for their implementation have been, or are being employed by Muslim groups and these are outlined below. The choice of these methods is, however, very much dependent upon the social and political conditions of a country in which an Islamic movement may be operating.

Change Through Popular Revolution

This approach aims to rally people for a popular uprising (revolution) against those in power, who are believed to be corrupt and unjust. However, this approach places less emphasis on preparing people and creating the right kind of social conditions prior to the revolution. Such an approach, therefore, does not usually lead to a smooth transition from one set of social conditions to another. Also, an inadequately planned or uncontrolled revolution is most likely to give rise to great social and economic disturbances and upheavals, and, hence, devastate the lives of thousands of people in the process.

Change Through Armed Struggle

This differs from the former approach in that a limited number of activists from a closed group are usually involved (obviously, because the operations have to be kept secret). In most cases, a few small reactionary or extremist groups are quick to adopt such methods for uprooting their corrupt governments. They aim to change their government, or those in power, through force by bringing about a military coup. Unfortunately, in this kind of approach, many innocent lives can be lost in the process and is, therefore, not encouraged by the well-established Islamic movements. However, in certain circumstances (for example, when a people are dominated by a foreign power or are ruled through force) such an approach may be the only alternative left for liberating a people from oppression. Even for such cases, change through armed struggle requires good planning, adequate preparation, and also great care needs to be exercised to ensure that the lives of ordinary people are not put into danger.

Change Through the Process of Elections

A few national Islamic movements, that are well rooted in their countries, work towards educating and nurturing better people and organising them for influencing society. In other words, they focus on preparing people for change, whilst at the same time they take on social and political issues. This engages them in campaigning for popular consent so as to gain political power through peaceful means, i.e. via the process of elections.

In summary, this Chapter has examined some issues regarding the application of the Islamic methodology. It is argued that an understanding of the social context and pragmatism are both essential for the effective application of the methodology. Social change is also normally advanced in a non-linear way, and, therefore, careful planning, wisdom and flexibility are required for applying the methodology. It also emphasises that the preparation of society prior to the introduction of laws is an important aspect of the Islamic methodology.

Notes:

1. According to some scholars (for example, Mawdudi, S.A., *The Meaning of the Quran*, Lahore: Islamic Publications, 1989), the Prophet Joseph had complete power of the state. However, others (for example, Ghannouchi, Rachid) argue that he was only in charge of managing the cultivation and distribution of food production.
2. Ghannouchi, Rachid, *Islam a Vision for Britain*, published by The Islamic Society of Britain, 1995, p.11.
3. For example: "*There is no compulsion and coercion in regard to religion. Truth stands out clear from falsehood ...*" (al-Baqara 2: 256), and "*say, the truth is from your Lord. Let him who will believe, and let him who will reject it...*" (al-Kahf 18: 29.)
4. See Mawdudi, S.A., *The Islamic Law and Constitution*, translated by Khurshid Ahmad, Lahore: Islamic Publications Ltd., 4th Edition, 1969.

CHAPTER IX

The Islamic Movement: A Vehicle for Social Change

This Chapter examines the characteristics of a social movement based on Islam more closely, since it is an important vehicle for change and reform in a society. It elaborates how an effective and dynamic social movement can be built in the light of Islamic guidance. The following key issues are examined: the need for an Islamic movement, general Islamic principles of organising, and the general characteristics of an Islamic movement.

The Need for an Islamic Movement

A social movement, in broad terms, is an organised body of people striving to introduce and mould change in some or all aspects of society. In general, a movement arises from a vision or out of a strong feeling against certain social injustices, beliefs or practices that may be deep-seated in society. Thus, it exists for a purpose and has a mission to accomplish. Also, members of a movement live, work and interact according to particular conventions, manners, codes and laws. These reflect the values and beliefs of the particular movement.

In view of this, an Islamic movement is an organised and disciplined social movement with a universal vision, even though it may initially act within a particular social context where it takes its birth. It is based upon the Islamic faith and operates according to Islamic social values. Its mission is to nurture and produce good people and a good society; in other words, its purpose is to eradicate social injustices and evils and to establish a God-conscious, balanced and just society and world. An Islamic movement derives its inspiration, motives, vision, guidance and a methodology of work from God's revealed guidance. The need to build a social movement to effect change is something which Islam lays great stress on. Umar bin Al-Khattab said[1]:

> *"There is no Islam without jama'a, there is no jama'a without leadership (Imarah), and there is no leadership without obedience."*

Thus, the sheer complexity and magnitude of the task of changing society and the world dictates that a *jama'a* or a movement comes into being. The Prophet Muhammad, himself, launched a very powerful social movement to transform and reform his society and world according to God's revealed guidance – *that movement was called Islam and its members were known as Muslims.*

> *"Let there arise from among you, a group, who would invite to all that is good, enjoining what is morally right, and forbidding what is unjust. They are the ones who would be successful."*
>
> (Ali-Imran 3: 104)

It follows, that it is not enough for people to put forward ideas only. Ideas are important, but on their own will affect little change. Irrespective of how attractive an idea may be, it will remain theoretical if people do not come together, organise themselves and strive for its realisation. Ideas can remain confined to books and within intellectual circles for centuries unless practical strategies are evolved and a social movement organised for its actualisation in social life. *Academic and theological discussions on their own cannot influence much societal change.*

General Islamic Principles of Organising

What are the organising principles that can bring people together for working to realise the vision of Islam in society and the world? Regarding this, the Prophet Muhammad has offered some guidelines and principles. In one of his famous saying, he stated:

> *"I enjoin on you five things: A collective life (jama'a), listening (sam'), obeying (ta'a), migration (hijra), and striving hard in Allah's way (jihad). He who secedes from the Jama'a (social movement) as much as a span has*

> *cast off the tie of Islam from his neck, unless he returns to its fold. And he who summons to what the pre-Islamic (jahiliya) people followed belongs to the assemblies of hell even if he fasts, offers prayers, and asserts that he is a Muslim."*
>
> (Ahmed and Tirmidhi)

In the above saying a couple of important general principles for organising are mentioned, which, if understood and applied, can aid in building a strong and dynamic Islamic movement.

Collective Life (Jama'a)

The Arabic word *jama'a* commonly refers to a community, an organisation or an Islamic social movement. *Jama'a* is, therefore, a collection of people who have come together around shared values and concerns, or for a common purpose and mission. Living a collective, organised and disciplined life in a movement offers many benefits. These are outlined below:

First, efforts for change become more co-ordinated, integrated, and hence effective. This is implied by the saying: *the sum of the total is greater than the sum of the parts*. By working together, people are able to pool their human and material resources. Furthermore, a movement provides leadership and *shura* (decision-making mechanisms). All these together increase the social and political capacity of a movement, and hence improve the effectiveness of actions for social change.

Second, a social movement strengthens inter-personal relationships and brotherhood and sisterhood, and through these provides the means for social support and encouragement to its members. It also inspires and motivates people and assists in cultivating steadfastness and fortitude. In addition, a movement establishes self-defence mechanisms, which become vital during hard times, and particularly if confrontation develops with those opposing the change efforts.

Third, a movement, through its work, becomes a model for the kind of change and reforms it is striving for. People, living and working together for a cause, establish a culture, social relationships, and a way of doing things. This creates an image in the eyes of the wider society about the movement and the kind of change it stands for. This is what the Quran implies when it appeals to the Muslim community to become witnesses before humanity:

> *"And, thus, We have made you a community of the middle way, so that you may be witnesses before humanity, and the Messenger a witness over yourselves ..."*
>
> (al-Baqara 2: 143)

Individuals on their own cannot become *effective witnesses* if they remain outside a social movement, as Islam has to be lived in one's personal and collective life. This is why the Prophet, as mentioned above, stressed that anyone who secedes from a social movement has practically left Islam.

Finally, and this is more important for a change based on Islam, the effective personal and social development of individuals can be enhanced through a movement (*tarbiya*). A movement brings its members forward to face societal and global challenges. This produces an awareness of social issues and cultivates courage, steadfastness and sharpens the intellect. Thus, individuals, by being involved in a social movement, acquire more knowledge and understanding of the message and work, learn from others peoples' experience, increase confidence and practical skills, and experience the benefits and joys of collective Islamic living and striving. For example, brotherhood and sisterhood, care, affection, generosity, social support, etc., all these blessings can only be experienced through collective living and work. They cannot be experienced outside a movement (see Chapter Ten for a further discussion on personal development).

Listening (Sam')

This is the second point enjoined by the Prophet Muhammad for collective work. Listening implies a number of things. First, members of a movement should willingly listen to their leadership and accept the decisions arrived at after a process of consultation. Second, the term 'listening' also suggests both vertical (i.e. between members and their leadership) and horizontal (i.e. between members themselves) communication and an effective organisational design.

Experience indicates that the structure of a movement can either facilitate or impede "listening". This point will be discussed in more detail later on.

Third, the command of the noble Prophet to "listen" advises that a social movement should work to cultivate a culture that fosters and encourages "listening". People should feel free to express their opinions, feelings and views regarding issues on a movement's agenda. Ideas and suggestions should be listened to with full respect, even though they may differ considerably from that of the leadership. No one should be cut-out or intimidated for the views they hold. Put another way, a social movement should allow free expression and establish a consultative process in all matters affecting its work. In general, *limited ideas lead to limited actions*. By encouraging "listening", the number and variety of ideas and views will expand and grow. Also, more ideas and opinions will stimulate creativity, both in approach and action. As a result, a movement becomes more dynamic and competent.

Fourth, for effective listening (i.e. communication) to take place, social relations based on genuine love, respect, understanding, and the observance of general communication etiquette need to be cultivated and established. In fact, these are a prerequisite for listening. Islam prohibits vain talk, back-biting, bad and abusive language, sarcasm, and so on, since these have an adverse effect on inter-personal relationships. Moreover, disrespect, a lack of openness and weak inter-personal relationships are not conducive to listening. Finally, listening also suggests giving ear to what's happening in society so that a movement can gather 'intelligence' and hence can respond more effectively to the challenges it may face from the social environment. Again this aspect is crucial for the viability of a movement.

Obeying **(Ta'a)**

Once listening has taken place, that is, after giving full consideration to all views and opinions on a collective matter, decisions have to be made within the Islamic framework. These decisions should then be accepted whole-heartedly by all members, even though they may not be in accordance with one's own opinions. Obedience to all decisions through this process leads to a strong movement. If decisions are not accepted or complied with, a social movement cannot remain strong, focused and disciplined. On the contrary, it can even fragment into smaller groups leading to infighting and weaknesses.

Incidentally, Islam stresses that obedience must be within the Islamic limits. Any decisions that conflict with the principles and values of Islam are null and void. No one is permitted, even the head of an Islamic society, to decide anything that goes against what has been revealed by Allah or instructed by His Messenger.

> "*Listening and obeying are the duty of a Muslim, both regarding what he likes and what he dislikes, as long as he is not commanded to perform an act of disobedience to Allah, in which case he must neither listen or obey.*"
>
> (Bukhari and Muslim)

Furthermore, obeying, like listening, has structural implications. When policies and decisions are agreed upon by a consultative body (*shura*), but mechanisms for filtering these decisions through the organisation are lacking, then obeying cannot be said to be implemented. It would not be proper to expect those to whom decisions have not been communicated to "obey". Thus, mechanisms for effective communication and filtering decisions through the whole social movement are necessary. This implies making the necessary structural improvements or adjustments to facilitate vertical and horizontal communication, and this point is elaborated upon later.

Migration (Hijra)

The fourth principle of effective organising as mentioned by the Prophet in his saying, is *hijra*. This usually refers to the migration which the Prophet Muhammad and his noble Companions made from Makka to Medina in 622 CE. This event also marks the starting point of the Islamic calendar. The event was so important that according to historians it was a great turning point in human history. After *hijra* (migration), the Prophet of Allah was able to establish an Islamic society in Medina from which, within a short period, a great part of the world was illumined with Islam. *Hijra*, was, thus, a strategic move made to pool resources and to consolidate power for social change.

However, *hijra* is not a one off event, but rather a constant action. The noble Prophet of Allah, when he was asked what the best *hijra* was, replied:

> *"The one by which you abandon that which your Lord dislikes."*
> (Mishkat)

Put another way, *hijra* is a constant effort to move away from what God dislikes towards what He enjoins upon people. It is a strategic move towards a direction that enables people to practice their faith more easily and in freedom. This gives the term *hijra* a wider meaning and multiple dimensions. An inner *hijra* moves a person away from false gods and rebellion against Allah towards giving unreserved allegiance, loyalty, love and obedience to Allah. A mental or intellectual *hijra* involves thinking, research and planning a move towards Allah and the establishment of His guidance. Physical *hijra* involves the actual execution of these plans; to find resources and power for Islam so that it can be practised in peace and freedom. In other words, *hijra* enables a person and a social movement to reach a higher level of their humanity, a level where they can feel more tranquillity, peace, freedom and dignity and are able to act independently. It liberates and uplifts a person and movement from the status-quo, and from territorial or national fixation when these conflict with Islamic values and principles.

Thus, *hijra* is not limited to a physical migration but has more profound implications for a social movement. It actually motivates a movement towards constant thinking and planning for making strategic moves that enable it to become independent, grow and become stronger in terms of people, resources and allies. It directs attention towards preparedness for achieving victory. This dimension of a social movement is generally neglected. By constantly seeking allies, resources and power-bases, a movement becomes more powerful and, hence, able to take more effective actions (*jihad*) for social change. Interestingly, the Quran always mentions *hijra* before *jihad*:

> *"Those who believe, do hijra (migration) and jihad, (strive) have the highest rank in the sight of Allah, and it is they who will achieve success."*
> (at-Tawba 9: 20)

Hijra is, therefore, about strategic moves made for consolidating resources and power to enable effective *jihad* to take place; to seek out opportunities and prepare for them. It is aimed at increasing a movement's social and political capacity and effectiveness. In this sense, *hijra* is indeed a pre-requisite to *jihad*, since without preparations, resources, and some form of strength and power (capacity), *jihad* cannot really be effective. In our opinion, it is for this reason that *hijra* is always mentioned before *jihad*.

Actions for Social Change (Jihad)

The next principle of organising mentioned by the Prophet Muhammad for building a strong movement is *jihad*. This literally means to strive ones utmost for an objective. As mentioned earlier, in Islamic usage, the term *jihad* aims at strategic, organised, co-ordinated and disciplined actions to eradicate oppression and injustice from society and open new avenues for Islamic *dawa*. In other words, *jihad* is about expending time, energies and resources in the Way of Allah. Listening, obeying and *hijra*, as discussed above, form the building blocks for effective *jihad*.

Jihad is the culmination of the work of an Islamic movement. It enables a movement to keep focused on its purpose and mission, and hence reduces the risk of deviation or going astray. Without striving to accomplish its purpose, the formation of a movement becomes meaningless. *Jihad* is, thus, the oxygen of an Islamic movement; without it, it will die. In view of this, the above saying of the Prophet Muhammad warns against seceding from a movement, that is from the struggle: "*He who secedes from the jama'a (social movement) as much as a span has cast off the tie of Islam from his neck, unless he returns to its fold...*" Put another way, anyone who withdraws from the struggle, the *jihad*, actually deviates from Islam itself.

Observance of Islamic Values and Principles

Finally, the Prophet cautioned Muslims not to adopt *jahiliya* (pre-Islamic ignorant ways). These ways were characterised by injustice, falsehood, tribalism, partisanship, and other evils. This implies that in every effort and work, adherence to the truth, Islamic morals and just principles is obligatory. In fact, the whole ethos of an Islamic movement should be built upon its moral teachings – and under no circumstances can Islamic principles be violated. Even under extreme opposition, abuse and persecution, Islam does not allow a movement to disregard its principles and values. As an illustration, during a war, if the enemy destroys land, rapes women, kills old people and civilians, or commits other atrocities, Muslims are not allowed to retaliate with the same. Many incidences to this effect can be cited from Muslim history. One example here suffices. Abu Bakr, the first Caliph, gave clear instructions to the Muslim army leaving for battle. A few of these are listed below[2]:

- *Always fear God because He knows what hearts conceal.*
- *Honour the representatives of your enemies.*
- *Always be truthful.*
- *Do not commit misappropriation or fraud nor be guilty of disobedience to the commander.*
- *Do not mutilate the limbs of any person.*
- *Do not kill old people, or women and children.*
- *Do not destroy the crops and date-palms nor burn them with fire.*
- *Slaughter not cattle except for purposes of food.*
- *You will pass people who live in monasteries. Do not disturb or harm them.*

Islam is a global movement, aiming at the eradication of corruption and wrong. It does not, therefore, permit its followers to resort to actions and behaviour that go against truth and justice under any circumstances.

One further important point emerges from this regarding the mobilisation of people for a cause. The words of the saying, "*And he who summons to what pre-Islamic people followed...*" actually prohibits a movement from mobilising people for wrong and unjust causes. On the contrary, a movement should work to awaken and mobilise people for just causes. Effective mobilisation in this context can be facilitated when a movement's work is entrenched in contemporary social issues and the political institutions of society. These efforts can also enable a movement to become more relevant, facilitate in building its resources and develop momentum for change.

In sum, organised people is power through which change can be effected. The above six principles for organising provide a framework for connecting people into a strong, dynamic and vibrant movement for advancing positive changes in society and the world.

General Characteristics of an Islamic Movement

An Islamic movement has unique distinguishing features. These are listed below:

1. God-oriented: both inward and outward.
2. Operates within a moral framework.
3. Service-oriented: striving to build a just society and serving humanity (and not for any personal ends).
4. Built-in dynamism (that is an Islamic movement is not fossilised. It is involved in a continuous process of revival and regeneration to keep pace with changing conditions in light of the Quran and *Sunna* – *ijtihad*).
5. Universal (or open) membership.
6. Non-sectarian: all-inclusive, ecumenical.
7. Balanced ethos.
8. Pragmatic in approach.
9. Power organisation.
10. Simple and integrated structure.
11. Competent leadership.

Some of these characteristics are self-explanatory, however others require some elaboration as is given below.

Universal Membership

Just as Islam is a universal faith, for all people, so is an Islamic movement universal. Its membership is open to anyone who believes in Islam and desires to work for realising its vision in individual and social life; whether he/she is from the east or the west, or whether black or white. The movement built by the Prophet Muhammad was universal. It embraced people from different backgrounds and walks of life, from different nations and tribes, and who collectively shared a wide range of skills and experiences. They were all united by the Islamic faith and vision. For example, Abu Bakr and Umar were Arabs, Suhaib was from Rome, Salman from Persia and Bilal was an Etheopian.

Membership of an Islamic movement cannot, therefore, be restricted to a particular group or class of people. It has to be open and broad-based. The criteria for joining and involvement should be faith, a common vision and purpose, and not any racial, geographical, linguistic or sectarian consideration. All Muslims must be approached and invited to join in the efforts for reform and change; the pious and the not so pious, the intellectuals and the illiterates, the young and old, men and women, black and white.

Restricting recruitment and involvement to a certain group of people to the exclusion of others cannot really win support from the general public for change. Furthermore, by confining membership to those who belong to a particular school of thought, social class, or those who hold particular opinions and views, would naturally root bias, restrict the generation and flow of ideas, and stifle creativity in a movement, and all these factors together can ultimately lead to extremism. Also, such criteria for membership generally leads to the formation of exclusive clubs and cults, rather than a mass movement for societal change. An Islamic movement must, therefore, be open and all views and opinions that are within Islamic limits respected and tolerated. In actual fact, diversity enriches a movement, and nurtures creativity and innovation, and these assist in surging it forward.

Balanced Ethos

This again is a very important characteristic of an Islamic movement. Islam enjoins wisdom, balance, moderation and tolerance in all affairs, and it condemns excessiveness, extravagance and fanatical attitudes. To cultivate a balanced ethos, Muslims are encouraged to understand the objectives of Islam, stay close to Islamic guidance, and give as much weight to an aspect of Islam as the noble Prophet of Allah and his faithful Companions gave, no more and no less.

Extremist attitudes, practices and customs, make their entrance into an organisation, community or groups, through various ways – through views based on ignorance, superficial knowledge, imbalanced understanding or impatience. It is cultivated when certain verses of the Quran, sayings of the noble Prophet or certain of his deeds are exaggerated or understood out of their context, or when they are over emphasised. It even arises from exaggerated love or hate of someone or something. Extremism is a disease and a means of leading a movement astray – and eventually to its decay and disintegration if not addressed. It deviates a people and movements from God's guidance. Also, exaggeration and extremism lead to intolerance, disrespect, inflexibility and cause conflicts amongst people. These, in the long-run, destroy communities and are, therefore, alien to Islam because Islam is the "middle" way.

> "*You are a community (Umma) of the middle way, so that you may be witnesses before Humanity ...*"
>
> (al-Baqara 2: 143)

> "*Allah intends every facility for you; He does not want to put you to difficulties*"
>
> (al-Baqara 2: 185)

Islam regards extremism in *din* (way of life) as a basic fault of the people before the advent of the Prophet Muhammad.

> "*O people of the Book, exceed not the limits in your religion…*"
>
> (al-Maida 5: 77)

> "*Beware, do not adopt extremism, because your predecessors got annihilated by adopting extremist attitudes in din.*"
>
> (Muslim)

Extremist, rigid and strict attitudes did not exist during the early period of Islam. The Prophet Muhammad himself, as can be gathered from documented evidence, was very tolerant, he listened to others with respect, avoided arguments and quarrels and adopted the best available course of action even though it may have been suggested by someone else. There was a balance between his personal, family, social and public life. He was always polite and pleasant to people and was noted for his compassion, mercy, kindness and generosity. He was involved in *dhikr* (remembrance of Allah), he offered prayers and observed fasting and always attended to his home and family. Along with all this, he led his community and worked for social change. He consulted his Companions and on numerous occasions accepted their views even though they were different to his. He encouraged the seeking of knowledge, earning a lawful livelihood, physical exercise and training, made peace agreements with his enemies, and held dialogues with people of other faiths. All this demonstrates his balanced way of life, thought and actions.

Acquiring a deep and balanced understanding of Islam assists in leading a balanced and moderate personal and social life. However, some people are found to give more emphasis to certain aspects of Islam over others, or they place unjustified burdens on themselves that have no reference in the Islamic sources of guidance. For example, emphasising certain rituals to the exclusion of others, giving much importance to customary practices and ceremonies, and introducing innovations in worship, or being too occupied with insignificant details. All these create bias, extremism and rigid attitudes and views. Idealists also sometimes tend to adopt extremist positions.

An extremist temperament is one of the major causes of Muslim disunity and weakness today. Cultivation of moderation and balance in peoples temperaments is required for reforming the affairs of the world according to Islam. In sum, Islamic workers must avoid extremism and rigidity, learn and observe the ethics of disagreement in Islam, and show respect and tolerance to differing views and opinions that are within the boundaries of Islam[3].

Pragmatic in Approach

Pragmatism, adaptability and flexibility arise out of broad experience, balanced knowledge and thinking. The Prophet Muhammad and his faithful Companions constantly remained open-minded, outward looking and alert. They were flexible in their approach and had no hesitation to learn and relearn, and adapt to the changes occurring in the external social environment, whilst holding fast to their faith and principles. They prepared themselves for any threats, made use of opportunities and kept themselves fully informed of the developing situation in their society. They did not create mind-guards or become inward looking.

Enslavement to structures, bureaucratic procedures, language and ways of working was not part of their style or attitude. In fact, such attitudes and rigidity stifles creativity and innovation, and can lead a movement towards stagnation and even to decay. This is why Muslims are enjoined not to be rigid or follow anyone blindly. They must only abide by, and work within the framework of the beliefs and principles encoded in the sources of Islam, i.e. the Quran and *Sunna*. Principles of Islamic jurisprudence highlight that anything outside the basic sources of Islamic guidance, including the opinions of scholars, is not sacred and subject to change, improvement or modification.

An analysis of movements indicates that through the passage of time, many successively become prisoners of their own decisions, thoughts and ideas. A particular style, terminology, practices and a culture-set are reinforced. Over time, these gradually begin to be considered sacred and are adhered to passionately. Members of these groups stop taking advice and feel threatened by any criticisms or suggestions which go against their norms, and they become imprisoned in their own thoughts (this is termed a psychic prison). The decay of a movement at this stage is certain. To prevent this from happening, a deep understanding of Islam, regular contact with the Quran and *Sunna*, admitting new members with new ideas more readily, adapting to the social environment and maintaining a flexible approach in the process of change is encouraged.

As a movement works and expands, it would inevitably come across new situations and problems and these must be addressed in the light of Islamic sources of guidance (*ijtihad*). No doubt, during decision making the opinions and decisions made by Muslims in the past need to be kept in mind, but a blind imitation of them cannot be prudent. For example, when Ali, the fourth Caliph, was faced with an extremely difficult political situation, he had no hesitation in shifting the Islamic capital from Medina to Kufa (657 CE), even though previous Caliphs had not done so. The point being stressed is that the important issue is not people, scholars, places or any material things, but whether a movement is moving towards its goal. The only criteria that Muslims have been asked to observe under all circumstances are the principles and values contained in the Quran and *Sunna* of the Prophet Muhammad.

Power Organisation

Power is crucial for advancing positive values and changes in society and for checking corruption and evil. However, it is only a means and not an objective in itself. Power is for Islam, for implementing Islamic values and justice, for the betterment of humanity and not for any personal or national vested interests. Islam stresses that power should be accountable and accessible, and not become an instrument of manipulation, persecution, aggression and injustice. With this in mind, power, employed positively and within the Islamic framework, enables the mobilisation of resources for the change efforts. It increases the social and political capacity of a movement and empowers it to work independently. With power, a movement can engage more effectively within society and influence the policy making processes. Relying too much on external sources for financial, military or political power, can hamper a movement's independence in the long-term. In fact, submission to Allah demands that Muslims put their trust in Him alone, learn to stand on their own feet, and build their own power base and resources. A movement which can mobilise considerable power cannot be easily manipulated, coerced, or black-mailed by corrupt forces or prevented from taking actions against social injustices.

It is a reality of our world that power only respects power. For transforming society and the world according to Islamic ideals, great power needs to be acquired and mobilised. This is why the Prophet Muhammad prayed and worked for gaining power and authority as mentioned in the Quran:

> *"and give me a sultan (i.e. power, authority, government) for my help..."*
> (al-Isra 17: 80)

> *"And against them make ready your strength to the utmost of your power, including steeds of war..."*
>
> (al-Anfal 8: 60)

> *"Prepare to meet them with as much strength as you can afford. Beware, strength consists in archery. Beware, strength consists in archery. Beware, strength consists in archery."*
>
> (Muslim)

Naturally, if power is held by corrupt people and institutions, efforts for changing the status quo will be frustrated, particularly if it goes against their self-interests. Also, weak people and movements cannot influence much change. As a matter of fact, powerless people and communities may themselves resort to corrupt practices in order to save and protect themselves from their immediate miserable state of affairs. Many can also be easily coerced and manipulated.

Power takes many forms and is generally distributed unevenly through society. Besides faith in Allah, determination, cohesion and moral power, other sources of power that can be mobilised by a movement include: money, material resources, technology, sources of information, media and political platforms, as well as skills and specialised knowledge. Being able to muster support from these sources is an indication of a movement's power. Islam instructs Muslims to seek means for strengthening themselves – they should endeavour to become strong in faith, strong spiritually and morally, strong socially, physically, intellectually, financially and militarily. Although corrupt elements did their utmost to eliminate the Prophet Muhammad and his Companions and resisted reforms and changes in society, he was however alert to their plots and prepared his social movement well to meet their aggressions and hostilities.

Unfortunately, for a long time Muslims have confined Islamic work to building faith, practising a few rituals, and developing moral and spiritual strength only. Gaining intellectual, financial, political and military power is given very little importance. This may be one reason why many Muslims countries have negligible industry, meagre and out-dated technology and means of production, possess few universities of renown, and despite having an abundance of resources possess very little economic muscle. In contrast, the early Muslims, who had a correct and balanced understanding of Islam, were different in their attitude. They encouraged the acquisition of knowledge and pioneered many technological innovations.

> *"To seek knowledge is compulsory on every man and woman."*
>
> (Ibn Maja)

> *"Allah likes a stronger believer more than a weaker one, although there is good in both."*
>
> (Muslim)

Movements that are serious about social change cannot afford to overlook this important aspect. Developing economic power through setting up industry and business enterprises, gaining knowledge in all fields of human learning and identifying allies in social, financial, military and political institutions are all essential strategies for building a power movement. Research groups and think tanks in various areas can be set up and a culture of aiming for excellence (*ihsan*) nurtured. Likewise, efforts need to be exerted for influencing economic and political platforms and institutions. Efforts towards this direction will enable an Islamic movement to play a constructive role in society and the world.

To muster support, the Prophet of Allah formed strategic alliances and made peace treaties with communities, groups and tribes who did not necessarily share his beliefs and vision. For example, the noble Prophet of Allah made a very comprehensive treaty with the Jewish tribes that lived in Medina soon after his migration to the city. The peace Treaty at Hudaybiyya (628 CE) with his arch enemies from Makka has already been mentioned. There is also evidence that he made treaties with other Arab tribes during the course of his mission. Further, he made alliances with individuals and groups to further his work. These were of a social, political and military nature. As examples, the Prophet had support from his uncle, Abu Talib in Makka. He also sent some of his Companions to Abbysinia (616 CE) to seek asylum in that country, which was ruled by a pious Christian king (who it is thought later became a Muslim).

Peace treaties and strategic alliances can assist in wining support, reduce resistance and provide strength to a social movement. Here, it is important to clarify that these alliances were not established with any kind of group, but rather with those who shared common values or concerns about society, or those who promised not to obstruct his reforms and spread corruption in society. History has shown that these peace treaties and alliances also greatly assisted in removing several misconceptions and fears about Islam and the changes it aimed to advance. These alliances enabled the Muslims to interact with people of different faiths and share their beliefs and values with them in dialogue, and hence influence them in many ways. Moreover, they assisted in building trust and provided access to more material, military and manpower resources for the work of the Islamic movement. Furthermore, friendly relationships, peace treaties and strategic alliances are important for influencing society for change. Groups that cut themselves off from the rest of society, under the delusion that everyone outside their group is misguided or evil, will not be able to affect much change in the wider society. A movement needs to actively seek out people, groups and communities who share common values and concerns, and establish strategic alliances for furthering the change efforts. The Quran emphasises that Muslims should co-operate amongst themselves and with others for the common good.

> *"And co-operate in righteousness and piety, but do not co-operate in sin and transgression…"*
>
> (al-Maida 5: 2)

Simple and Integrated Structure

This is also another important characteristic of an Islamic movement. A movement's structure is defined by the way effort, people and resources are organised and co-ordinated to achieve its objectives. It affects the flow of information and ideas, communication processes, the co-ordination of plans and resources, the way people interact and deal with each other, and the development and involvement of individuals. In fact, an organisational structure affects the very culture of an organisation. It can either facilitate or impede the development of the Islamic characteristics of a movement. Thus, the way a movement is structured requires careful consideration if it is to evolve into a strong and dynamic force for social change.

The social movement organised by the Prophet Muhammad was simple and integrated, and hence effective. It was not too formal, rigid or bureaucratic, and there was little central control. In fact, it mapped the natural setting and organisation of people at that time, i.e. the network of families bound into tribes. However, at the same time, the Prophet ensured that any un-Islamic structural characteristics and elements such as the division of people into Arabs, non-Arabs, social classes, etc., were not embodied into his organisational model. Moreover, people, tribes and communities were granted autonomy to manage their affairs, address their own social problems, and make their decisions within a set framework outlined in the Quran and using the guidelines from the noble Prophet himself. The involvement of people was further facilitated and enhanced through allowing a great deal of flexibility. This enabled individuals to take initiatives and feel empowered and more responsible. This, in turn, increased their commitment and contribution. In addition, the noble Prophet, not only gave instructions, he also encouraged suggestions and ideas. In other words, communication was not one way, top-down, but rather people were encouraged to come forward, express themselves freely, be involved in decision making, and contribute with their suggestions and opinions.

Thus, the structure of a movement should be simple and integrated, enable vertical and horizontal communication, have the least layers of hierarchy so as to empower people to take initiatives and to speed up the decision-making process. Experience indicates that too many rules, strict procedures and rigid discipline leads to inflexibility and can actually hamper the change efforts. In order to manage change effectively, a movement requires versatility. The best and most effective way to work should decide the structure.

Incidentally, a culture evolves from the combined effect of the type of organisational structure and the leadership style. In view of this, an Islamic movement must ensure that its structure and style of leadership actually assists in creating a caring culture, which builds an atmosphere of tolerance and kindness – a kind of culture that gives a sense of belonging, involves people, encourages team spirit, and provides moral and material support to its members. An autocratic style of leadership usually leads to an hierarchical structure which segments members into sections or levels, roots rigid procedures and creates a tense and uncaring culture. Such a structure prevents capable and talented people from joining a social movement simply because of the rigidity and unnecessary rules and procedures. An hierarchical and segmentalist structure can also impede the flow of information, adversely effect communication processes, and hence threaten the viability of a movement.

In the light of Islamic guidance, organisational structure is a means to an end, and not an end in itself. *It cannot, therefore, be treated as sacred.* Rather, it must evolve and change as an organisation grows and expands. It must be kept as 'simple', 'flat' and 'flexible' as possible to ensure the maximum interaction of the membership, and to facilitate adaptation to the changes occurring in the external social environment. Rigid hierarchical structures usually result in placing power and control in the hands of a few people (elitist group), and this can lead to a great many organisational problems. An Islamic movement cannot allow any kind of elitism to flourish in its organisation; neither social, political nor religious.

Finally, a structure must have built-in mechanisms for decision making and for resolving any disputes, differences or personality clashes. Social cohesion and discipline within the rank and file is crucial if a movement is to surge forward with its programme of change in society and the world. Undoubtedly, in any normal group of people there will be differences of opinions and views on issues. A structure should cater for these differences and allow them to surface in a healthy way for attention and consideration. If views, particularly those that conflict with the leadership, are quashed without any justification, then such practices will inevitably lead to frustration and ultimately to the weakening of a movement. The noble Prophet of Allah allowed anyone to express themselves freely, even though their views or opinions were different from his own. He gave everyone due respect and considered carefully their views and suggestions. After discussion and consultation, these views were either accepted or discarded in an admirable and amicable way. By preventing dissenters, or opposing views to surface, politicking and the rising of groupings are most likely to result and subsequently conflicts will arise within a movement.

Competent Leadership

Paying attention to the development of effective and competent leadership is also essential if a movement desires to surge forward towards realising its vision in society and the world. Good leadership is vital for the success of any movement. It is instrumental in steering an organisation wisely and effectively towards its goal. In contrast, by having incompetent leaders at the helm of affairs, a movement may well either stagnate or be led astray.

The qualities of Islamic leadership, the way leaders are chosen, the mechanisms for consultation, and the responsibilities of leadership, are all significant issues and are addressed below.

1. In the light of Islamic guidance, leadership requires deep faith, clarity of vision, a sound understanding of Islam and its process of social change, strength of will, confidence, a spirit of sacrifice, and a burning desire to live for the Islamic mission. Moreover, good leaders must be pious, compassionate and have a pleasant character. They should exhibit patience and perseverance in all situations (*sabr*). Ideally, the leaders of an Islamic movement should be able to inspire people to action, maintain support and generate confidence.

   In addition to these personal qualities, prudence, foresight and insight into social and political affairs is essential for practical reasons. Further, leaders require a fairly high level of competence in communication, planning and organising, together with political maturity and an ability to take responsibility seriously. These qualities and abilities are crucial since leaders provide direction and strategies.
2. According to Islam, leaders cannot be imposed. On the contrary, people have a God given right to choose their leadership. All the Rightly Guided Caliphs were chosen by the general body

of Muslims, although different selection methods were employed for each. This is, therefore, an important principle of Islam.

> *"Your best leaders are those whom you love and who love you., on whom you invoke blessings and who invoke blessings on you; and your worst leaders are those whom you hate and who hate you, whom you curse and who curse you…"*
>
> (Muslim)

An Islamic movement requires proper procedures for choosing its leaders and for accountability. A lack of reasonable checks and balances in organisations regarding these issues is a recipe for corruption and abuse of power. History informs us of the fact, that after the period of the Rightly Guided Caliphs (the first four Caliphs of the Muslim *Umma*) many Muslim leaders were imposed upon the people instead of their being chosen. This led to abuse of power and corruption, and subsequently to moral degeneration amongst the leadership.

3. Effective mechanisms for consultation are essential. *Shura*, or the process of consultation and policy making with a body of representatives is another important principle for collective life in Islam (as has been discussed earlier in Chapter Two). Consultation generates ideas, provides multiple view-points for a problem situation, and offers more creative and pragmatic solutions. If effectively implemented, *shura* can enable the formation of a dynamic movement. Incidentally, in Islam, a leader is definitely not a dictator or a boss who orders people about. Rather he is a person who leads a movement in the cause of Islam, and, in the process, motivates, inspires and encourages people to take part in actions for a better social life. A good leader encourages consultation and participation and also values people. According to some Islamic scholars the decisions arrived at by the consultative body, *shura*, are binding on a leader.[4]

> *"Those who hearken to their Lord, and establish prayer; and who (conduct) their affairs by mutual consultation; who spend out of what We bestow on them ..."*
>
> (ash-Shura 42: 38)

For practical purposes, a *shura*, or the consultative body, can adopt either a direct or a representative model. In a direct *shura* model, all members, or the majority of adults at least, of the organisation or community are involved in the decision-making process. However, such a model, ideal as it may be, is usually only practical for small communities. It is difficult to implement such a model in a situation where the numbers of people run into millions. For such a case, Islamic movements have formulated a representative *shura* model. In this model, the membership elects a representative body for participating in the decision-making process and for holding the executive accountable for its actions. The representative body can include scholars from various fields of learning, specialists, wise and experienced people, local representative and special interest-group representatives (for example, women, youth and minorities).

4. Finally, leadership is a responsibility and all leaders, in whatever capacity, are accountable for their actions and decisions. The Prophet Muhammad said:

> *"Each one of you is a shepherd and is responsible for what he is a shepherd of."*
>
> (Bukhari and Muslim)

Islamic leaders must fulfil their duties and responsibilities sincerely and to the best of their abilities. The four Rightly Guided Caliphs – the ideal leaders for Muslims – were all God-conscious, stood for justice, and were held accountable for all their actions and how they conducted the affairs of society. In fact, consultation with the people and accountability to them and to Allah were the values they strongly adhered to.

> *"Ali reported Allah's Messenger as saying "No obedience is to be given (to a leader) in the case of an act of disobedience to Allah, obedience is to be given only regarding what is reputable."*
>
> (Bukhari and Muslim)

Islam asserts that a leader must not attempt to become an idol, expect blind following or deceive his people; rather he should strive to become a role model of justice and piety.

> *"The one who will be dearest to Allah and nearest to Him in station on the day of resurrection will be a just leader..."*
>
> (Tirmidhi and Mishkat)

In summary, this Chapter has discussed some general principles underlying the organisation of an Islamic movement. These are listening, obeying, migration, effective actions, and observance of Islamic values. It also stresses some important characteristics such as being universal, moderate, pragmatic, developing strength and power, and having an effective structure and leadership, all of which are essential in ensuring the effectiveness, relevance and viability of a movement for change. If they are observed and implemented, a dynamic and strong social movement for changing social life according to Islam will result.

An Islamic movement should strive to recruit, develop, involve, organise and train people, and also in building alliances in order to increase its capacity for change. Such efforts will extend its strength and power, and ensure its growth, expansion and advancement in society. This Chapter has stressed that individuals on their own cannot effect much change and, thus, collective efforts are essential. Furthermore, if a social movement is lacking in any of the important characteristics mentioned, it will not be effective in its efforts.

Notes:

1. Quoted from al-Qurtubi, Yusuf ibn Abd al-Barr, *Jami Bayan al-Ilm wa Fadluh*, Madina: al-Maktabah al-Ilmiyyah, n.d., Vol. 1, p.62.
2. Quoted from: Khan, Muhammad Habibur Rahman, *Life of Abu Bakr, First Caliph of Islam*, translated by Syed Moinul Haq, Lahore: Ashraf Publications, 1973, pp.55–6; and; Khan, Majid Ali, *The Pious Caliphs*, Kuwait: Islamic Book Publishers, 1978, p.44.
3. See for example Alwani, Taha Jabir, *The Ethics of Disagreement in Islam*, Herndon (USA): The International Institute of Islamic Thought, 1993.
4. See El-Awa, Muhammad S., *On the Political System of the Islamic State*, Indiana: American Trust Publications, 1980, pp 92–7.

CHAPTER X

Agents of Change: A Framework for Personal Development

Throughout this book the personal development and on-going training of the agents of change has been emphasised. According to the Glorious Quran, an important task of the Prophet Muhammad was to enlighten people through purifying their inner-selves and teaching them Allah's guidance and wisdom.

> *"Indeed Allah conferred a great favour on the believers when He sent among them a Messenger (Muhammad) from amongst themselves, reciting to them His verses, and purifying them, and instructing them in the Book and wisdom, while before that they had been in manifest error."*
>
> (Ali-Imran 3: 164)

This Chapter examines self-development and training more closely within the context of an Islamic movement. In particular it deals with the scope and objectives of personal development, offers a framework for a self-development programme, and addresses other issues which need to be taken into consideration when implementing such a programme.

Scope and Objectives of Personal Development

The process of on-going personal development and training can nurture moral and pious individuals and produces competent agents for change. This is why contemporary Islamic movements consider personal development an important priority. The more knowledgeable, refined, skilful and cultured members become, the more likely they are to understand issues, analyse and solve problems creatively, relate to others in a more mature manner, and be morally upright. Furthermore, continuous self-development, which is integrated into all aspects of life, can assist people towards becoming active citizens and good leaders of society. This, in turn, makes a movement more dynamic, competent and effective in pursuing its programme for a moral, God-conscious and fair society.

From an Islamic perspective, the scope of personal development is both wide and deep; it incorporates both inner and outer dimensions. It is not confined to the acquisition of knowledge, learning a few instructions, or practising a few rituals. In addition, it encompasses the following:

1. Producing inner change: This includes the cultivation of Islamic faith, values and morals, better attitudes and an upright character, purification of the soul from greed, hatred, envy and other negative emotions, sincere intentions, a spirit of sacrifice and brotherhood and sisterhood.
2. Clarification of the Islamic vision and developing a sense of mission.
3. Developing knowledge and understanding of Islam, society and the physical environment.
4. Developing social and practical skills, experience and wisdom.
5. Developing leadership skills and competencies.

In the light of the above, the objectives of personal development become clear; they are to nurture and produce the following inner and outer qualities and characteristics that arise from a Muslim's faith and values (these are elucidated by the Quran in numerous places):

- *Muslim*, one who submits to Allah alone.
- *Mumin*, one who has strong faith and conviction in Allah.
- *Muttaqi*, one who is God-conscious and exercises self-restraint.
- *Muhsin*, one who excels in good works and aims for excellence in all actions and deeds.
- *Mujahid*, one who strives for God's cause with sincerity and devotion.

- *Salih*, one who lives a righteous life.
- *Siddiq*, one who is truthful and honest in all actions and dealings.
- *Shahid*, one who is a witness of Islam.
- *Daiya*, one who invites people to Islam through their words and good actions.

> *"For Muslim men and women, for believing men and women, for devout men and women, for truthful men and women, for men and women who are patient and constant, for men and women who humble themselves (before Allah), for men and women who give in charity, for men and women who fast, for men and women who guard their chastity, and for men and women who engage much in Allah's remembrance – for them Allah has prepared forgiveness and great reward."*
>
> (al-Ahzab 33: 35)

Thus, personal development from an Islamic perspective is broad and balanced and incorporates the enhancement of human qualities and potential to the full, for the service of humanity. Its objective is to facilitate people in becoming effective and exemplary witnesses of Islam in society.

A Framework for Personal Development

An Islamic movement should formulate an effective yet flexible training and development programme, one that ensures the balanced and on-going advancement of its leaders and workers. Such a programme must be comprehensive, contextually relevant, and take into consideration the psychology of training and development. This implies that designers of training programmes must know how the human mind learns, and the different styles, methods and techniques that can be employed to increase the effectiveness of training. Moreover, teaching and learning strategies must be formulated prior to any programme implementation.

What follows is a suggested framework, comprised of five dimensions, for producing a balanced and flexible, yet comprehensive, personal development programme:

1. Basic Islamic development (faith, morals, basic practices, knowledge and character development).
2. Spiritual development (inner change and purification).
3. Human resource development (producing competitive competence, developing skills and specialisation, and gaining a deep understanding of society and its functioning).
4. Social development (development of strong inter-personal relations and social skills)
5. Movement training (i.e. organisational training which includes self discipline, accountability, adherence to organisational procedures, *shura* skills (effective consultation and meeting skills), strengthening of the brotherhood and sisterhood, and making sincere sacrifices and efforts for advancing positive change).

Figure 2 shows how this framework can be translated into an appropriate programme of learning for a given group of people and in a given context.

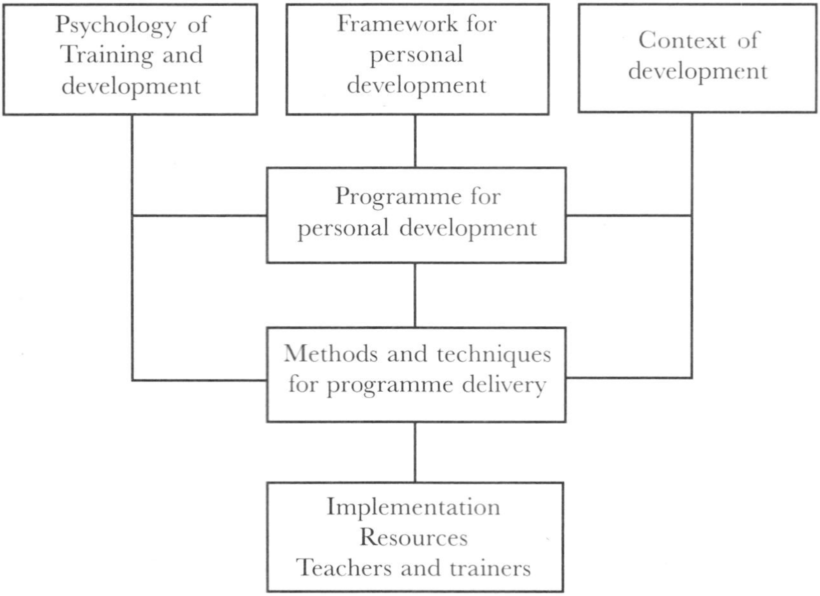

Figure 2.

Each component of the personal development framework is detailed below.

Basic Islamic Development

The focus of this dimension of personal development is on developing the basic knowledge of Islam and producing refined and moral individuals through stimulating their human qualities. Islamic workers must endeavour to acquire a basic knowledge and understanding of the Islamic faith and values. They need to understand what is obligatory (*fard* and *wajib*) and prohibited (*haram*), how to perform the basic acts of worship, and be familiar with the life and basic teachings of the Prophet Muhammad. Moreover, agents of change must cultivate good manners, attitudes and behaviour (*akhlaq*) in their character. Islam also instructs individuals to purify their intentions and work solely for seeking the pleasure of Allah and not for any other motive.

> *"Verily actions will be judged according to intentions ..."*
>
> (Bukhari and Muslim)

In short, a strong faith, moral character, deep knowledge and an integrated personality are the basis of this dimension of personal development. According to Islam, these can only be correctly cultivated through developing complete devotion and commitment to Allah alone. In other words, individuals must have a single loyalty – an unreserved loyalty to Allah alone. Divided loyalties lead to a disintegrated personality. The general symptoms of a disintegrated personality are temperamental imbalance, outward piety, confused priorities and impious intentions. These symptoms create lack of focus, distress, low morale, impatience, depression and even psychological disorder amongst individuals. Therefore, every loyalty, other than that to Allah, must be cast away from the depths of one's heart if one is to nurture an integrated and balanced personality and achieve inner peace and tranquillity.

In addition, individuals are required to keep a check on basic human faults and weaknesses and not allow these to dominate their character.

Such faults include bad language, spying, backbiting, disrespect for others and being involved in other things that are prohibited.

Spiritual Development

This second dimension of personal development overlaps to some extent with what has been discussed above. The objectives of spiritual development are:

1. Creating an awareness of self and of God, and an understanding of the meaning and purpose of life.
2. Creating a yearning for communion with God (*dua*), turning to Him constantly (*tawba*) and desiring to worship and serve Him alone (*ibada*).
3. Developing a deep sense of gratitude (*shukr*) to God for all His blessings and mercy, and an inner devotion and humbleness (*khushu*).
4. Creating a higher and noble vision; raising oneself above the self and material things.
5. Creating a compassionate, merciful and soft heart for other people; a deep desire to support and care for others.
6. Controlling negative emotions and feelings (for example, arrogance, greed, selfishness, envy, etc.) that harden and corrupt the soul, character and conduct.

> *"Successful are those who purify it* (i.e. their soul), *and the losers will be those who corrupt it"*
>
> (ash-Shams 91: 9–10)

The method laid down by Islam for spiritual development[1] is through:

1. Acts of worship, reading of the Quran, remembrance of Allah, night vigilance (*qiyam al-layl*) and spending resources, time, wealth, etc., in the way of Allah, with an emphasis on their inner dimensions[2]. In other words, how the soul, heart and mind should be engaged in acts of worship and in developing a feeling of God-consciousness.

2. Personal efforts for inner change and improvement through self-discipline, a regular check on intentions and motives, regular self analysis, creating a sense of time and time management, and attempting to obtain constant feedback from others. The aim of these exercises is to eradicate inner evils such as arrogance and a superiority complex, selfishness, hate, greed and love of material things, anger for wrong purposes, pretence and show, stubbornness, low-spiritedness and lack of perseverance, fear, and the pursuit of vain desires. At the same time, a person must endeavour to cultivate inner virtues such as faith, sincerity, piety, humbleness, gratitude, a sense of purpose and mission in life, remembrance and love of God, His Prophets and believers, concern for the Hereafter, softness of heart, control of the ego, and a burning desire to realise the vision of Islam.

Throughout his mission, the noble Prophet Muhammad endeavoured to be closer to Allah. Besides the five times daily prayers, it was his practice to spend long hours during the night in prayer and recitation of the Quran. This was his way of showing his gratitude to Allah. He remembered Allah often; in all his words and deeds. The noble Prophet constantly praised Allah, was thankful to Him, turned to Him for help in all his problems and prayed for His mercy. His faith in Allah and conviction in Islam as the hope for humanity was unshakeable. He also had faith in the fact that victory and success comes only from Allah. Obviously, those who sincerely strive to be closer to Allah and seek His aid will have their prayers answered and be entitled to His Mercy, Forgiveness and Help.

> "*When my servants ask of me, tell them that I am near, and I listen to them ...*"
>
> (al-Baqara 2: 186)

> "*Your Lord has said: Call upon me and I shall answer you.*"
>
> (Ghafir 40: 60)

The closer one is to Allah, the more one draws from His Infinite Knowledge and Wisdom. Consequently, the more knowledge of reality and wisdom an individual and a group gains, the more effective they are in introducing reforms and improvements in societies.

Put another way, from an Islamic perspective, successful change is not only dependant upon intelligence, effective strategies or even on efforts and resources. In addition, the Help and Mercy of Allah must be sought, since all change is in His hands. Hence, Islam asserts that individuals must strive, in addition to their efforts for a better society, to get closer to Allah, secure a strong attachment to His revealed guidance, and constantly pray for His forgiveness, mercy and help. With this dimension missing, the change desired by Islam cannot be accomplished. If change agents forget Allah, then they are most likely to neglect His guidance and lose a sense of accountability to Him. In such cases, good moral actions cannot normally be sustained.

> *"And be not like those who forgot Allah, and He caused them to forget themselves. They are the transgressors."*
>
> (al-Hashr 59: 19)

To ensure that individuals and movements do not forget Allah, which is an essential ingredient for successful change, they are instructed to offer prayers five times a day, keep fasts during the month of *Ramadan* (the 9th month of the Islamic calendar), give *zakat* (poor due), perform pilgrimage, read and understand the Quran, keep up remembrance of Allah, engage in self-reflection and self analysis, and regularly supplicate to Allah alone. This method, as prescribed by Islam, is most effective in nurturing God-consciousness.

> *"Establish regular prayer from dawn till the darkness of the night; and the morning prayer, recite the Quran ..."*
>
> (al-Isra 17: 78)

A God-conscious heart is in actual fact a driving force for positive action. God-consciousness and a sense of accountability to Allah are also fundamental prerequisites for self-purification (*tazkiyat an-nafs*), self-inspiration, self-motivation, and for selfless sacrifices and contributions. These are all, in turn, necessary requirements for striving for the Islamic cause. They assist in maintaining hope in hard times, bringing peace and tranquillity to hearts, creating energy in individuals for righteous action, forging brotherhood and sisterhood and cultivating team spirit. Without God-consciousness and piety (*taqwa*), an Islamic movement cannot sustain itself and it will inevitably disintegrate or become ineffective in its efforts.

Human Resource Development

This third dimension of personal development concerns itself with producing competitive competence. It focuses on building a capacity to understand and face challenges, so that the agents of change are able to bring to bear a methodology that is superior to the corrupt forces in society. Put another way, an Islamic movement should increase its capacity to such a level that it is capable of meeting challenges from any opposing force in the social environment in a competent and effective manner. Thus, human resource development encompasses the learning of appropriate and necessary skills, knowledge and the development of specialisation. It is obvious that good and pious people who lack social and political awareness and maturity, and who posses meagre skills and knowledge, are not likely to be competent enough in understanding and addressing societal challenges. This is why it is incumbent upon all Muslims to work continually at developing skills that are required for social and political participation and action.

The knowledge and skills required will naturally depend upon the kind and magnitude of the resistance and challenges faced by a movement. They are also dependent upon the communication methods and technologies in vogue, the economic and political climate, the moral and intellectual level of the people being addressed, and the overall social context. As an illustration, in the contemporary Western context, Islamic workers need to cultivate strategic thought, understand the roots of Western civilisation and the prevalent ideologies and way of life, increase local and global political awareness, and have good communication and media skills, which includes listening, speaking, writing and presentation. Furthermore, social, managerial, leadership, problem solving, organising, planning and information technology skills are vital[3].

The Prophet Muhammad invited his faithful Companions to acquire knowledge, develop expertise and skills, and aim for excellence in their chosen areas (*ihsan*). They practised archery, sword-fighting, horse riding and oratory, since these were imperative at that time. In addition, reading, writing, memorisation of the Quran, learning *ahadith* (sayings of the Prophet), planning, and other skills required for that time and age were greatly encouraged.

Social Development

The social development dimension of the personal development framework aims to cultivate Islamic social values and skills, including good inter-personal relations and a strong brotherhood and sisterhood. These assist in gelling members of a movement into a cohesive force and enables them to become good witnesses of Islam. Members of a movement should, therefore, be instructed in being truthful, honest and fair in all works and dealings, and in endeavouring to establish mutual friendship, trust and respect. Moreover, they should be sensitive to each other's feelings and situations, and offer their assistance and support to others on all occasions, especially during difficulties and hardships. To achieve social cohesion, Islamic principles and etiquettes of collective life should be established in the organisational culture. These include showing respect, politeness and hospitality, having a balanced temperament, being forgiving, kind and merciful, and avoiding harshness and insults, and so on. If socially harmful attitudes and practices such as hatred, jealousy, intolerance, backbiting and feuds over small issues are allowed to flourish, then social disintegration and decay is most definite.

> *"O believers, let not some men among you laugh at others, it may be that the (latter) are better than the (former). Nor let not some women among you laugh at others, it may be that the (latter) are better than the (former). Nor defame, nor be sarcastic to each other, nor call each other by offensive (nicknames). Ill-seeming is a name connoting wickedness (to be used of one) after one has believed. And those who do not desist are (indeed) doing wrong. O believers, avoid suspicion as much (as possible). For suspicion in some cases is a sin. And spy not on each other, nor speak ill of each other behind their backs..."*
>
> (al-Hujurat 49: 11–12)

Movement Training

Finally, this aspect of the personal development framework focuses attention on organisational and political training in the context of an Islamic movement. Its aim is to orient members of a movement towards living a disciplined collective life and to sincerely engage in its work. First, members of a movement must gain a firm understanding of the organisational structure, norms, procedures and processes for consultation, decision-making, the selection of leaders, accountability and making complaints. Second, they should clearly comprehend the Islamic movement's vision, objectives, and methodology. Third, they must be familiar with the movement's policies and programme of work (*manhaj*)[4]. Finally, they need to be politically aware and mature so as to understand societal issues and challenges, and to identify allies and resources for advancing efforts for social change. Thus, movement training is crucial for getting the best out of the membership, maintaining discipline and order, keeping a movement intact and strong, and for precluding any dissension, groupings, power struggles or ill-feelings in the rank and file.

> *"Truly Allah loves those who strive in His way in ranks (i.e. organised) as though they are a solid cemented structure."*
>
> (as-Saff 61: 4)

Change efforts require that people be single minded and completely loyal and devoted to the change efforts. Active participation and co-operation, obedience to the decisions that have been collectively made through a process of consultation, care for other members, and sacrifice of time and energies, are all essential ingredients for building a strong movement. These qualities and characteristics must, therefore, be nurtured. Those who are weak in determination, lack political maturity and self-discipline or have selfish motives (for example, desiring status, position, fame, or working to acquire power and influence within a movement) cannot genuinely strive long for the cause of Islam. In the light of this, an Islamic movement must be constantly alert and active in checking temperamental imbalance, and impious intentions and motives, since these are the seeds of inter-personal and organisational problems.

Implementation of the Development Programme

Finally, the practical implementation of a personal development programme requires some deliberation. The following points are deemed important in this respect:

A Personal Responsibility

Though an Islamic movement must make every possible effort to facilitate personal development, nevertheless, this duty must be considered as a personal responsibility and obligation. It cannot be left to others. Self-development is not a one-off event, but a life-long process. Individuals should be motivated to learn, mature, and correct and improve themselves constantly. More importantly, they need to learn how to learn by themselves, using the programmes and facilities offered by organisations and institutions. The following proverb articulates this point: *Give a man a fish, and you will feed him for a day. Teach a man to fish, and you will feed him for his life.*

However, if individuals do not assume this responsibility themselves, then the provision of instructional material and other learning facilities will not be of much assistance in self-development. In fact, members who are not determined and require spoon feeding or rely too much on the organisation for their training requirements, actually become a burden to a movement rather than an asset. According to Khurram Murad[5], for effective self-development, individuals must:

- be determined,
- make effort,
- aim for excellence,
- be regular, and
- integrate self-development into one's daily life.

A Degree of Flexibility

The personal development programme should be designed in a way that it offers a certain degree of choice and flexibility in its implementation. This is a substantial point since members of a movement are most likely to be of different ages and genders, and may perhaps have differing levels of knowledge and understanding. Also different people learn in different ways, at different paces and have divergent learning needs and interests. Thought should, therefore, be given to this aspect during the design stage of a personal development programme. A modular personal development programme, having many hundreds of small core and optional units (for example, on Quran reading, memorisation, prayers, character development, political awareness, writing skills, etc.) could allow for such flexibility and offer a degree of choice to Islamic workers. Core modules can cover the essential elements of Islam and its teachings for collective work, and these should, therefore, be compulsory. Optional modules, on the other hand can offer a choice to cater for divergent interests and facilitate specialisation. Furthermore, members with greater knowledge and experience should be integrated with those who possess little of these. This will not only speed up the personal development of new members but also prevent elitism forming in a movement.

Involvement in Practical Work

The practice of the Prophet Muhammad clearly indicates personal development was not seen in a narrow sense of teachers, books, syllabi, training programmes, etc. Rather, it was viewed in a much broader framework and incorporated practical involvement in the social life and work of a movement. Practical involvement is crucial since it provides a context for personal development, enables the application of knowledge to real issues, and makes the developmental process purposeful and relevant. This is why the Prophets of Allah did not place their followers in a classroom or academic type of environment, nor did they adopt inflexible and uniform methods for everyone.

Experience shows that the outcomes of education and personal development programmes are maximised if they are integrated into family and community life. For example, through home study and discussions, worship with family and community members, learning from seniors and elders, increasing practical experience through community involvement, and taking up community projects, etc. Thus, for an effective implementation of the personal development programme, a combination of methods can be employed such as direct teaching and training, encouraging and involving members in team work, challenging issues and organisational problems.

To boost personal development, members need to be involved in the everyday affairs of a movement, in discussions, decision making, problem solving and planning, since these require intellectual exertion and the application of knowledge to real issues. Simply spoon-feeding the members, or giving them tasks that do not sufficiently challenge or stimulate their thoughts, cannot really produce confident and competent agents of change. Through involving people and trusting them with responsibility, not only can more work be accomplished, but also the level of understanding of those involved can increase as a result. Subsequently, the greater the understanding gained, the greater will be the conviction, concern, commitment, sacrifice and striving for the cause of helping and serving humanity.

> "*Those who strive in Our (cause), We will certainly guide them to Our path...*"
>
> (al-Ankabut 29: 69)

> "*And they were youth who had faith in their Lord, and We increased them in guidance*"
>
> (an-Nahl 16: 13)

Theory and Practice

Although the Prophet Muhammad endeavoured to ensure the development of knowledge of his Companions, he did not allow his movement to reduce into a school or an academic institution. This is because on-going learning and development are a means, crucial as they may be, and not the objective of Islamic work. The noble Prophet managed to maintain a good balance between knowledge development on the one hand, and practical efforts for change on the other. He did not consider these two issues separately, but rather in an integrated way. The choice is, therefore, not of either knowledge development or practical efforts for social change, but both aspects being considered and addressed simultaneously. They are mutually interdependent. Practical work draws on knowledge and it also develops experience and wisdom.

Thus, personal development cannot be de-coupled and isolated from everyday work, actions and civic duties. In other words, personal development in Islam is not conceivable without engagement in practical social actions. Enjoying enormous knowledge and good character, and not applying these in efforts to improve society is meaningless. Furthermore, although a corrupt and immoral society affects the piety and character of all individuals who live in it to some extent, those who are inactive are, however, more vulnerable. It is, generally, through practical work that individuals and a movement matures and makes progress. By doing, working and taking up challenges, a movement grows and becomes strong and cohesive, and also the knowledge and experience of its members increases in the process. This point is very elegantly made by the following saying: *"I hear and I forget, I see and I remember, I do, and I understand."*

A continuous emphasis on theoretical learning, without giving due attention to practical work, can actually cause a movement to become inward looking, and progressively irrelevant to society. In such cases neither the individuals nor the movement develop much. To counteract this, the development of role models can be encouraged, so that through them members can be inspired to reach high levels of knowledge, skills and character. In addition, the establishment of Islam's system of worship (i.e. prayers, fasting, etc.), together with creating a culture of piety can all aid in the personal development process. With these systems and mechanisms in place, self-development does not require much attention, and a movement can largely be free to concentrate on its actual mission.

Quality and Quantity Issue

Linked with this is another issue concerning the quality and quantity of people in a movement. Some argue that a movement should work on a few people and focus on their personal development rather than expand at the cost of lowering the quality of the individuals. However, practical experience points to the contrary. It is clear from the life example of the Prophet Muhammad that he never concentrated on a few individuals. Rather he tried to approach as many people as possible with the Islamic message and recruit them into his movement. It follows from this, that by aiming for quantity, the quality of people in a movement can actually improve. This is because society has people with all kinds of skills, knowledge, talents, specialisation and experiences. As more and more people join a movement, the more enriched it becomes. More people bring in greater diversity, knowledge, new and varied experiences and skills and this subsequently leads to intellectual and cultural richness.

To summarise, this Chapter has highlighted the importance of personal development and training. It outlines a framework to ensure the balanced development and training of individuals. This framework incorporates basic Islamic development, spiritual development, human resource development, involving and empowering individuals, and social development. All these are essential elements for nurturing good people and building a strong and competent Islamic movement for social change. Undoubtedly, people are the most important resource of an organisation and of a nation, and hence this resource needs to be organised, developed and put into effective use. Those organisations that are able to utilise and develop peoples' potential effectively are more successful than those that do not.

Notes:

1. See Islahi, Amin Hasan, *How to Attain True Piety and Righteousness*, translated by Sharif Ahmed Khan, Safat (Kuwait): Islamic Book Publishers, 1982, and Mawdudi, S.A., *Guidelines for Workers*, translated by S. Naqvi Ali, Lahore: Islamic Publications Ltd., 1981.
2. See Al-Ghazali, *Inner Dimensions of Islamic Worship*, translated by Muhtar Holland, Leicester: The Islamic Foundation, 1983.
3. See Altalib, Hisham, *Training Guide for Islamic Workers*, 2nd revised edition, Herndon (USA): The International Institute of Islamic Thought, 1992.
4. See Mawdudi, S.A., *Islamic Movement. Pre-requistes for Success*, 3rd Edition, Aligarh (India): Crescent Publishing Co., 1980, and Al-Qardawi, Yusuf, *Islamic Education and Hasan Al-Banna*, Calcutta: Hilal Publications, 1983.
5. Murad, Khurram, *Self Development*, edited by Arif Jihad, 2nd edition, Amanah Publications, 1994.

CHAPTER XI

A Practical Framework for Positive Change in a Western Context

"Indeed, you have only three possible futures. First, to be assimilated and absorbed in the secular culture here (in the West), receiving in return, a niche where you can practice your private customs and festivals. Second, to face genocide, or extermination, like the Muslims in Spain and Bosnia, and the Jews in Germany. And third, to bring Islam to the West and the West to Islam. Again, the choice is yours... Being Muslims, desiring to live as Muslims, do you really have a choice? Certainly not. There is only one choice for you and it is quite obvious... make a resolve today... to cry out and carry on the message of the Prophet, from every home and market square, to every man, woman and child, so that they may live in true submission, to your Lord..."

(Khurram Murad, 1932–96)[1]

This Chapter draws together material covered in earlier Chapters so as to offer a practical framework; a framework to advance the Islamic message and its values in a Western context. This framework consists of three major components: the development of Muslim community life, sharing the message of Islam with the indigenous population, and playing a constructive role in society. Each of these components will need to be translated by the Islamic movement into a programme of action.

Muslims in the West: A Unique Situation

Historically, Muslims have lived and even established themselves on Western soil on a number of occasions, and in cases, for long periods of time. They were in Spain for over 700 years (711–1492 CE), and from there they even moved as far as southern France, where they stayed for a short while. In Spain, they established a brilliant civilisation, and this contributed much to the material progress of the West. In addition, the Muslims were in Sicily (and in a few parts of southern Italy) for over 200 years (831–1091 CE) before the conquest of the Normans. Furthermore, the indigenous people of eastern Europe, mainly from present day Bulgaria, Romania, Austria, the Balkans (for example, Bosnia, Kosovo and Albania) and Turkey, actually started to accept the Islamic faith from as early as the 13th and 14th centuries CE[2].

The present day situation of Muslims in the West, as compared to the earlier periods, is however, unique and challenging in many ways. During the early days when Islam had reached many parts of the world, the Muslim world-community was well organised and in a powerful and dominant position. There was a thriving and vibrant Islamic civilisation which stretched from Morocco to Indonesia, and Muslims were admired and looked up to for leadership and guidance. Their culture and system of governance was far advanced and superior than other systems that existed. In comparison, the Muslim world-community today, in general, is unfortunately suffering from backwardness, despondency and disunity. Many Muslim countries are imitating the culture and way of life that is prevalent in the West, and have adopted secular ideologies and systems of government to administer their collective affairs.

Looking further back in time, when the Prophet Muhammad started his Islamic mission in Arabia, the corrupt forces of his time were not as organised and equipped with such huge and potent resources as they are today. Neither did so many myths and misrepresentations exist about Islam and the Muslim community during his time as they do today, particularly in the West. Furthermore, the noble Prophet was an Arab and he addressed his own people in their own language. Also, since he understood the culture, traditions and the dominant way of life, he was skilful and competent in operating within the context of his society. In contrast, Muslims in the West today, the vast majority of them, are migrants. Thus, they are not on the whole seen by the indigenous populations as part and parcel of Western societies. Primarily, their origins are from non-Western countries; predominantly from the East, such as Pakistan, Bangladesh, the Middle East, Turkey, and Malaysia. Many of them, therefore, particularly the early migrants, do not sufficiently understand the culture and way of life of Western people.

Moreover, many Muslim migrants have brought with them to the West numerous negative elements: their sectarian tensions and conflicts, together with their political, national and tribal allegiances, and in some cases a few local customs and practices that actually conflict with Islam. In addition, unlike the early followers of Islam, the work of striving for a fair society and living for the mission of Islam are not priorities for many Muslims since they did not, in general, come to the West for these objectives. All these factors only assisted in reinforcing negative images of Islam, hindering the West from gaining a true understanding of its faith and culture, and causing many tensions and group conflicts amongst the Muslims themselves.

Thus, as a result of the unfortunate present day local and global situation of the Muslim people, together with the historical misunderstandings of Islam that exist, the West does not see Islam as appealing, beneficial, or relevant. Muslims are also not, on the whole, seen as examples of good behaviour with a high level of spirituality and morality. In fact, Islamophobia is deep rooted in the West's perception of Islam and Muslims are viewed with suspicion.

Against this background, those who desire to live by Islam, promote its message and values, and contribute positively towards their society, are indeed placed in a very uncomfortable, awkward and difficult position. So where can one begin to promote a change based on Islam? Here, the Islamic framework and the methodology for change, as detailed in earlier Chapters, provide guidance on moving forward. These indicate that the chief ingredients for improving social life are to share Islam's message and values (*dawa*), build an exemplary Muslim community life in order to witness Islam before the Western public, and to contribute positively towards the spiritual, moral and social progress of society. In the light of this, the agents of change need to organise themselves and produce a practical programme of action based on these ingredients. This programme, should be pragmatic and take into consideration the present day situation of the Muslims, together with the West's attitudes towards Islam. Moreover, efforts in this direction must of course be underpinned by sincerity, a right frame of mind and a genuine concern for society. A framework to assist in the formulation of an effective, yet pragmatic, programme of action for advancing the Islamic message and values is proposed in the subsequent sections of this Chapter.

A Genuine Concern for Society

This has to be the starting point since a genuine concern for society and compassion towards fellow human beings aids in shaping a right frame of mind and attitudes that are required for co-existence, interaction, co-operation and positive contribution. Put another way, change agents must see themselves as being part and parcel of society and the indigenous population as their own people[3].

Being solely concerned with the immediate needs and issues of the Muslim community, without giving due regard to mainstream issues, cannot earnestly cultivate a genuine concern for society. Also, indifference to one's own society, whilst engaging in activities that revolve around issues in Muslim countries, in the Middle East for example, cannot logically win significant support or respect for Islam in the West. Of course, an awareness of what's happening in Muslim countries is undoubtedly important since Muslims are part of a world-community. However, this should not by any means distract attention away from the immediate environment in which one lives. Unfortunately, the indigenous population of Western societies are considered by some as the infidels (*Kuffar*), who are all enemies of Islam. This, in our opinion, is a flawed perspective and one that can lead to hostile attitudes, tensions, conflicts and extremist behaviour. The fact of the matter is that the vast majority of the West's population have never had an opportunity to know what Islam is really about. They must, therefore, be given this opportunity. With regard to this, Khurshid Ahmad has something important to contribute. He suggests:

> "Muslim community [in the West] should evolve a new pattern of Islamic life and culture in the context of the Western society... they should live as full participants and not as pseudo-citizens. They have to develop a new mode of life, in consonance with the values and norms of Islam in the context of local conditions, and not transplanted from their countries of origin."[4]

Thus, anyone who has a concern for humanity cannot really remain detached or indifferent to societal issues and problems. Currently, the West faces a number of momentous problems and issues, which should all be cause for alarm. These include: the erosion of morals, the break-down of family life, the decline of the community, the increasing gap between the rich and poor, the negative and harmful influence of the media, rising institutional and political corruption, organised crime, the destruction of our environment, and the huge profits made by the alcohol, gambling, pornography, drug, fashion, and other similar industries to the detriment of society. These are significant issues that propel society along a very hazardous course and, hence, they require urgent attention. Without a genuine concern for society, one cannot even begin to address these.

A Practical Framework to Guide Positive Change

Development of Practical Strategies

Indeed, having a genuine concern for people and society is most likely to motivate a person to work for the common good. In order to carry out this obligation effectively, the formulation of a well thought out, long-term strategy and programme for action is deemed necessary. This will help in focusing, guiding and channelling energies and resources towards realising the vision of Islam. The following are suggested guidelines to aid the strategy formulation process:

1. First, change agents require a deep understanding of Islam's vision for society and the world (see Chapter Two), and a clear direction for realising this vision. As the saying goes: "*If you don't know where you are going, then any road will take you there.*" A vision and direction are, thus, necessary for focusing thoughts, energies and resources.
2. A good grasp of the ideologies, beliefs, attitudes and life-styles dominant in the West is essential (see Chapter Four). An understanding of these will aid in identifying those aspects which must be altered if the contemporary social conditions are to be improved. This can be gained through an in-depth study and analysis of the prevalent social, technological, economic, legal, political and environmental factors. In addition, social and political values, hierarchies and processes that are rooted in social systems need to be understood since these can either facilitate or hinder the diffusion and dissemination of ideas through society. Furthermore, an awareness of the developments in information and communication technologies is also crucial as these increasingly determine the methods and techniques for the dissemination of ideas and information, both locally and globally.
3. An understanding of the Islamic framework and methodology for social change (see Chapters Six to Ten) is also necessary. The Islamic methodology must be applied prudently, keeping the Western context in view. This is important since the approaches, methods and strategies that are employed in Muslim countries of the East, may not be relevant or have much impact and appeal in the West. Thus, a fresh approach and working models, derived from the Islamic sources of guidance, suited to a Western context are

required for pragmatic reasons. Islam is a universal coherent system of life and it cannot be presented as a foreign or imported religion. It must be seen and accepted as an indigenous movement working for a moral and God-conscious person and a fair society.

4. Finally, change agents in an Islamic movement, must assess their own strengths and weaknesses, possess good judgement of the kinds of knowledge and skills that are necessary for effective work, and gain a correct estimation of the resources they can mobilise for playing a constructive role in societal affairs (see Chapter Nine and Ten).

A defensive strategy, which is commonly employed by communities living as minorities, aims at securing basic needs (for example, obtaining Muslim schools, mosques and *halal* food) and finding small corners for safeguarding and practising their faith. Though such a strategy appears to be advantageous in the short-term, nevertheless it may not prove prudent in the long-term. This is simply because the influence of the dominant culture in a society is far too large for a minority culture to sustain itself it. Further, such a strategy encourages isolation and could perhaps prevent Muslims from playing a constructive role in the affairs of main stream society. In view of this, a multi-pronged strategy for moving forward with Islamic ideals is suggested. This implies that in addition to addressing the immediate and short-term needs and issues of the Muslim community in the West, efforts must be exerted in parallel, towards building a powerful Islamic movement, sharing the Islamic message and teachings, and influencing society positively in the light of Islamic guidance. In other words, efforts need to focus on raising the moral and spiritual level of the Muslim community, while simultaneously engaging in societal affairs through social and political participation.

In the light of this, a practical framework to guide strategy formulation is offered in Figure 3. This framework comprises of three main areas of concern: community development, sharing the message of Islam, and contributing positively towards society. These areas are further elaborated overleaf.

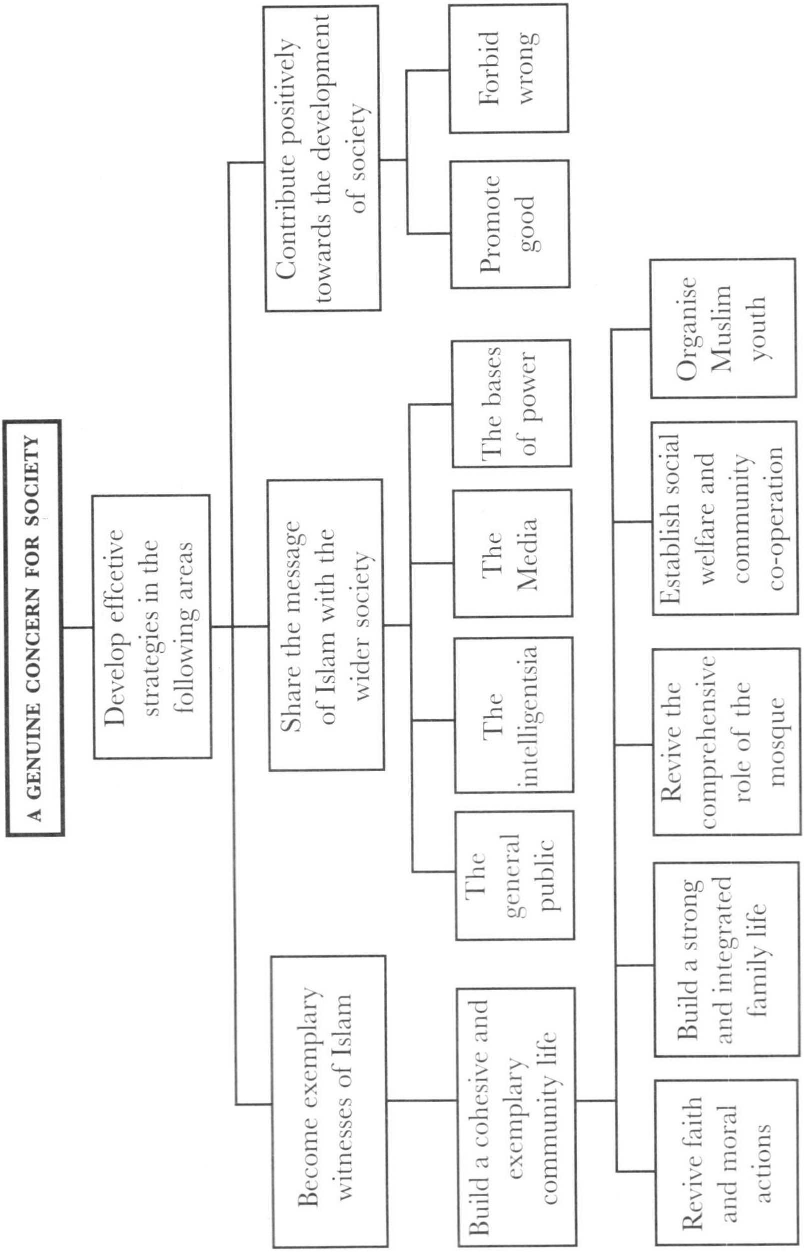

Figure 3: A Practical Framework for Positive Change in a Western Context

Development of Muslim Community Life

Human beings have a social inclination and they, thus, find meaning, purpose and fullness in community life. This is why Islam denounces monasticism and enjoins family, social integration, co-operation and respect. By living together in an organised, cohesive and active community life, Muslims can become good witnesses of Islam in the West. Such a community life can be built through a process of cultivating Islamic moral values, discipline and strong relationships amongst community members.

Currently, there are numerous pockets of Muslim communities scattered throughout the West, but unfortunately, they are not so cohesive, organised, or up to the moral and spiritual standards they ought to be. In fact, in certain cases, Muslim communities, like other communities, are actually weakening and fragmenting. Thus, the challenge for change agents is to organise these communities and provide them with the relevant intellectual and moral support for addressing their problems and weaknesses so that they emerge as better models of Islam. This is an essential but very complex and challenging assignment. Bringing people together, organising them and providing them with a common purpose is not such an easy task to accomplish as it might first appear. Change agents may experience many problems such as: resistance to the change efforts, sectarian and group conflicts, lack of tolerance, weak faith, poor character and conduct, selfish attitudes, personality clashes between community members, unemployment, poor housing, and some specific social problems such as those faced by old-people, women, youth, and so on.

Therefore, we suggest that a focus on the following areas can assist in laying down the foundations for a strong, vibrant and God-conscious community life:

1. Affecting an inner change in the lives of Muslims; revival of faith, piety and morality.
2. Rebuilding an integrated and strong family life.
3. Reviving the comprehensive role of the mosque.
4. Establishing systems for on-going community development and welfare.
5. Organising the Muslim youth.

These points are elucidated upon below:

Revival of Faith, Piety and Morals

According to Islam, the starting point for the revival and development of a community is to focus attention on the root problems that prevent people from connecting to each other, and not on treating the symptoms. The root problems for social issues are not poor housing, unemployment, lack of buildings, mosques, resources, social security, and so on. Rather, as Islam argues, they stem from a lack of faith, morality and a sense of a noble and higher purpose in life. This may explain why all the great Prophets of Allah worked so hard to cultivate these essential ingredients which are in essence prerequisites for a healthy community life.

Islamic morality, if imbibed and adhered to, sets an order in human relationships and as a result bring people closer together in trust and co-operation. Morals are nurtured on strong faith and piety, and these in turn are cultivated through the establishment of God's worship (the five pillars of Islam), reading of the Quran, remembrance of Allah, night vigilance (*qiyam al-layl*) and spending resources (time and wealth, etc.) in the way of Allah. Thus, to revive Islamic faith, piety and morality, efforts should be made to establish the pillars of Islam wherever pockets of the Muslim communities exist. Moreover, Muslims' relationship with Allah and His Book, the Quran, together with love of the Prophet Muhammad and his Sunna must be strengthened.

In reflecting over the five pillars of Islam (i.e. basic beliefs, prayers five times a day, alms giving, fasting and pilgrimage) we are of the opinion that they are in effect the five pillars of "community life". They are the glue that keeps Muslims together in a community. Each pillar, if understood and practised properly, can help in the purification and development of the inner self as well as in social development. They bring community members together (rich and poor), aid in the cultivation of a strong relationship with Allah, affect attitudes positively and strengthen relationships between members of the community. All these are the seeds for effective community development.

An Integrated and Strong Family Life

Islam considers a family to be the most important unit of society. If this building block is diseased or weak, then consequently social life will be the same. This is why Islam pays a great deal of attention to the affairs of the family. The family facilitates the building of human personality and moulds social and cultural values. It caters for the emotional, spiritual and personal needs of individuals. A good and proper functioning family life can provide warmth, love, affection and care. It can also assist in protecting the young from harmful social influences and provide a healthy forum for their cultural development. Ideally, Islam enjoins a kind of family in which both parents live in love and harmony, who impart Islamic values and teachings to their children, and who observe piety and moderation in their life-style. In fact, a family shaped by Islam can become a strong force for positive social change. The challenge for building an integrated and strong Muslim family in the West arises from:

- some of the un-Islamic family practices and customs that have become part of the inherited culture from Muslims' countries of origin.
- the influence of family values from a secular-materialistic culture.

Both these challenges can be addressed through a balanced Islamic education and the careful observance and establishment of Islamic values and practices in family life.

Firstly, the role of husband and wife and their relationship with each other need to be shaped according to Islamic guidelines. Unfortunately, due to the influences of the dominant secular culture, these roles are being confused and as a result many problems are arising in family life. An over emphasis on rights has led to a negligence of duties and responsibilities, and this, in turn, breeds other unhealthy attitudes. Efforts to gain greater independence, freedom and a larger private space (i.e. 'to do what I want to do' attitude), are leaving less and less time for inter-personal contact. By both parents working outside the home for long hours (to pursue their careers) and frequently eating out, opportunities for family members to interact, converse, share feelings and strengthen family ties has been greatly reduced. People are living together, yet remain strangers. Indeed these lifestyles hinder the positive development of a happy family life. Due to their jobs, both husband and wife are unable to fulfil their duties towards each other, and as a consequence, family affection, trust and relationships are impaired. The proper nurturing of children, a crucial parental responsibility, is being overlooked, and in cases, even neglected. No wonder, the breakdown of the family, divorce and juvenile delinquency are on the rise. In addition, the social and emotional costs of these lifestyles are incalculable.

Men and women due to their biological differences are assigned different primary, but complementary, roles by Islam, and any confusion in these roles will inevitably lead to internal tensions and a decline in the family. This differentiation of primary roles, not only facilitates the distribution and sharing of responsibilities and tasks and hence alleviates mundane pressures, but also makes the husband and wife more dependent on each other, which in turn strengthens their relationship. As a norm, men are the bread-winners and women attend to the children and domestic work. However, in addition to fulfilling their primary roles, both partners, if they wish to do so, can mutually agree amongst themselves to perform extras roles in community life within the Islamic limits.

Second, Islam asserts that parents should endeavour to become good examples for their children. They also have a responsibility to impart knowledge and foster morals, good behaviour and manners in their children so that they grow up to be responsible and good citizens of society, and become excellent ambassadors of Islam in the West. This duty can only be fulfilled if children are given time, proper attention and love by their parents. Baby-sitters and nannies, no matter how affectionate and capable they may be, cannot be a substitute for natural parents in this respect.

> *"O believers, save yourselves and you children from the fire of Hell..."*
> (at-Tahrim 66: 6)

Undoubtedly there are many pressures exerted on families in Western societies and these are preventing proper and healthy development. In fact, social and economic forces strain the marriage bond. In addition to unemployment, inflation, bills, taxation, and so on, there are many other social pressures as well. The negative influence of TV, a consumer culture, rapid changes in fashion and goods, pressure on women to work outside the home, extravagant customs and life-styles, and so on, all these only assist in aggravating the problems further. However, by rebuilding extended families, many of the family pressures can be alleviated.

Further, motherhood and home life are unfortunately not given much value; the societal emphasis has shifted from home life to the office and factory floor. Due to this, and as current social trends indicate, the traditional family system in Western societies is crumbling. Thus, by setting a good example of a family and home life, the blessings and joys of a family based on Islamic values can be witnessed to by society. This will further help in protecting and promoting the institution of the family in society as a whole.

Revival of the Role of Mosques

The mosque is another important social and religious institution in the lives of Muslims. Re-vitalising the mosques is an essential requisite for producing a God-conscious and moral community. In fact, mosques were intended to be centres of community life, and through the centuries they have played a key role in reviving people, nurturing active citizens, and assisting the spiritual, moral and social development of Muslim communities. They were not only places of worship, but also acted as centres of learning, social welfare and public spaces where community issues and problems were addressed. During the early days when Islam was established in its full glory, planning, preparation, and the co-ordination of efforts for social improvement and development also took place in mosques. Moreover, they assist in breaking down social barriers and hierarchies, since all people, rich and poor, black and white, scholars and illiterates, all come together to worship their Lord and Creator, and, hence, meet and interact with each other. Furthermore, mosques can be quite effective for the dissemination of ideas, news and information.

However, through the passage of time, the role of mosques has gradually been reduced to places of worship only; for the remembrance of Allah, prayers, invocation, supplication, reading of the Quran and for holding marriages and funerals. People are not encouraged to use them for socialising, for discussing social issues and problems, and for social welfare. In the light of this, by endeavouring to revive the comprehensive role of mosques, a great contribution can be made towards the strengthening of Muslim community life. Regular daily attendance, large congregations, together with facilities for socialising and exchanging information and concerns in mosques, can greatly contribute towards a better community life. All community issues need to be brought to the mosques, discussed, and plans developed for addressing them.

Social Development and Welfare

Issues related to education, social welfare and co-operation between the various Muslim organisations and mosques also requires on-going attention. These are important areas for building strong and dynamic communities that can enable Muslims to become exemplary witnesses of Islam and a force for positive change in the West.

The provision of comprehensive education is vital for human and social development, and hence for the health and viability of a community. Islam enjoins all members of a community, men, women and children, to make efforts for acquiring knowledge and developing skills and competencies that are required for active citizenship and proficient Islamic workers. Unfortunately, however, education is sometimes viewed in a limited and narrow way; restricted to rote learning and the curriculum. For example, Muslim children, in many places, are mainly taught how to recite the Quran in Arabic and there are meagre efforts for imparting knowledge and understanding its message, spiritual and cultural values, and showing its relevance to today's world. Continuing in this direction will be detrimental. It will fail to cultivate their Islamic faith and mould their character and attitudes. This in turn can lead to more social problems, not least behavioural. Education must, therefore, be viewed in a comprehensive way. It must begin from homes, be carried through into community life, and be integrated in all aspects of social life and activity. Educational programmes can also be delivered in a variety of ways, both through formal and informal methods such as via one-to-one engagements, family study circles, sitting with scholars and elders, private reading, group study, lecture programmes, short courses offered on audio, video and computer, correspondence courses, and so on, or through mosques and schools.

Likewise, social welfare is an important responsibility of a Muslim community. Islam enjoins care for the elderly, the orphans, the needy and the unemployed.

> *"It is not righteousness that you turn your faces towards the East or the West. But it is righteousness to believe in Allah, the last day, the angels, the book, and the Messengers. And to spend your wealth out of love of Allah, for your kin, orphans, for the needy, for the wayfarer, for those who ask..."*
>
> (al-Baqara 2: 177)

Being indifferent or careless in this matter and leaving such communal issues to local authorities and social service departments, definitely breeds social irresponsibility and, hence, weakens social links. As a matter of fact, support and grants from the state for these purposes have actually contributed to a weakening of social relationships and community life. This is because people no longer feel a need to turn to each other for help and social support – instead they turn to the local authorities for their social welfare needs. In contrast, inter-community care and support improves communication and builds social cohesion.

In addition, establishing co-operation between mosques, groups and organisations is also a crucial part of community development. Through social cohesion and co-operation, communities can become more organised and, thus, be able to act effectively on social issues. This can also increase their social capacity and provide an infrastructure for further community development and social welfare.

Organising the Muslim Youth

Last, but not least, the Muslim community is obliged to give serious attention to the plight of the young. Because of their age, they are more vulnerable to the materialistic and immoral temptations presented by society. This makes it more crucial to give the young the urgent attention they deserve.

Since the young are the future of any community, they need to be inspired by Islam and given a better understanding of its message and way of life. By organising and providing them with a sense of mission and direction, they can become instrumental for societal change and reform in the West. They need to fully understand their duties and responsibilities as Muslims and what constructive role they can play in the West. Further, since they understand Western culture and are able to speak Western languages more fluently than their elders, this makes them more suited to interaction with the wider society and they can contribute positively and creatively towards its well-being. Here, parents, teachers and mosques can play an active role in organising the young. They should provide them with all the necessary support and encouragement for their moral, intellectual and spiritual development.

Sharing the Message of Islam with Society

This is the second important strategic concern for Islamic workers. As discussed above, organised, and disciplined Muslim community life is crucial for becoming better witnesses of Islam. In addition, the Islamic methodology prescribes that Islam has to be presented and shared with the public at large (*dawa*). This task is a major challenge for the Muslim community living in the West. This evidently requires Muslims to be engaged with mainstream society. Naturally, by working to share Islam, Muslims will be brought into close contact with the general public, academics, the media and various social and political institutions and bodies. This close contact will provide ample opportunities for them to share their faith and present positive and correct information on Islam and the political circumstances surrounding the Muslim people. Through this interaction, numerous fears, myths and prejudices can be removed and mutual trust generated. Also better relations can be established between Muslims and other citizens, and as a result everyone can experience the peace and happiness of living together in a multi-cultural society with dignity and respect.

Sharing the message of Islam effectively (*dawa*) assumes both freedom of speech and a right to be heard. A society may allow people to speak freely, however, they can be prevented from being heard. This maybe due to a deliberate policy, or may simply exist because of the sheer complexity of modern social processes and arrangements that have been instituted in society. Further, those who direct societal affairs can quite easily place mechanisms and rules in social and political processes in order to effectively prevent certain messages from being heard or receiving attention. Indeed, they have the means to control the public agenda and debate, and can reinforce, through state apparatus, certain values and beliefs in a society, as well as prevent others. Thus, people can be actively engaged in sharing their ideas, views and message through all kinds of methods and techniques (for example, use of the media, books, advertisements, leaflets and posters, demonstrations and public rallies, etc.), but all this can fall on deaf ears. An Islamic movement, therefore, must not only give thought on how its message can be propagated, but also identify platforms, mechanisms and power bases which will carry and enable its voice to be heard and taken seriously by society. As mentioned earlier, social and political hierarchies play an important role in controlling and channelling the diffusion and dissemination of ideas and beliefs through society. To understand these and build networks across social and political divides is crucial.

Thus, for effective *dawa*, the building of social, political, legal, and economic networks is necessary. It is such networks that provide strategic contacts, access to societal power, information, and influence for positive social change. Most Prophets of Allah established networks to assist them in their efforts for social change. However, this is not as easy as it may appear. The way societies in the West are structured, building networks across social divides is beset with many obstacles. People at the lower end of the social ladder simply do not have the resources (money, language or interests) of the upper classes, which makes the building of social networks difficult.

In our view, to present Islam effectively in the West, thought needs to be given to the following questions:

- how can the message of Islam be effectively translated into a language which can be understood in current times, particularly by Western minds?

- how can this message be made relevant to today's society and world?
- how can this message be communicated in a logical and methodical way using appropriate and effective means?

The Islamic methodology further prescribes that Islam must be presented in peaceful, and in the best and most gracious ways possible; through interaction, communication, and social and political participation. This implies that the Islamic message and way of life is to be shared and discussed and not thrust onto people. In this respect, the Quran gives many guidelines on how best to do this. One very comprehensive verse stresses the use of wisdom.

> *"Call to the Way of your Lord with wisdom and beautiful preaching; and reason with them in ways that are best and most gracious..."*
>
> (an-Nahl 16: 125)

This verse, already discussed in Chapter Seven, emphasises the use of wisdom and offers guidance on engaging with society. Wisdom implies being careful with the use of words, proper planning of the intended communication, and employing appropriate and suitable means, all within the social context in which the dialogue is taking place. Furthermore, the verse stresses that the call is to Allah and not to the self or group. This indicates that dialogue should be free from any hidden or personal agenda. With respect to this point, in many inter-faith dialogues there is usually a hidden agenda to some degree, either by one party or both. Through such dialogue the aim is either to convert people of other faiths, or to weaken their conviction and even confuse them. However, for Muslims, to engage in a dialogue, there must be no such thing. Rather it must be genuine and sincere, and the sole intention should be to share and to create respect and tolerance between themselves and people of other community faiths. A dialogue should be an encounter and communication in an atmosphere of mutual trust and acceptance[5]. The aim should be to remove fears, misunderstandings and historical prejudices and animosities that exist between Islam and the West. It should also aim at discovering possibilities for co-operation and working together for the common good[6].

Sharing the message of Islam requires a genuine and sincere communication with the ordinary citizens as well as social and political institutions. In particular, communication needs to be established with the following sections of society:

1. The general public.
2. The intelligentsia.
3. The media.
4. Powerful people and institutions.

The General Public

Establishing communication with the general public can facilitate understanding, and develop tolerance and respect. Thus, efforts aimed at sharing Islam with neighbours, friends and colleagues, general members of the public, together with teachers, doctors and other professionals, are required. The objectives of these efforts should be to dispel Islamophobia and relate Islam's message to the current issues of society. It is believed that such endeavours can assist people in understanding Islam and its perspective on social issues. One-to-one contacts, the distribution of literature and audio-videos, displaying exhibitions, holding cultural awareness programmes, organising public gatherings and using the media are some of the methods that can be employed for sharing Islam with the public.

The Intelligentsia

The Islamic framework for social change indicates that Godless materialistic world-views and systems of life that dominate society must be challenged since they are the root cause of problems and social crisis. Islam, as a viable alternative, must be presented and its guidance made relevant to society. One way of achieving this is through establishing communication with thinkers and academics since they influence thought in society. These efforts would contribute towards placing Islam onto the intellectual agenda of the West.

Intellectuals ponder over the 'why', 'what' and 'how' of things. They influence a people's perception of reality and set trends in thought.

Philosophers, social scientists, political analysts, and other academics concerned with social affairs, research, think and write many papers and books on issues, moral dilemmas and crises facing our society. They also advise government and policy makers on how to best address these issues. Thus, establishing communication, through conferences and other means, with this community of people is vital if Islam is to influence the thought and culture of the West. For this purpose, seminars and conferences can be organised, and papers related to ideological, cultural and social issues can be published in journals that are widely read by thinkers and academics. All such approaches would undoubtedly impact and influence the thought and ideas of Western thinkers and assist in sharing with them the Islamic perspective on social, economic and political issues.

Furthermore, change agents need to draw the attention of historians, sociologists and academics from other fields of knowledge, to the immense contributions made by Islam and Muslims towards the development of Western societies. The Muslims established a great civilisation in Spain, and they were also in Sicily for more than two hundred years. Furthermore, their presence in the Balkans and Turkey has been evident for more than five centuries. History records that the West greatly benefited from the presence of Muslims in Europe. The social systems and the intellectual, scientific and technological developments during the times when Muslims ruled these areas had a lasting effect on Western thought and these became the seeds for material progress[7]. By highlighting these contributions perhaps a change in attitudes towards Islam can be affected.

The Media

By media, all the means of mass communication are implied. These include newspapers, magazines, radio, TV, cable, satellite and the Internet. It is a very powerful and effective tool for communicating and disseminating concepts, ideas, culture, thought and information to the general public. Whoever has influence and control over the media is definitely very powerful.

Without doubt, the media contributes a great deal in shaping and directing society. It puts issues before the public's attention and aids in framing peoples' behaviour, attitudes and culture. It sets trends in lifestyles and fashion, has embedded consumerism in society by being the most powerful vehicle for advertising, and it controls the public debate and agenda. Unfortunately, the media thrives on violence, war, sex and fantasy. All these provide entertainment and escapism, and regrettably such things have become the central values of society. Furthermore, the way the media is exploited is dehumanising in so many ways. For example, people are portrayed as biological machines and programmes are on the whole designed to appeal to the baser feelings and emotions of people.

Incidentally, every Prophet of Allah attempted to employ the (mass) media of their time. Examples include Abraham talking in the court of Nimrod, Moses talking to Pharaoh before an audience of many thousands, Jesus giving his sermon on the Mount, and the Prophet Muhammad addressing his people on Mount Safa in Makka to share his message. In every case the audience included many hundreds of people, if not thousands.

So far, the media in general, has not proved to be very favourable to Islam or the Muslims. It generally portrays very negative, cruel and hostile images of the Muslim community, both at the international and local levels. Whether this is done deliberately or not, the outcomes are not conducive to religious tolerance and social harmony in our society. It breeds suspicion, misgiving and even fear and hatred. It is, therefore, crucial for Muslims not to sit back and moan about the attitude of the media. They should actively engage with the media and encourage the removing of negative stereotypes and images of Islam. Representation on all significant media forums, bodies and organisations must be encouraged in order to be heard and respected. Such platforms provide opportunities for raising concerns and offering ideas for the delivery of good programmes representing religious and community values. The reason for this should not solely be for influencing the media in giving a true image of Islam and the Muslim community, but also to voice concerns on the harmful effects of the media on society in general. Many initiatives could be taken in this respect. For example, by establishing public forums and organisations that hold the media companies accountable for their actions, programmes and products, and by joining hands with other media interest groups, which may share similar concerns, to exert political pressure.

The Powerful Elite

These are also a very important community of people with whom communication is necessary. They direct and influence social values and conditions. They are behind the formulation of long-term strategies and policies that affect everyone. However, those holding power and influence are not very accountable or visible. The government does hold some power, but it is not where all power is concentrated. Financial institutions, the media, secret organisations, large business corporations, political institutions, Quangos (quasi non-government organisations) and so on, wield a considerable amount of power, and in some cases a great deal more than the elected government. They are the real "movers and shakers" of society.

This is why the noble Prophets of Allah addressed the leaders and powerful elite of their societies to submit to Allah. Abraham went to Nimrod, Moses to Pharaoh, Jesus to the Pharisees and Scribes and even to the Roman officials, and Muhammad to the leaders of the Quraish and neighbouring kings and emperors. If powerful people submit to God's guidance, then society is most likely to follow.

The concern is that those who wield power do not always have the best interests of society in mind. They generally attempt to further their own interests and strive to consolidate more power for themselves, and in most cases this can be to the detriment of society. Thus, it is crucial that powerful people and institutions be approached and lobbied for support in efforts for the common good.

Positive Contributions Towards Society

Finally, in addition to sharing Islam with society, the Islamic methodology directs change agents towards exerting efforts for enjoining good and forbidding wrong in society and the state.

"You are the best community raised for humanity, you enjoin good and forbid wrong and you believe in Allah ..."

(Ali-Imran 3: 110)

Enjoining good includes the promotion of Islamic values in society such as: truth, honesty, chastity, family values, respect and care for the elderly, care and proper upbringing for the young, a moral and balanced education, just social policies, the equitable distribution of wealth, care for orphans and support for the poor. Furthermore, acting on such good in one's private life is not enough according to Islam. Public life and the state must also conform to equitable and moral principles. In fact, anything that is not firmly established in collective life cannot be sustained for long in the private sphere. This is why all the Messengers of Allah, according to Islam, did not solely preach individual morality, they also strove to build public life on strong faith and Islamic moral code.

Thus, in the light of Islamic guidance, crime, corruption and social evils should not only be the concern of the victims or the police, rather they must be everyone's concern. To sit back and be indifferent to immorality and wrong can only assist in the spread of these social evils. Thus, Islam enjoins upon Muslims to act for raising their voice and concern against all forms of wrong and immorality. They are duty bound to rid society of immoral, depraved, dishonest and unjust practices. All forms of corruption, injustice and acts of oppression have to be fought against – this includes gambling, prostitution, pornography, alcohol, drugs, political corruption, economic injustice, and harmful legislation and social policies.

Resistance to Social Change

Enjoining good and forbidding wrong is such a task that it inevitably invites a huge amount of resistance and opposition. It is sometimes difficult to imagine the enormous resistance that change agents can face during their efforts. The Quran states:

"Do you think that you will attain Paradise without such (trials) as came to those who passed away before you? They encountered suffering and

adversity, and were so shaken in spirit that even the Messenger and those of faith who were with him cried: "When (will come) the help of Allah". Say verily, the help of Allah is (always) near."

(al-Baqara 2: 215)

As an illustration, underground drug dealers and the drug distribution network involves many thousands of people across many countries. It is presumed that in some cases even state officials and banks may be involved in this immoral activity. Together, they make millions, if not billions of pounds of illegal money every year. Imagine, if people of good-will were able to mobilise support for eradicating such an evil from society? Would the drug pushers remain passive spectators to the liquidation of their major source of income? Indeed they would not. On the contrary, they are most likely to obstruct such efforts, and may even go as far as to murder those leaders and activists who are involved in such efforts. This illustration can be applied to other detrimental products and activities generally found in present day societies such as gambling, indecent literature, magazines and films, alcohol, etc. Ironically, each of these are given free reign to flourish, and as a result they have turned into enormous industrial empires and make billions of pounds profit annually. However, every year millions of lives are shattered, families are broken, and social life in general brought into disorder because of these immoral activities.

Thus, working to rid society of immoral ways inevitably invites a huge amount of organised resistance. Further, people behind such activities usually exert considerable influence on the state apparatus. Put another way, even governments may resist efforts to hinder the marketing and use of such products or services. This is why many Prophets, when they started to strive against evil practices, were vehemently opposed by those whose interests were threatened, and at times even attempts were made to slay them. However, the Quran repeatedly states that those who are working for positive social change must not fear anyone or anything, no matter how great the resistance is. They must put their full trust in Allah and continue with their efforts to eradicate all immoral, unjust and harmful elements from society. Resistance must not be invited, but if it comes in the way of improving society, then it must be faced courageously.

According to the Quran, Allah helps people of good-will in their endeavours if they work sincerely for seeking His pleasure alone. The most a society can do is offer resistance or even attempt to eliminate the agents of change. However, Islam teaches that such people, if they are slain as a result of their sincere efforts, become martyrs. They will be amongst those on the Day of Judgement who have the highest rank in the sight of Allah, and they will have the best of rewards. It is this faith and conviction that motivates believers to continue in their efforts for a better social life and to face resistance with great courage. When a people are ready to die for such a cause, then there can be no power on earth that can stop them in their efforts.

> *"O believers seek help (from Allah) with patient perseverance and prayers. For Allah is with those who patiently persevere. And say not of those who are slain in Allah's way, they are dead. No they are living, though you perceive it not. Be sure We will test you with something of fear, and hunger, some loss in goods or lives or fruits (of your toil), but give glad tidings to those who patiently persevere. Who say when afflicted with calamity: To Allah we belong, and to Him is our return."*
>
> (al-Baqara 2: 153–6)

Notes:

1. A quote from an article by Murad, Khurram, in *Convention '95* brochure produced by the Islamic society of Britain, July 1995.
2. Hasan, Masudul, *History of Islam*, Revised Edition, Delhi: Adam Publishers and Distributors, Vol. 2, 1995.
3. For example, the Quran mentions in many verses that the noble Prophets addressed their people as: "O my people".
4. Quoted from Siddiqui, Ataullah, *Christian-Muslim Dialogue in the Twentieth Century*, London: Macmillan Press Ltd, 1997, p.132.
5. Ibid., pp.30–1.
6. Ibid.
7. See for example: Ahmed, K. Jamil, *Heritage of Islam*, Lahore: Ferozsons, 1956., and Watt, W.M., *The Influence of Islam in Medieval Europe*, Edinburgh: Edinburgh University Press, 1972.

CHAPTER XII

Conclusion

A basic overview of Islam has been presented in the preceding Chapters, with a particular emphasis on the kind of society that would emerge if its message and teachings were to be applied in social life. The purpose and mission of the Muslim world-community was also elucidated, and the major contemporary intellectual and practical challenges that face the agents of change in building a God-conscious, moral and just society were highlighted. The book further expounded the Islamic framework and methodology to guide thought and actions for social change. It stressed that care and thought must be given while applying the methodology in a given social context. Moreover, some guidance was offered for building a cohesive and powerful Islamic movement, which is an essential vehicle for societal change. Finally, a practical framework for a Western context was put forward to aid in the formulation of a programme of action.

In conclusion, the following points require special emphasis. First, having a clear Islamic vision and a deep understanding of its objectives and priorities for individual and social life is deemed crucial since this will underpin any effort for societal reform and change. Islam, the Way of God, is for all people and for all times. It does not belong to any particular group of people; rather it is a universal message of hope and liberation for the whole of humanity. It is also a comprehensive and balanced system of life that encompasses both the inner (i.e. spiritual and moral) and socio-political dimensions of human life and society. Islam puts forward a set of universal beliefs, values and principles that provide a coherent framework for life. This framework inspires people towards virtue and focuses, guides and channels their enthusiasm and energies towards constructive and positive work. Islam offers a methodology that guides the process of nurturing and producing good individuals and building better societies that are free from the domination of elitist groups and oppressive elements.

Second, throughout this book, it has been emphasised that the followers of Islam are charged with a mission; a mission to realise the vision of Islam in social life and the state. Being Muslims, they cannot remain indifferent. On the contrary, they must be concerned about the future of society and the world. Islam instructs them to rise above selfish interests and to come out of their private and narrow worlds and engage with society, striving to the utmost of their abilities in the process. They must strive to re-link faith and power in order to place power in an active moral framework. Today, where secular-materialism has segmented, compartmentalised, disintegrated, corroded and hence weakened the social fabric, agents of positive change must work to re-build and reintegrate social life in order to eliminate the contradictions and conflicts that have arisen from the disintegration. Endeavours to this end are desperately needed, today more than ever. Social concerns and issues should be raised at every level of society and a movement launched for this purpose. People and organisations of good-will must be identified and mobilised for support. Strategic alliances must be forged for this cause, and people and power mobilised in order to enhance the capacity for positive social action. In other words, a well thought-out programme of change must be formulated in the light of Islamic guidance and actively pursued. This programme should include the following three essential dimensions: to invite people to Islam; its beliefs, values and principles (*dawa*). To bring about an inner change in those who respond to the call; a change in their world-view, orientation, character and behaviour so that they become exemplary models of virtue (*tarbiya*). And finally, to initiate systematic changes and improvements in social and political institutions and processes of society.

If Muslims sincerely commit themselves to Allah's way and strive to the best of their abilities to transform their world into a better place, as the Quran instructs them to do, then Allah promises them success in this world and in the Hereafter.

> *"Allah has promised to those among you who believe and practise righteous deeds that He will surely establish them in the land, as He established those before them ..."*
>
> (an-Nur 24: 54)

However, at the same time, Islam cautions that efforts for change should be motivated by a strong faith in Allah, to win His good pleasure, and a deep concern and love for humanity. They must not be based on greed, hatred, revenge or any other negative emotions or vested selfish interests.

The following saying makes an important point:

- If you are planning for a year, plant grains.
- If you are planning for a decade, plant trees.
- If you are planning for a millennium, plant men (people).

The Prophets of Allah came to plant better men – to build a better future by building moral individuals and a just social order. They achieved this through planting in people Islamic beliefs and values. They nourished people with Islamic morals and ideals. They created a healthy atmosphere through establishing just systems so that individuals could grow and mature into models of righteousness, goodness, uprightness, integrity, prudence and virtue. Thus, to build a better tomorrow, society must invest in people. People should be provided with a clear, inspiring and challenging vision of a just and better world, organised into a social movement and involved in efforts for social change.

Finally, the following verse from God's Glorious Book, the Quran, very eloquently and concisely summarises the contents of this book:

> *"By time, humans are at a loss (Khasara). Except those who have faith (Iman), and (are involved in) righteous actions. And those who exhort each other to the truth and to perseverance."*
>
> (al-Asr 103:1–3)

The Arabic word *Iman*, used for faith in the above verse, is very comprehensive in its meaning. It implies people having faith and a deep conviction in Allah and whose vision is shaped by Islamic beliefs and values. It is such *Iman* that inspires and moves individuals to organise themselves into an Islamic movement for engaging in righteous actions for positive social change. In the process they must always adhere to the principles of truth and justice and persevere in their efforts. Once *Iman* and righteous actions are rooted, then social reform and progress becomes unstoppable.

The verse also states that 'time' – past, present (and even future) – is a witness to the fact that people have continued to be in a loss, are in a loss, and will be in a loss, except those who are involved in efforts for a better social life. The word 'loss' implies the opposite to what humans value. People value all such things as success, progress, benefit, dignity, justice, peace, pleasure, happiness, love, respect, affection, kindness, friendship, etc. Therefore, anything that harms these is loss (*khasara*). *Khasara* disturbs and depresses souls, which in turn breeds negative emotions and attitudes, and these consequently bring harm to inter-personal relationships, leads to social problems and tensions, intellectual and material set-backs, and to the general degeneration of society. Today, due to the rejection of the natural principles mentioned in the above Quranic verse, people as individuals and as communities are moving towards personal and social loss. They are losing their sublime human qualities and hence our personal and social miseries.

To overcome this loss, Islam urges humanity to change its direction and its attitude towards God's revealed guidance. People, as individuals and as communities, should accept the message brought by the noble Prophets and build their societies on its foundation. They must promote values such as family, community, care and support, and nurturing in a world that is filled with greed, selfishness and indifference. It is only then that we can have a better social life and see social harmony, justice and peace prevail in our societies and in the world.

> *"O our Lord, give us all that is good and beneficial in this world, and all that is good in the world Hereafter, and save us from the torments of the Hellfire".*
>
> (al-Baqarah 2: 201)

Bibliography

1. Process of Social Change

Ahmad, Khurshid, and Ansari, Zafar Ishaq (eds.), *Islamic Perspectives, Studies in Honour of Sayyid Abul A'la Mawdudi*, Leicester: The Islamic Foundation, 1979.

Al-Banna, Hasan, *Memoirs of Hasan Al Banna Shaheed*, translated by N.M. Shaikh, Karachi: International Islamic Publishers, 1982.

Al-Faruqi, Isma'il, *Islamic Dawa, Its Nature and Demands*, Washington: American Trust Publications, 1986.

Al-Rashid, Mahmood, 'Faruqi's Conception of the Islamic State', in *Al-Mizan: The Balance*, Vol.1, No. 2, pp 23–30, 1995.

Al-Alwani, Taha Jabir, *Research Monograph No. 1: Usul Al Fiqh Al Islami, Source Methodology in Islamic Jurisprudence*, USA: International Institute of Islamic Thought, 1990.

Chapra, M.U., *Islam and the Economic Challenge* Leicester: The Islamic Foundation and the International Institute of Islamic Thought, 1992.

Fukuyama, Francis, *The End of History and the Last Man*, London: Hamish Hamilton Ltd, 1992.

Idris, Ghafar Sheikh, *The Process of Islamization*, USA & Canada: The Muslim Students' Association, 1977.

Iqbal, Muhammad, *Reconstruction of Religious Thought in Islam*, Lahore: Muhammad Ashraf, 1960.

Islahi, Amin, Ahsan, *Call to Islam and How the Holy Prophets Preached*, Kuwait: Islamic Book Publishers, 1978.

Kamali, Mohammad Hashim, *Principles of Islamic Jurisprudence*, Cambridge: The Islamic Texts Society, 1991.

Mawdudi, S.A., *The process of Islamic revolution*, Lahore: Islamic Publications Ltd., 7th edition, 1979.

Mawdudi, S.A., *The Islamic Movement Dynamics of Values Power and Change*, edited by K. Murad. Leicester: The Islamic Foundation, 1984.

Mawdudi, S.A., *Nations, Rise and Fall – Why?*, Lahore: Islamic Publications Ltd., 2nd edition, 1978.

——, *A Short History of the Revivalist Movement in Islam*, Lahore: Islamic Publications Ltd. 5th Edition, 1981.

——, *Witnesses Unto Mankind. The Purpose and Duty of the Muslim Ummah*, edited and translated by Khurram Murad, Leicester: The Islamic Foundation, 1986.

——, *The Islamic Law and Constitution*, translated by Khurshid Ahmad, Lahore: Islamic Publications Ltd., 4th Edition, 1969.

——, *Come Let Us Change this World*, compiled by Kaukab Siddiq, Lahore: Islamic Publications Ltd., 1982.

Murad, Khurram, *Shari'ah The Way of Justice*, Leicester: The Islamic Foundation, 1981.

Siddiqi, Shamim A., *Methodology of Dawa*, New York: The Forum Publication, 1989.

Sztompka, Piotr, *The Sociology of Social Change*, Oxford: Blackwell Publishers, 1993.

Strasser, Hermann, and Randall, Susan C., *An Introduction to Theories of Social Change*, London: Routledge & Kegan Paul, 1981.

Yakan, Fathi, *Islamic Movement, Problems and Perspectives*, translated by Maneh al-Johani, Indiana: American Trust Publications, 1984.

2. Islam and the West

Ahmad, Khurshid, *Islam and the West*, Lahore: Islamic Publications (PVT) Limited, 5th edition, 1986.

Baumer, Franklin Le Van (editor), *Main Currents of Western Thought*, 4th edition, London: Yale University Press, 1978.

Esposito, John, L., *The Islamic Threat, Myth or Reality*, Oxford: Oxford University Press, 1992.

Huntington, Samuel P., Clash of Civilisations?, *Foreign Affairs*, Vol. 72, No. 3 (Summer 1993).

Izetbegovic, Alija Ali, *Islam between East and West*, Indianapolis: American Trust Publications, 1993.

Lamartine, *Histore de la Turquie*, Paris 1854, Vol. II, p.277.

Nadwi, Abul Hasan, *Islam and the World*, Kuwait: International Islamic Federation of Student Organisations, 1977.

Qutb, Muhammad, *Islam & the Modern Materialistic Thought*, Delhi: Hindustan Publications, 1985.

Siddiqui, Ataullah, *Christian-Muslim Dialogue in the Twentieth Century*, London: Macmillan Press Ltd, 1997.

Watt, W.M., *The Influence of Islam in Medieval Europe*, Edinburgh: Edinburgh University Press, 1972.

3. Sira, Islamic History and Heritage

Abdur Rauf, *Illustrated History of Islam*, Lahore: Ferozsons (Pvt.) Ltd, 1994.

Ahmed, K. Jamil, *Heritage of Islam*, Lahore: Ferozsons, 1956.

Bashir, Z., *Sunshine at Madinah*, Leicester: Islamic Foundation, 1990

Briffault, Robert, *The Making of Humanity*. London: G. Allen and Unwin Ltd., 1919.

Denffer, Ahmed Von, *Ulum Al-Quran. An Introduction to the Sciences of the Quran*, Leicester: The Islamic Foundation, 1983.

Hasan, Masudul, *History of Islam*, Revised Edition, Delhi: Adam Publishers and Distributors, Vol. 2, 1995.

Hitti, Philip, K., *History of the Arabs*, London: Macmillian and Co., 5th Edition, 1951

Haykal, Muhammad Hussein, *The Life of Muhammad*, translated by Ismaeel Al-Faruqi, London: Shorouk International, 1983.

Khan, Muhammad Habibur Rahman, *Life of Abu Bakr, First Caliph of Islam*. Lahore: Ashraf Publications, 1973.

Lings, Martin, *Muhammad*, London: George Allen & Unwin Ltd. and the Islamic Texts Society, 1983.

Salahi, Adil, *Muhammad: Man and Prophet*, Shaftsbury (UK): Elements Books Limited, 1998.

Siddiqui, Abdul Hameed, *The Life of Muhammad*, Lahore: Islamic Publications, 1969.

4. Personal Development

Ahmad, Khurshid, *Principles of Islamic Education*, 7th edition, Lahore: Islamic Publications Ltd., 1984.

Al-Qardawi, Yusuf, *Islamic Education and Hassan Al Banna*, Calcutta: Hilal Publications, 1983.

Al-Ghazali, *Inner Dimensions of Islamic Worship*, translated by Muhtar Holland, Leicester: The Islamic Foundation, 1983.

Altalib, Hisham, *Training Guide for Islamic Workers*, 2nd revised edition, Herndon (USA): The International Institute of Islamic Thought, 1992.

Alwani, Taha Jabir, *The Ethics of Disagreement in Islam*, Herndon (USA): The International Institute of Islamic Thought, 1993.

Ibn Taymiyyah, *The Diseases of the Hearts and their Cures*, compiled by Ibraaheem bin Abdullaah al-Haazimee, translated by Abu Rumaysah, Birmingham (UK): Al-Hidaayah Publishing and Distribution, 1998.

Islahi, Amin Hasan, *How to Attain True Piety and Righteousness*, translated by Sharif Ahmed Khan, Safat (Kuwait): Islamic Book Publishers, 1982.

Murad, Khurram, *Self Development*, edited by Arif Jihad, 2nd edition, Amanah Publication, 1994.

Mawdudi, S.,A., *Guidelines for Workers*, Lahore: Islamic Publications Ltd., 1981.

Mawdudi, S.A., *Islamic Movement. Pre-requisites for Success*, 3rd Edition, Aligarh (India): Crescent Publishing Co., 1980.

Glossary

AH — After *Hijra* (migration). *Hijra* marks the beginning of the Islamic calendar.

Ahkam — Commands of Allah, legal rulings.

Akhira — The Life Hereafter.

Akhlaq — Morals and manners.

Aqida — Islamic creed.

Bashir — Bearer of glad tidings.

Daiya — One who invites people to Islam through his words and good actions.

Dawa — Inviting to Islam.

Din — Religion or Way of life.

Dhikr — Remembrance of Allah.

Dhimmi — Literally, one who is protected. It refers to a non-Muslim living under the protection of an Islamic state.

Fard — Obligatory acts or duties.

Fasad — Corruption, mischief.

Fiqh — Islamic jurisprudence.

Hadith (pl. Ahadith) — A narrative. It refers to the sayings, deeds and approvals of Prophet Muhammad (peace and blessings of Allah be upon him).

Hajj — The once-in-a-life time obligation of pilgrimage during the month of *Hajj* to the Holy Kaba (in the city of Makka).

Halal — Lawful.

Haram — Prohibited or unlawful.

Hijra	Migration. It refers to the migration of Prophet Muhammad (peace and blessings of Allah be upon him) from Makka to Medina.
Ibada	Prescribed acts of Worship and obedience to Allah.
Ihsan	Moral excellence or benevolence.
Ijtihad	Exertion for independent judgement in light of Islamic guidance.
Iman	Faith.
Iqamat ad-Din	Establishment of God's Way in Human life.
Jama'a	Group, community or congregation.
Jahiliya	Ignorance (of Divine guidance).
Jihad	Striving against vice, evil and unjust systems of life in order to influence positive change.
Khasara	Loss.
Khushu	Devotion, humbleness and concentration in prayer.
Khalifa	Vicegerent, trustee or successor.
Kafir/Kuffar (pl)	Literally, this means to cover. In Islamic terminology, it refers to those who reject Islam despite the fact that they know it is the truth.
Makruh	Abominable, reprehensible.
Mandub	Commendable.
Manhaj	Method and process.
Maruf	Something that is universally accepted as good.
Mumin	One who believes in Allah.
Muhsin	One who excels in good work.
Mubah	Permissible.
Mujahid	One who strives or struggles in the way of Islam.
Munir	Something that is lit.
Munkar	Something that is universally recognised as bad or detestable.
Muslim	One who submits to God Alone.
Muttaqi	One who is God-conscious.

Nafal	Optional acts of worship (which are encouraged but not obligatory).
Nazir	A Warner.
Qiyam al-layl	Night vigilance or night prayer.
Ramadan	The 9th month of the Islamic calendar; the month of fasting for Muslims.
Riba	Usury.
Sabr	Patience, fortitude, steadfastness.
Salat	Prayers five times a day.
Salihin	Those who live righteously.
Sam'	Listening.
Sawm	Fasting.
Sira	The life or biography of the Prophet Muhammad (peace and blessings of Allah be upon him).
Shahada	Islamic declaration of faith or martyrdom.
Shahid	One who is a witness to Islam or a martyr.
Sharia	Path or way. Generally used to refer to Islamic laws and rules.
Shirk	Associating partners with God, worshipping other than God.
Shukr	Gratitude.
Shura	Consultation. A body (of representatives) for consultation and decision-making.
Siddiq	One who is truthful.
Sufi	Muslim mystic.
Sunna	The established way of the Prophet Muhammad (peace and blessings of Allah be upon him).
Ta'a	Obedience.
Tafsir	Explanation or commentary of the Quran.
Taghoot	Highest form of transgression against God
Taqlid	Imitation, following the views and opinions of others (especially in following a particular school of thought in matters of *Fiqh*).

Taqwa	God-consciousness.
Tarbiya	Nurturing. Moral, spiritual, intellectual and physical development.
Tawba	Constantly turning towards God and asking for His forgiveness.
Tawhid	The Oneness of God.
Tazkiyat an-nafs	Purification of the soul or of hearts and minds from evil.
Umma	The Muslim world-community.
Usul al-Fiqh	Methodology and rules for addressing issues in the light of Islamic sources of guidance.
Wajib	Required acts.
Zakat	The obligatory Poor due.

Index

Printed in Spain
APIPE Artes Gráficas
tel: 00 34 609 54 07 01
fax:00 34 937 53 09 87